Julian Symons is primarily remenof crime writing. However, in his an enormously varied body of work. Social and military ...., biography and criticism were all subjects he touched upon with remarkable success, and he held a distinguished reputation in each field.

His novels were consistently highly individual and expertly crafted, raising him above other crime writers of his day. It is for this that he was awarded various prizes, and, in 1982, named as Grand Master of the Mystery Writers of America – an honour accorded to only three other English writers before him: Graham Greene, Eric Ambler and Daphne du Maurier. He succeeded Agatha Christie as the president of Britain's Detection Club, a position he held from 1976 to 1985, and in 1990 he was awarded the Cartier Diamond Dagger from the British Crime Writers for his lifetime's achievement in crime fiction.

Symons died in 1994.

BY THE SAME AUTHOR
ALL PUBLISHED BY HOUSE OF STRATUS

CRIME/SUSPENSE

THE 31ST FEBRUARY

THE BELTING INHERITANCE

BLAND BEGINNING

THE BROKEN PENNY

THE COLOUR OF MURDER

THE END OF SOLOMON GRUNDY

THE GIGANTIC SHADOW

THE IMMATERIAL MURDER CASE

THE KILLING OF FRANCIE LAKE

A MAN CALLED JONES

THE MAN WHO KILLED HIMSELF

THE MAN WHO LOST HIS WIFE

THE MAN WHOSE DREAMS CAME TRUE

THE NARROWING CIRCLE

THE PAPER CHASE

THE PLAYERS AND THE GAME

THE PLOT AGAINST ROGER RIDER

THE PROGRESS OF A CRIME

A THREE PIPE PROBLEM

HISTORY/CRITICISM

THE TELL-TALE HEART: THE LIFE AND
   WORKS OF EDGAR ALLEN POE

ENGLAND'S PRIDE

THE GENERAL STRIKE

HORATIO BOTTOMLEY

THE THIRTIES

THOMAS CARLYLE

Buller's Campaign

Julian Symons

HOUSE OF
STRATUS

Copyright © 1963, 2001 Julian Symons
Introduction Copyright © 2001 H R F Keating

All rights reserved. No part of this publication may be reproduced, stored in a retrieval system, or transmitted, in any form, or by any means (electronic, mechanical, photocopying, recording, or otherwise), without the prior permission of the publisher. Any person who does any unauthorised act in relation to this publication may be liable to criminal prosecution and civil claims for damages.

The right of Julian Symons to be identified as the author of this work has been asserted in accordance with sections 77 and 78 of the Copyright, Designs and Patents Act 1988.

This edition published in 2001 by House of Stratus, an imprint of Stratus Holdings plc, 24c Old Burlington Street, London, W1X 1RL, UK.

www.houseofstratus.com

Typeset, printed and bound by House of Stratus.

A catalogue record for this book is available from the British Library.

ISBN 1-84232-934-0

This book is sold subject to the condition that it shall not be lent, resold, hired out, or otherwise circulated without the publisher's express prior consent in any form of binding, or cover, other than the original as herein published and without a similar condition being imposed on any subsequent purchaser, or bona fide possessor.

FOR
FREDA BOARD

CONTENTS

INTRODUCTION

The French call a typewriter *une machine á ècrire*. It is a description that could well be applied to Julian Symons, except the writing he produced had nothing about it smelling of the mechanical. The greater part of his life was devoted to putting pen to paper. Appearing in 1938, his first book was a volume of poetry, *Confusions About X*. In 1996, after his death, there came his final crime novel, *A Sort of Virtue* (written even though he knew he was under sentence from an inoperable cancer) beautifully embodying the painful come-by lesson that it is possible to achieve at least a degree of good in life.

His crime fiction put him most noticeably into the public eye, but he wrote in many forms: biographies, a memorable piece of autobiography (*Notes from Another Country*), poetry, social history, literary criticism coupled with year-on-year reviewing and two volumes of military history, and one string thread runs through it all. Everywhere there is a hatred of hypocrisy, hatred even when it aroused the delighted fascination with which he chronicled the siren schemes of that notorious jingoist swindler, Horatio Bottomley, both in his biography of the man and fictionally in *The Paper Chase* and *The Killing of Francie Lake*.

That hatred, however, was not a spew but a well-spring. It lay behind what he wrote and gave it force, yet it was always tempered by a need to speak the truth. Whether he was writing about people as fiction or as fact, if he had a low opinion of them he simply told the truth as he saw it, no more and no less.

i

This adherence to truth fills his novels with images of the mask. Often it is the mask of hypocrisy. When, as in *Death's Darkest Face* or *Something Like a Love Affair*, he chose to use a plot of dazzling legerdemain, the masks of cunning are startlingly ripped away.

The masks he ripped off most effectively were perhaps those which people put on their true faces when sex was in the air or under the exterior. 'Lift the stone, and sex crawls out from under,' says a character in that relentless hunt for truth, *The Progress of a Crime*, a book that achieved the rare feat for a British author, winning Symons the US Edgar Allen Poe Award.

Julian was indeed something of a pioneer in the fifties and sixties bringing into the almost sexless world of the detective story the truths of sexual situations. 'To exclude realism of description and language from the crime novel' he writes in *Critical Occasions*, 'is almost to prevent its practitioners from attempting any serious work.' And then the need to unmask deep-hidden secrecies of every sort was almost as necessary at the end of his crime-writing life as it had been at the beginning. Not for nothing was his last book subtitled *A Political Thriller*.

H R F Keating
London, 2001

PREFACE

This book sprang from a good deal of research, over a period of several years, into the whole of the South African War. It was my intention to write a book about the War, looking quite a long way before and after the actual fighting, and dealing with its political and economic, as well as its military, aspects. But I was too slow or too idle, and within the last five years two books have been published, *The Boer War* by Edgar Holt and *Goodbye, Dolly Gray* by Rayne Kruger, which made me feel that it was not worth producing a third book which must go over much of the same ground, although in more detail. I gave up altogether the idea of writing about the War, until last year it occurred to me that it might be possible to make an interesting book out of the Natal campaign, which was a more or less self-contained story within the larger framework of the War.

Such a plan proved easier to outline than to execute. I found that in order to deal with the Natal campaign intelligibly I had to show the remarkable ascendancy that the Commander-in-Chief of the Natal Field Army, Sir Redvers Buller, retained over his soldiers after his defeats, and to do that it was necessary to say something about Buller's career and position at the War Office and about the little-remembered struggle between the 'Wolseley Ring' and the 'Roberts Ring', which had so much effect on events in South Africa. Then, also, it seemed that I must at least sketch in the background of the events leading to the War, so that the haphazard choice of Ladysmith as a position might be made clear. All this, as it seemed to me, threw light upon Buller and his actions. I tried to bear in mind also, however, that it was not my purpose to write a history of the War, nor even of the first few months of it, and that I must reject everything outside my theme. So there is nothing here about Roberts' campaign in South Africa, nothing about the defence of Mafeking and of Kimberley, very little about the War in its political and social aspects, and only an explanatory minimum about Boer attitudes and actions. To deal with Roberts' campaign, except so far as it concerned Buller's, would have changed the shape of the book.

Perhaps a note on sources, and on the use of original material, may come in here, rather than appended to individual chapters or in the form of footnotes. A good deal of the material about Wolseley, particularly in the first part of the book, comes from the letters written to his wife, which are in the Royal United Services Institution. I am grateful to the Institution for permitting me to use the letters, and to its Director, Brigadier J Stephenson, for his patience in dealing with my queries. A selection from them, called *The Letters of Lord and Lady Wolseley, 1870–1911*, was published in 1924, but the editor, Sir George Arthur, was so excessively pious and unscholarly that he changed words and phrases freely, and ran letters into one another without giving any indication of what he had done. I have, obviously, used only a tiny fraction of these fascinating letters, and I must ask the reader to take my word for it that the extracts I have quoted fairly represent Wolseley's feelings about Roberts.

Some of the letters quoted to and from Spenser Wilkinson come from papers provided by the Ogilby Museum, but most of them are from Lord Roberts' papers, which are in the hands of the National Register of Archives. My use of the Roberts papers throws a rather different light on one or two matters (in particular Roberts' persistent angling for a command in South Africa) from that cast by his official biographer, Mr David James. I am grateful to the officials of the Ogilby Museum and the National Register of Archives, and in particular to Mrs Lamb of the latter body, for the help they have given me. The activities and character of Lord Milner play only a small part in this book, although he would of course be one of the two or three major figures in any complete account of the War, but

I have used a little new material from the Milner Papers in New College.

Anybody who writes about the military side of the War must be in debt to the masterly *Times History of the War*, all of which was edited and much of which was written by Leopold Amery. His descriptions of military engagements are of a lucidity and brilliance that could hardly be bettered. A good deal of new information in the form of memoirs and reminiscences has become available since Amery wrote, and I have used this, but although we now know much more about individual actions and motives than we did half a century ago, Amery's general assessments of military actions seem to need very little amendment.

I have been able to find few personal papers relating to Buller, although there is some useful material, including the letter to his brother Tremayne, in the Public Record Office, which also contains Wolseley's correspondence with Sir John Ardagh. In the end, though, the character of Buller both as an individual and as a representative of the British military tradition of his era, came to stand for me at the heart of the book. Nobody in his senses could possibly try to justify Buller's military actions during the Natal campaign, but I hope that this book will show that so far from being the simple dunderhead of legend he was an intricate and interesting character.

I owe a special debt of gratitude to Mr Kenneth Griffith, for permitting me to use his extensive collection of Boer War material, including the letter from Sir Redvers Buller, and for reading the proofs.

The late Viscountess Milner took a generous and lively interest in the book, and it was through her kindness that I was allowed to examine the Milner Papers at New College.

J S

PART ONE

THE TRIUMPH OF WOLSELEY

'I never expected to reach the age of 60, and have always regarded it as the last corner round which we turn before delivering up our bodies to that most hateful of all God's creatures, the undertaker. Once round that corner you have a steep hill in front of you, but it is no longer a hill hard to climb, but a steep descent down which you go as in a toboggan. I wish I could have had one more good struggle at the uphill work before I passed the corner, but God has willed it otherwise.'

VISCOUNT WOLSELEY to his Wife,
on his sixtieth birthday, 4 June, 1893.

Chapter One *Wolseley*

In April 1895, Garnet Joseph Wolseley, Viscount Wolseley of Cairo and Wolseley, County Stafford, Field-Marshal of the British Empire, and at this time commander of the British forces in Ireland, paid a visit to London, partly for official reasons and partly to discover the truth of the rumours he had heard that the Duke of Cambridge, after spending thirty-nine years in supreme command of the British Army, was at last prepared to retire. Wolseley wrote to his wife, who was making one of the frequent visits to Germany which she paid perhaps as much to escape the tedium of life in Ireland as to take the waters: 'The Duke of Cambridge was extremely civil and said the papers were filled with stories of the Commander-in-Chief – I turned the conversation and said I had not remarked it... I think the feeling is that his reign is nearly over and I think it is generally agreed that I shall soon be in the War Office once again.'

But was it to be as simple as that? As Wolseley talked to his friends in the War Office and made a boring obligatory round of Regimental and official dinners he found no certainty that he was to be the new Commander-in-Chief, or even any assurance of the Duke's retirement. A Liberal Government was in office, and although Wolseley expressed support of no political party, he was proud to call himself a Jingo. At some times he thought of Gladstone as the dark fiend himself and at others regarded him simply as an infamous old man, 'the worst and basest of mortals'. Nor did he feel much more kindly towards the other leading Liberals. How pleasant it would be, he wrote to his wife, to sit with her upon some sunny bench and read about Caesar's passage of the Rhine. 'How delightful it is to read about the great men of the world when one has had to dine with figures like Asquith or to hear first ministers of State like Rosebery hold forth in nothings at a banquet.' Why, after all, should the Government favour a man who had openly expressed contempt for them? Wolseley returned to Ireland in one of his frequent fits of deep depression. This was a little alleviated when his wife sent him as a birthday gift a portrait of Bismarck, whom he regarded as the greatest man alive, 'the strong man, the great patriot who scoffs at cosmopolitanism, at the idolatry of human life and at all those fads and clap-trap bunkum which are the stock in trade of little politicians like Mr Gladstone'. But more often he brooded on the way in which, during the past ten years, everything seemed to have gone wrong for him, so that now, in his early sixties, he was relegated to the comparatively unimportant command in Ireland. As the days passed he became convinced that, if the Duke did retire, he would be passed over. 'If I am rejected I shall give up all thought of my profession and will take to literature.'

Happiness is a matter of temperament. Wolseley's career had been one of success almost unalloyed, yet it is doubtful if he had ever been really happy except during the course of actively fighting those campaigns of his youth and manhood in which he had expected, and even hoped, to die. Intellectually all other British soldiers of the Victorian age were pygmies compared to him. He combined a capacity for making quick and correct decisions on the field of battle with extraordinary personal courage. These qualities had brought him to the front, but it was the tactical brilliance shown in his African and Egyptian campaigns that had led to his being named, in the eighteen-seventies, 'our only General'.

The Wolseley family had a strong military tradition. A Brigadier-General Wolseley had ridden beside William III at the Battle of the Boyne, had raised a troop of cavalry called 'Wolseley's Horse', which later became the Inniskilling Dragoons, and had become Master-General of the Ordnance. Garnet Wolseley belonged to the Irish branch of this Staffordshire family, and was born in Dublin on 4 June 1883. His father was a Major, who sold out his commission because he lacked money to buy a promotion, and was sick of garrison duty in the West Indies. He died when his eldest son Garnet was seven years old, leaving little but a military legend to his wife and children. The legend would have been enough to make Garnet Wolseley a soldier, but he was moved also by a feeling that the mother whom he worshipped liked him less than she liked her other children. 'I always felt that she did not love me as she loved some of her other children,' he wrote in his old age. 'I have no doubt she had good reason for this, for I am sure I was a trial to her in many ways, but I always felt, and felt it then deeply, that I was not understood and that others were put before me.' Just before he was nineteen years old, Wolseley received an ensign's commission in the 80th Foot. There was no money to buy him a commission, but he was given it in consideration of his father's services.

Wolseley's history as a soldier up to a point resembles closely that of other Victorian military heroes. He had, as he said, a sort of manly and mad fury to rise in his profession, and this ambition was expressed by actions of extreme gallantry. Within a few months he had been shot through the upper part of the thigh in leading an assault on a stockaded village on the Irrawaddy. During the Crimean War he exposed himself so constantly in the trenches and behaved with such reckless daring that he was wounded three times within a few weeks (on the third occasion a ball lifted his forage cap from his head), and then nearly three months later was struck in the face and leg by a bursting shell. The facial wound cost him the effective sight of one eye, and caused periodical agonizing headaches, to which he found no antidote. He served in India during the Mutiny, and distinguished himself by leading an unauthorized attack on the Motee Mahal Palace in Lucknow. He was mentioned five times in despatches, and received the brevet of Lieutenant Colonel before he was twenty-seven years old.

During the sixties Colonel Wolseley spent nine years in Canada as Assistant Quartermaster-General. The military engagements in which he was involved were trivial, and he had a good deal of time on his hands. He outraged the Army tradition of his day by spending it in a deep and serious course of reading. In Canada he wrote the *Soldier's Pocket Book*, an attempt to induce soldiers to consider the problems that they would face when actually involved in war: a rudimentary enough compendium, as it seems now, but in its day a revolutionary document. It was as a direct result of this publication that Mr Cardwell, the recently-appointed Secretary of State for War, invited Wolseley to become Assistant Adjutant-General at the War Office, and so began his quarter-century battle with the Duke of Cambridge.

George Frederick William, second Duke of Cambridge, had been placed in supreme command of all British forces in 1856, after the disastrous Crimean War. A burly, pepper-tongued but basically amiable man, he was deeply attached to ceremonial parades, field days, and glamorous uniforms. The high point of the year came for the Duke, not at any kind of manoeuvre, for no organized manoeuvres were held in the British Army for years under his régime, but in what was called 'Duke's inspection'. On this annual occasion the Guards battalions formed up in Hyde Park in review order, facing Park Lane. The Duke moved on to the ground and was received with a Royal salute. Various complicated evolutions were performed, and they were succeeded by a brigade attack upon an imaginary enemy, who was always to be found along the Bayswater Road. To defeat him hundreds of bear-skinned Guardsmen deployed across the park at the double, driving crowds of spectators before them, and firing the five blank rounds issued to each man. The show ended with bayonet exercise in quick time, two or three thousand bayonets flashing as one. Then the Duke congratulated the commanding officers and everybody went home, the officers to 'first leave' which lasted from the end of July until the end of November. It was a gentleman's army in those days.

Wolseley annoyed the Duke by his frequent failure to attend Duke's inspection, which was, he said often and clearly, a complete waste of time. The Duke, for his part, delighted the old guard of Army officers by referring scornfully at dinners to the apostles of 'Pwogwess' (he had a little trouble with his r's). He was greatly concerned to preserve all possible power for the Commander-in-Chief, and distrusted any change in organization. Every change under his regime, the Duke said once, had been made at the right time, and the right time was when the change could no longer be avoided. The Duke's objectives were, quite simply, not to give way

6

upon any point of organization or procedure, because it was self-evident that all changes must tend to destroy the Army's traditions and its independence. The removal of Army headquarters from the Horse Guards to Pall Mall, where it was under one roof with the War Office, is one of many instances in which a reform completely justified in the sense that it helped to make Army organization more efficient, was opposed by the Duke because he feared that it would have the effect of weakening the Army as an independent force. He expressed his 'grave objections' in 'the most forcible manner in my power' to the move. He called the change a degradation, pleaded that it was quite easy to send messengers from the Horse Guards to Pall Mall, even offered to stroll down himself and have a chat with the civilian authorities at the War Office when necessary. All in vain. He was compelled, in 1871, to suffer degradation and move to Pall Mall, where he complained continually of the discomfort and awkwardness of his quarters.

A great impulsion was given to Cardwell's reforms by the Franco-Prussian War. The Prussian military system, with its short service conscript Army and its emphasis on the importance of a General Staff, became a model for study by all advanced military thinkers in this country. Cardwell gathered such thinkers round him as his advisers, and Wolseley soon emerged as, intellectually at least, the chief among them. His own eventual objectives were far from being identical with Cardwell's, but at this time the problems of Army reform were urgent, while those of the Army's possible subordination to the civil power seemed much more distant. The reforms upon which Cardwell concentrated were the abolition of the system by which officers purchased their commissions, the establishment of a short service system more elaborate and ingenious than the Prussian, and of course devised upon a voluntary basis, and the organization of enlistment in terms of districts, with the country divided into twelve separate commands. All of these reforms were strongly opposed by the Duke, and all were enacted, after bitter struggles, with more or less success.

The system by which young men paid cash for their commissions and sold them to the highest bidder when they wished to leave the Army, was not only unjust but also a cause of appalling inefficiency.

A Lieutenant or Captain who had no money to buy further preferment might be senior to every other officer in his regiment. A man who had the money to put down could buy himself a Lieutenant-Colonelcy, and although the prices were officially fixed – at £14,000 for a Lieutenant-Colonelcy in the Cavalry and half of that in a Regiment of the line – those prepared to pay a premium could usually get what they wanted. The Duke himself found it difficult to defend such a system, but he was opposed to any change because he thought that 'however theoretically objectionable, it has worked favourably in the interests of the Service'. The other innovations, however, were resented not only by the Duke, but by the majority of the Army's officers. This was particularly true of the system devised by a 'Localisation Committee' set up by the Government, through which many of the Infantry Line Regiments were linked with others, and named by districts instead of by numbers. Several Regiments lost their identities altogether, or were merged with others and so deprived of their particular dress and facings. The linking was done with care, and a real attempt was made to preserve Regimental traditions, but the change caused deep and lasting anger, which was directed chiefly against Wolseley. Nothing better could have been expected of a civilian Secretary of State for War, but Wolseley seemed to many officers nothing less than a traitor to his own kind, a man bent upon destroying the Army in pursuit of personal power. There was enough truth in the criticisms to make them strike home. Like many reformers conscious that right is on their side, Wolseley identified his cause with his own leadership of it. When, in 1873, he was chosen to lead an expedition against King Koffee of the Ashantis, he carefully selected thirty-five young officers to accompany him. There was an aloofness, a detachment, about Wolseley that forbade any demonstration of affection even upon the part of those who considered themselves his close friends, but almost all of these officers regarded him with admiration tinged with awe. They were the instruments by which he moved towards power, the men he would push forward at any turn into positions of importance. They were known as the Ashanti Ring, the Wolseley Ring, even at last the Wolseley gang, and some of their names, like those of Lieutenant-

Colonel Evelyn Wood, Captain Redvers Buller and Captain William Butler, will recur in this book.

Almost all of the Colonial wars in Queen Victoria's time impress us by their triviality. The troops engaged never numbered more than a few thousand, they were opposed by natives whose arms were spears and old-fashioned rifles, and whose idea of tactics rarely went beyond a series of direct frontal charges. It would have been difficult not to defeat such enemies, and it seems surprising that these encounters should have carried with them much glory for the victor. But such thoughts ignore the strength of Victorian belief in the civilizing mission of the British Empire. By many people in Britain it was accepted as a matter of course that a Briton was superior in every way to a man of any other nation. They might not feel, as Wolseley did, that they would be perfectly indifferent if every Frenchman died tomorrow, but they certainly regarded themselves as being almost as much superior to Frenchmen and Russians as they were to Zulus and Kaffirs. It followed that the speedy triumph achieved over King Koffee was greeted with as much enthusiasm as would have been a victory over a European army. When Wolseley returned to Britain the Queen reviewed his troops at Windsor, the House of Commons gave him a grant of £25,000, both Oxford and Cambridge conferred honorary degrees upon him, and he was entertained by the Lord Mayor at the Guildhall. He received a KCB and was promoted Major-General. The honours were absurdly disproportionate to the achievement, which had consisted chiefly in the efficient organization of transport. They reflected a national desire to create the myth of a great general. It was not long before Wolseley was called 'our only general', meaning the only one certain of success in the field. It was a label he was not inclined to reject, and during the decade that followed he was always victorious, subduing a Bantu tribe in Natal, putting the finishing touches to the Zulu Wars (although the vital victory at Ulundi which marked the end of serious fighting was won, to his annoyance, by the general he had come to replace, Lord Chelmsford), and routing the army of Arabi in Egypt, by means of a brilliant and spectacular night attack at Tel-el-Kebir. This three weeks' campaign, a miniature modern *blitzkrieg*, brought him a barony and a grant of £30,000.

Wolseley had reached his position in the face of almost continuous hostility from the Duke, who had two main grounds of complaint, the first purely military and the second partly political. Knowing that a frontal attack on the Horse Guards' citadel had no chance of success, Wolseley often tried to circumvent his adversary's move in advance by presenting him with an accomplished fact or appointment. The Duke was justifiably annoyed when without consulting him the Cabinet put Wolseley in command at the time of the Zulu Wars, angrier still when he discovered that Wolseley had arranged for a group from the 'ring' to accompany him on the expedition. Wolseley reacted with characteristic sharpness when he was rebuked. 'I am not the Pope, and like all other men, must therefore make mistakes occasionally, but as a rule I am tolerably successful in my selection,' he wrote. The Duke replied with unwonted mildness: 'I cannot see that the public service is benefited by our going out of our way to put some officers permanently forward on all occasions, when there are others available quite equal to perform good service also.' His criticism of the short service system was revived at this time, when he found that Wolseley would have to rely on the raw young soldiers who had recently been enlisted, since many of the long service troops had gone into the Army Reserve. He accused Wolseley of ruining the morale of the Army by his 'damned newfangled methods'. The letters sent back by the successful commander must have added to his irritation:

> I am sure Your Royal Highness will be glad to hear from one who had commanded and personally led the soldiers under the old system and under our existing organization, that I have never seen our men steadier in action than they were last Friday.

A few weeks later the intransigent Wolseley was threatening to resign because the war was to be deemed to have ended with the battle of Ulundi, and the Zululand clasp was to be restricted to men engaged in activities up to that time. This, he said, was a personal insult. 'No honours or rewards would ever compensate me for a loss of military reputation, and as I cannot sit quiet under a General

Order emanating from Your Royal Highness which would sensibly damage that reputation, it will be necessary for me to return home without delay.' About this, too, the Duke gave way, but his complaints to his cousin the Queen were frequent and bitter. Was not Wolseley perfectly insufferable? The Queen consulted Disraeli. 'It is quite true that Wolseley is an egoist and a braggart. So was Nelson,' he replied, and a little later he wrote to Lady Bradford: 'Nothing can give you an idea of the jealousy, hatred, and all uncharitableness of the Horse Guards against our only soldier.'

The Duke was constantly irritated also by Wolseley's use of the press to make his views known in relation to any matter over which he had suffered temporary defeat. In this, as in so many other things, Wolseley was a soldier much in advance of his time. He believed, as he told a surprised young friend, Lord Melgund, that 'the press has become a power, which a man should try to manage for himself, that it is an influence, which one cannot deny, and therefore should try to make one's own'. The articles Wolseley wrote often gave deep offence to the Duke and when, in 1881, another Liberal Secretary of State for War, Childers, proposed that Wolseley should be appointed Adjutant-General, the Duke said positively that he could not recommend the appointment. The Queen, advised by the Duke, said that it would really never do. Childers insisted, and Wolseley had a long interview with the Duke in which he denied that he had inspired recent press criticism of the Commander-in-Chief and retorted by complaining of his own treatment. 'His Royal Highness has showered good things upon others round me: every appointment *I* get, every honour *I* receive, I am made to feel comes to me from other quarters than from the Commander-in-Chief to whom I would fain look for some recognition of my services, but I have hitherto looked in vain.' The Duke, without expressing positive approval of Wolseley, gave way again and accepted him.

The Queen's distrust of Wolseley had been much modified by his praise of the conduct of her son, Arthur Duke of Connaught, in the Egyptian campaign, and even more by Arthur's warm appreciation of Wolseley. Perhaps, she suggested, 'this *really* great General' would be tactful in future, and would refrain from making injudicious speeches. 'His friends should warn him against this!' The Duke agreed that Wolseley could be pleasant enough when he wished to be. 'His great fault is that he is so *very ambitious*, and that he has only a certain number of officers in whom he has any real confidence. If we could only modify these two feelings, he would be of twice the value he is to his country.'

For the time being, Wolseley's reputation was so great that little could be done against him. 'All Sir Garnet' became a Cockney phrase for all correct, and in the first London production of *The Pirates of Penzance* George Grossmith appeared in a garb unmistakably Wolseleyan, wearing the famous waxed moustaches that he adopted at this time, and sang:

> I am the very pattern of a modern Major-General,
> I've information vegetable, animal and mineral;
> I know the Kings of England, I quote the fights historical,
> From Marathon to Waterloo, in order categorical.

If Wolseley was to achieve his ambition – and there is no doubt that from the beginning of the eighteen-eighties he regarded the succession to the post of Commander-in-Chief as belonging rightly to him and to him alone – it was essential that he should succeed in everything he undertook. Any failure would raise up against him not only those who disliked the increasing power of the Wolseley Ring, nor the Indian Army officers who blamed Wolseley and his henchmen for the neglect they suffered when any important promotion was in question, nor those who suffered from the sharp tongue that, in the presence of friends, called the Duke the Great German Sausage: perhaps his most potent enemies were to be found among those politicians and men of affairs who, admiring his military talents, found his egotism intolerable and his social pretensions ridiculous. The Wolseleys lived and entertained upon a scale quite incommensurate with the lack of a private fortune, and in spite of those handsome grants from the House of Commons, they were often in need of money. The failure of the Gordon Relief Expedition, with Wolseley at its head, gave his enemies the chance they needed.

No doubt the delay of the Liberal Government in sending out any sort of expedition for the relief of Gordon was inexcusable, yet Wolseley's planning was so much that of a man who conceived the operation as a kind of display that could be used for his own glorification that he must bear a part of the blame. With memories of the Red River Expedition, which he had successfully undertaken in Canada long ago, he insisted on going up the Nile in boats, rather than marching across the desert to Berber as all the local experts advised. He sent to Canada for a group of the *voyageurs* who had helped to get through the rapids sixteen years before. Ian Hamilton wrote afterwards, ironically, that nobody but Wolseley could, in the days of railways, have persuaded cautious Liberal politicians to revert to the methods of the ninth century by going up the Nile in boats. The River Column, however, was only a minor feature of the Expedition. When the boats had passed the Third Cataract and reached Korti, a land force mounted on camels was to make a dash across the desert to relieve Gordon at Khartoum. This Camel Corps was made up of assorted officers and men from various favoured Regiments, in direct contradiction of all the tenets adhered to by the Duke, who bitterly resented this idea of skimming the cream from various Cavalry Regiments. Such a blending of irreconcilables confirmed the Duke in his view that Wolseley had no understanding of military tradition. And of course the officers chosen to command were all members of the Ring: Colonel Redvers Buller, Chief of the Staff, Grenfell, Brackenbury, Butler, Ardagh, Grove, Stewart, Wood. Ian Hamilton, an Indian Army officer who was determined to take part in the Expedition, managed to get to Cairo, and there saw Ardagh, who was Base Commandant. The interview went well until Ardagh learned that Hamilton was on the personal staff of Sir Frederick Roberts, Commander-in-Chief of the Indian Army. Then Ardagh, monocled and generally imperturbable, looked distressed. 'You won't mind if I speak plainly,' he said. 'I fear you might be regarded as an intruder.' But when a wire was sent to Buller, he agreed that Hamilton should be attached to the Gordons. Perhaps the Ring was not so inflexible as the Indian Army officers thought it.

The failure of the Expedition, and its subsequent withdrawal by the Government, is a story many times told. Different reasons have been found for it at different times: Buller's neglect in failing to keep sufficient camels in readiness for the Desert Column; the fact that control of the Desert Column passed to Sir Charles Wilson, a 'political' rather than a fighting General, after the deaths of Herbert Stewart and the dashing Burnaby; a similar neglect of the importance of a fighting General in relation to the River Column when General Brackenbury, a brilliant bureaucrat, was allowed to succeed General Earle, and sounded 'Retreat' instead of 'Advance'. Wolseley himself sent a famous memorandum direct to Lord Hartington, in which he complained that there were serving under him some regimental Lieutenant-Colonels who were entirely unfit for their positions, 'men who, although entrusted by Regulations with the command of over 800 soldiers of all ranks, could not, with due regard for the lives of these soldiers and the honour and interest of the State, be allowed any independent command before an enemy'. He used the occasion for an eloquent plea that Army promotion should no longer be automatically by seniority, but should be made through selection boards. The move would be supported, he said, by 'the young, the able, and the vigorous throughout the services'; and, with them on one side, why should administrators fear the complaints of those not allowed 'to learn the first rudiments of war at the expense of the lives of the gallant soldiers who have the misfortune to be under their command' on the other? But however blame should be apportioned, the Expedition's failure had the effect of destroying the image of Wolseley as infallible. On the surface all remained as it had been. Wolseley was still Adjutant-General, he still warred with the Duke about the importance of full military training, published outspoken articles which brought rebukes, threatened resignation. His friends moved further up the ladder of power, Evelyn Wood being placed in command at Aldershot, Brackenbury taking on the Intelligence Department which Wolseley had induced the Duke to enlarge, Buller becoming Adjutant-General when, in 1890, Wolseley accepted the Irish command. Yet the Great German Sausage presided still over the Army's affairs, and now found it much more easy to resist suggested reforms. Even the minor reforms Wolseley suggested in cutting down the unnecessarily large staff in Ireland and in attempting to modernize the Yeomanry proved unacceptable. The Duke was prepared, he said, to tell the Yeomanry to attend more to their carbines than to their swords, but any attempt to turn them into Mounted Infantry would take all the heart out of them. 'I am afraid you don't believe in *sentiment*, but I do so *strongly*, especially in military matters,' he said sadly.

In this the Duke was wrong. Behind Wolseley's exterior of ice and iron was a deep sentiment for martial glory, and an endless longing for love which found almost its sole expression in the letters he wrote to his wife, whom he addressed as his dearest Snipe or his little Runterfoozle. They were separated during several months of the year, when he was on manoeuvres or visiting military establishments and she was taking the waters in Germany or staying with friends, and at these times he wrote her long letters every day. 'You are the only person I have ever known except my mother who did not bore me,' he wrote to her once and in these letters, by turns loving, ironical and bitter, some of them decorated with little drawings like that showing the broad-bottomed Prince of Wales seated on an even broader-bottomed horse at the Aldershot review ('A chair was produced to enable him to mount at the saluting point, to which he had driven in a carriage'), Wolseley put down his thoughts about the present and future of Britain, and dissected his own life and errors. He wrote with the ardour of a man who longed for military glory, combined with the arrogance of an intellectual conscious that his gifts have never been fully used. He was glad that she wept on Trafalgar Day, and confessed that he had piped his own eye. Often he told her of his regret that he had not died as he had hoped in battle, 'in the open air with my face to some enemy of England's'. What was left to him now but the dull routine of Army life? His defeat had been caused only in part, he thought, by the ignorant obstruction of the Great German Sausage. The politicians who had frustrated and tricked him were also to blame, and beyond the politicians, beyond even the wickedness and treachery of Gladstone, Wolseley found that his defeat had been caused by the cosmopolitan vulgarity of British life. 'Vulgar' was his final word of condemnation, and it was comprehensively used. Words like *wee* and *bonny* were vulgar – why could English people not say *small* and *pretty*? Radicals were vulgar fellows. Horse racing was a cruel and vulgar sport. A preference for town over country life was vulgar, and most vulgar of all was the kind of life lived by the upper class in society:

> The ordinary, I may call it the vulgar life of the English best class of society is odious to all people of thought and refinement who are not thorough-paced snobs... It is horrible to say so, but I feel that a country living under our present form of Government and whose classes, that is the rich as well as the old county families, live as the Prince of Wales and all his abominable set of men and women do, can only be saved from annihilation by some such periodical upheaval as a great war.

Brooding, in the draughty Royal Hospital, Dublin, the heart of hateful Ireland, on his mistakes and defeats, he thought that such a war would not come in his lifetime.

Chapter Two *Roberts*

It will be understood that the prospect of the Duke's retirement gave new hope to Wolseley. The vision of personal power, and the prospect of moving back from Irish exile, excited him deeply. He longed for authentic news, and as the first flushes of certainty and despair faded, began seriously to assess the prospects of the various candidates for office. There were three besides himself: the Queen's son, Arthur, Duke of Connaught, Buller – who was now a General and Sir Redvers – and Lord Roberts, who had come home in 1893, after forty-one years' Indian service, as Commander-in-Chief of the Indian Army. Of these Wolseley in his mind brushed aside the Duke of Connaught, forgetting both the strength of the Queen's feeling that the Commander-in-Chief should be directly linked with the Royal family and the fact that, desperate to get the Duke of Cambridge out of the way, he had himself a few months earlier proposed the Duke of Connaught's appointment. Would it be his own protegé Buller, who as Adjutant-General was in a very strong position? Or would it be, could it possibly be, Roberts? The very possibility was almost more than he could contemplate.

'If Buller be fairly selected to supersede me without any scheming on his part I should of course accept this selection as one I could not cavil at,' he wrote to his wife. 'But to be superseded by a man older than myself, as Roberts is, and by a man of whose abilities I have a poor opinion is trying indeed... It is the venom of possible defeat which I am sure rankles more in my mind at present, and defeat by a man whom I know to be a very inferior fellow.'

He went on trying to get some news of the Government's intentions through his correspondents in London, but without success.

In the meantime Roberts, unemployed and on half-pay, was chafing in his home at Grove Park, near Hendon, almost as sorely as Wolseley. The antagonism between them sprang originally from the widespread feeling among Indian Army officers that the Wolseley men at the War Office denied them promotion whenever possible. When, for example, Ian Hamilton was chosen by Roberts to be his Assistant Military Secretary, and the Duke of Cambridge refused to confirm the appointment, Hamilton laid the blame on Redvers Buller, whom he regarded as the Ring's evil genius. In course of time there came to be a Roberts Ring, which was set up in opposition to the Wolseleyites. There was this difference between them: that Wolseley had deliberately organized his Ring as a means of favouring certain officers and obtaining personal power, whereas the Roberts Ring was set up by the officers themselves, no doubt with Roberts' consent but without his active co-operation. There was the difference, also, that during the eighties and nineties the Wolseleyites had all the trump cards in their hands.

Lord Melgund, who was friendly with both men, confided optimistically to his Journal the hope that he might introduce them to each other, and that they might become friends. 'It will do much good if they show that there is room in the world for two great men, and that though they may differ in opinion they are at any rate above petty jealousies,' he wrote. 'Both men are very much to be admired: Wolseley, I should say, the better read of the two, very agreeable and the best of friends; but with all his good fellowship I never think he inspires the individual love of everyone as Roberts does... The men worship Roberts. I doubt if they care much for Wolseley personally.' Melgund never effected this introduction, but had he done so it is most unlikely that his purpose would have been achieved, for Wolseley felt a dislike, and almost hatred, of Roberts, which finds frequent expression in his letters. Partly, no doubt, this sprang from Roberts' opposition to many of the Wolseley-Cardwell reforms, including short service and the idea of linked battalions, and from the fact that the two men advocated different policies in

18

relation to India. The conditions of Indian service were very different from those in the Home Army, and it is likely that Roberts did not clearly understand the need for a reserve of trained soldiers which was so apparent to Wolseley. Shortly after his return from India, Roberts also became an advocate of short service. But it is difficult to escape the conclusion that the prime cause of Wolseley's dislike was jealousy of Roberts' increasing fame. Many years earlier he had written to Melgund, 'I have watched Roberts' career now for a long time, and I'll tell you what it is, he is a very fine fellow.' That, however, had been before Roberts' famous march from Kabul to Kandahar, and before he had become known as 'our only other General'. When Roberts came home from India he was fêted by the press in a way that must have been peculiarly galling to Wolseley. Kipling's ballad, published soon after his return as Baron Roberts of Kandahar, both expressed and enhanced the feeling of a Victorian public always alert for a hero:

> Now they've made a bloomin' Lord
> > Outer Bobs,
> Which was but 'is fair reward –
> > Weren't it, Bobs?
> So 'e'll wear a coronet
> Where 'is 'elmet used to set;
> But we know you won't forget –
> > Will yer, Bobs?

> Then 'ere's to little Bobs Bahadur – little Bobs,
> > > Bobs, Bobs
> > Pocket-Wellington an arder –
> > Fightin' Bobs, Bobs, Bobs!
> > This ain't no bloomin' ode,
> > But you've 'elped the soldier's load,
> > An' for benefits bestowed,
> > > Bless yer, Bobs!

There is no indication that Roberts reciprocated Wolseley's dislike, although he had some reason to feel slighted. After the

Ashanti War Wolseley had been given £25,000 and received promotion; after the Afghan campaign Roberts was given half that sum, without a promotion. In 1889 he had been offered the Adjutant General's post, and then the offer had been withdrawn because the Prime Minister, Lord Salisbury, refused to let the Duke of Connaught take over the Indian command. At the end of his time as Commander-in-Chief in India he had hoped to be appointed Viceroy, and was bitterly disappointed when this post went to Lord Elgin. Instead, when the noise of his return had died down, he was offered the badly paid and comparatively unimportant position of Governor of Malta or Gibraltar. Roberts, like Wolseley, was without private means. He replied that he could not afford to take up either post, and in the course of an interview with the Secretary of State for War, Campbell-Bannerman, complained that it seemed clear from the manner towards him both of the Duke of Cambridge and of Buller, that there was no intention of employing him. He said that he was very reluctant to accept the peerage offered him, and that unless his pay was somehow increased he would not be able to live in London or even to attend the House of Lords. Campbell-Bannerman was sympathetic. Would Roberts like to be a Field-Marshal? Roberts said that he would, but that he primarily wanted employment. He asked for Aldershot, which was the most important and influential position outside the Horse Guards. But the Duke of Connaught again proved an insurmountable obstacle. The Queen was determined that her son should have the Aldershot command, and Roberts was told by Campbell-Bannerman that the officer in command there was 'peculiarly at the beck and call of the officers at Head Quarters', and that one who had been Commander-in-Chief in his own right must not be exposed to this humiliation. Roberts might have appreciated this solicitude more had it been accompanied by the offer of some more lucrative and important post than Malta or Gibraltar. He ignored Campbell-Bannerman's strong recommendation that he should accept one or other of these, and found himself unemployed and apparently unemployable. He was made a Field-Marshal in 1895, a year after Wolseley.

Roberts had been determined from childhood to become a soldier, and he had overcome the handicaps of his own extreme smallness, of much ill health in adolescence and of the loss of sight in one eye in childhood through illness. In many ways he was a model of what a soldier, or indeed any man, should be. His temper was gentle, his patience exemplary, his observation keen. His own habits were temperate, and he was a supporter of Army temperance organizations. To alleviate the boredom, which he saw as the prime cause of heavy drinking in the army, he provided recreation rooms and relaxed routine restrictions for the men under his command. The men liked him, and those who were on his staff truly loved him. He was 'so charming, so considerate, so even in his temper', that he commanded a degree of personal allegiance from his staff far greater than that of any other British soldier in his time. He was a much pleasanter man than Wolseley, but only as a field commander was he Wolseley's equal. His intellectual powers can hardly be mentioned in the same breath with those shown equally in Wolseley's private letters and official minutes, nor did he have the far-seeing intelligence that made Wolseley remark that in a century's time the future of the world might rest with America and China. He lacked, too, the capacity for imaginative large-scale organization in which Wolseley was unique in the British Army of the period. His personality was flexible rather than strong, and although Wolseley was wrong in saying that Roberts' only talent was for self-advertisement (nor was he the man to say it), certainly he did obtain a good deal of publicity through the activities of his ambitious staff officers.

The most pertinacious of these was Colonel William Nicholson, who had been for three years Roberts' Military Secretary. The strange Army career of this able administrator reached its culmination when in 1911 he, who had never commanded a unit in peace or war, was made a Field-Marshal for the part he had played in reorganizing the Army. But this was a far distant prospect in the early nineties for a Nicholson home on leave, bitterly discontented with his lot, and determined to obtain promotion or throw up the Army altogether. From his home, at the centre of things in Hove, Nicholson sent to Roberts at Grove Park a stream of letters analysing the situation in relation to Wolseley, Cambridge, Connaught, Buller, passing on rumours he had heard from junior figures at the Horse Guards, freely conjecturing about motives and attributing always the most sinister intentions to the political and military figures in power.

The Court, Nicholson told Roberts, wanted Wolseley as Commander-in-Chief for five years. He would then be succeeded by the Duke of Connaught. The object of the military authorities would be 'to relegate your Lordship to some post where you will have as little power and responsibility as possible'. One cunning stroke might be the offer to him of the Irish command, which he should be very chary of accepting. Or possibly – the number of possibilities struck Nicholson as almost infinite – Roberts might be offered the post of Adjutant-General, or Chief of the Staff under Wolseley. Should he accept? Perhaps not. 'Your Lordship might prefer not to be brought into close official association with Wolseley.' Then again, he might be asked to serve under the Duke of Connaught. 'I see no great objection to this provided you are the Chief of the Staff, and the virtual head of the Army.' And what about Buller? Nicholson had heard that neither Buller nor Evelyn Wood, who was now Quartermaster-General, wanted to see Wolseley in power. In a letter to a famous military correspondent named Spenser Wilkinson, who favoured the Roberts ring, he attributed a cunning plan to Buller:

'Buller is personally on friendly terms with Campbell-Bannerman. His plan is that his own tenure of the Adjutant-Generalship should be extended from 1 October for two years, and that he should then be succeeded by Evelyn Wood. Wolseley would become unemployed on 1 October 1895, and be succeeded in the Irish Command by Roberts. When the favourable moment arrives, the Duke of Connaught would replace his uncle as C-in-C. By this means Roberts and Wolseley would be practically shelved, the real power would remain in the hands of the present Horse Guards clique, and the Royal family would retain control over the Army.'

Nicholson's inveterate pushing of Roberts' cause, and his attempt to get 'inspired' articles into the press, at last became an embarrassment to Roberts, who wrote to Spenser Wilkinson:

I have never had occasion to ask for an appointment, and I would not for the world do anything myself; or ask my friends to do anything to help me in the future. I should like to go to the Horse Guards because I think I would do some good for the Army, but if I am not to be made Adjutant General, well and good. I shall be quite happy and contented.

It was not quite true that Roberts had never asked for an appointment. He had asked for the Aldershot Command, and was to ask for other appointments too. But if he thought that it was useless to stake a claim this time, he was right. The appointment of the new Commander-in-Chief had already been settled by Lord Rosebery's Liberal Government.

Chapter Three *The Government's Defeat*

The paradox has already been observed by which Wolseley, working for Army reform, found his allies most often among Liberals who had in their minds the very different end of transferring control of the Army from the military to the civil power. A Commission set up in 1888 under the presidency of Lord Hartington recommended that the post of Commander-in-Chief should be abolished, and that his functions should be carried out by a Chief of the Staff who would be chief military adviser to the Secretary of State for War, an Adjutant-General responsible for discipline, training and education, a Quartermaster-General handling supplies and transport, a Director of Artillery and an Inspector of Fortifications. The Chief of the Staff would have no access to the Cabinet, and effective control of the Army would pass completely into civilian hands.

The Duke of Cambridge, however, was an immovable pillar in the way of the Hartington reforms, which in any case had not been recommended unanimously by the Commission. Nothing could be done while he remained Commander-in-Chief, and he reacted coldly to suggestions that it was time for him to move into the shadows of retirement. In 1895 the Duke was only seventy-six years old. He felt himself to be in the prime of life and perfectly able to carry out his duties, and he responded to the request that he should retire (for the suggestions at last became a request) by demanding that if attacks were made upon him in the House, the Government should be called upon to defend him. Queen Victoria was intent both to preserve the position of Commander-in-Chief as nearly intact as possible, and also to ensure that it should pass to her son. She was distressed to be told by Rosebery that he thought it undesirable for one member of the Royal family to succeed another. The Duke of Connaught was, no doubt, Rosebery tactfully said, the right person, but he thought it better that the Duke of Cambridge's successor should be Sir Redvers Buller, and then – the Queen noted in her Journal – 'after three or four years Arthur would be hailed with acclamation.' Reluctantly she agreed, but she asked for an assurance that the Duke of Connaught would not later be debarred from office. Rosebery replied in terms more dextrous than reassuring: his own opinion, and that of Campbell-Bannerman, he said, was that the later chances of the Duke of Connaught would be positively improved by the intermediate appointment of Buller to succeed the Duke of Cambridge. Everything seemed to be settled. Lieutenant-Colonel Bigge (later Lord Stamfordham), who had recently been appointed Private Secretary to the Queen, went down to Aldershot and explained things to the Duke of Connaught, who was 'dignified and sensible'. His wife, a greater realist, said that it was now or never, and she was no doubt right in thinking that the Liberal Government intended that it should be never. Campbell-Bannerman, Buller and the Duke of Cambridge talked the whole thing over, and the Duke, although he would not resign, agreed to 'give up office' at the Queen's request, and to recommend Buller as his successor. The Queen wrote an 'as painful to me as it is to you' letter to dear George, and her dutiful cousin George replied with great pain and deep sorrow.

This was in mid-May, and Rosebery and Campbell-Bannerman must have congratulated themselves on having got rid at last of the Great German Sausage. Not at all. Three weeks later the Duke rebelled against the politicians who had thought him finally disposed of. He refused to accept a statement drafted for his signature in which it was said that he 'desired' to resign, and made it perfectly clear that he did not want to resign at all. Rosebery described their correspondence as 'painful', and begged off a dinner which he was to attend, and at which the Duke was also to be present. But the thing was to be done, and the Queen had now become impatient and was prepared to do it. 'Think Duke wrong not to have retired some years ago, and that it is undignified to cling to office,' she said in a cypher telegram to Bigge. And in reply to a telegram in which Bigge asked whether she would approve informally of Buller, as both Rosebery and the Duke favoured him, she wired back: 'Approve of Sir R Buller.'

On 21 June Campbell-Bannerman rose in the House of Commons to announce the Duke's retirement, which was to take effect from 1 October. He could not, he said, make the announcement without emotion. He would try to disengage himself 'from the influence of his most attractive personality, and from the power he possesses beyond most men of winning for himself the regard, I would say even the affection, of those with whom he is brought into contact'. Campbell-Bannerman would not even mention, he said, the Duke's technical attainments and his extraordinary familiarity with all the details of the military profession, but he must speak of the common sense and knowledge of the world which had enabled the Duke to avoid jealousy, difficulty and general friction during his thirty-nine years' reign. The speech, a model of untruthful propriety, gave great pleasure to both the Queen and the Duke. About the name of the Duke's successor, Campbell-Bannerman was tantalizingly reticent. He was asked whether the appointment was to be 'an ornamental one' given to 'a person who had little experience in war', but to this hit at the Duke of Connaught he made no reply. The announcement had been made as preliminary to a debate on the Army Estimates, and St John Brodrick, the Unionist member for West Surrey, now rose and attacked the dangerously low state of the country's small arm ammunition. There was, he said, practically no reserve of it. We were drifting into a position of grave national danger, and he moved to reduce the salary of the Secretary of State for War by £100. In spite of Campbell-Bannerman's assurance, given in terms worthy of Ramsay MacDonald, that the ammunition reserve was 'better this year than last, better last year than it had been the year before, and would be considerably better at the end of the financial year than it was now', the Government unexpectedly lost the Division by 132 votes to 125. On the following day they resigned.

Buller's appointment had not been announced because the Cabinet considered that too long a period would elapse between the announcement and the Duke's retirement, and that this might prove embarrassing both to Buller and the Duke. The fact that he had been chosen and approved was known only to the Cabinet, and to the circle around the Queen. Nothing irreversible had been done. The incoming government of Lord Salisbury could make their own choice. The only military men who knew the secret were Buller and the Duke of Cambridge, and they kept close counsel.

Chapter Four *Buller*

In 1895 Redvers Henry Buller was at the height of his power and influence in the British Army. He had been Adjutant-General for five years, after three years as Quartermaster-General, and it was known that the Duke found his personality sympathetic, and greatly relied upon him. It would be too much to say that Buller was the effective Commander-in-Chief, but in almost all important matters relating to Army organization he got his own way. This disciple of Wolseley exerted more power in the Horse Guards than his master had ever achieved, and it is strange that neither Wolseley nor Roberts' correspondents should have realized how likely it was that the appointment would go to the man in possession.

Buller was six years younger than Wolseley, seven years younger than Roberts, and the gap in age made him seem of a different generation. He was differentiated also by the fact that his father was a wealthy Devonshire squire and his mother a Howard and the niece of the Duke of Norfolk, where Wolseley's father was a penniless Major and Roberts' an Indian Army General, who managed to send his son to Eton and Sandhurst, but was able to give him little financial support thereafter, so that he was never free from debt until he became a Major-General. James Wentworth Buller was a Liberal Member of Parliament and a staunch Free Trader, who represented Exeter in 1830, lost his seat in 1835 because of the unpopularity of his anti-Corn Law views, and regained a place in Parliament twenty-two years later as member for the Northern Division of Devon. Like his father young Redvers prided himself on his independence, got on well with working people, and expressed himself with a bluntness regarded by many as being simply rude.

The Buller family were eleven in number, and Redvers was the second of seven sons. He grew up in a tight family circle, with a shy father who took very seriously his duties as squire of Downes, and a simple and pious mother. James Buller was in Victorian terms an ideal landlord, one who took great care for his tenants' welfare, rebuilt their cottages when they were in bad condition, and was said to know every tenant's character and the number of his children. His wife, although a member of the great Catholic Howard family, was a strict Evangelical, who founded a Free School and paid the teacher's salaries out of her own income. A powerful atmosphere of loving piety expressed through good works surrounded the children, and certainly left a mark upon Redvers. Within the limits of this piety the young Bullers had a good deal of freedom, and Redvers became known at home as formidable in argument, not from the logic with which his case was put, but from the persistence of his advocacy. The common Victorian process of beating obstinacy and disobedience out of children began for him at the age of seven, when he was sent to a private school presided over by a master who walked about the classroom flicking the boys with a driving whip. At this school Redvers was 'thrashed within an inch of his life' for ringing all the doorbells in a street; he was invited to leave the family school, Harrow, after some trouble about painting several doors red; and, sent from Harrow to Eton, survived the rest of his schooldays without conspicuous trouble or any particular distinction. He remained a thickset red-faced country bumpkin, whose significant life was spent during the holidays at Downes, where he learnt carpentry and worked in the smithy. From early childhood he had been called by the family Murad the Unlucky, because of his propensity to accidents, and when he was seventeen he cut his leg so badly when lopping a branch from a tree, that the local doctor wanted to amputate it. Redvers refused, and retained the leg, although from that time onwards his movements were always slightly hampered.

When Redvers was sixteen, his mother died. She was taken ill at the Exeter railway station, St David's, and remained in a bed at the station waiting room for three days, during which it is said that Redvers stayed beside her, until her death. Six months later his sister Julia, the only girl in the family older than Redvers, died. He had been devoted both to his mother and his sister, and their deaths played an important part in moulding his character. The Bullers were not a military family, although there was a distant cousin who had become a General and a grand-uncle who had been commander of the 27th Foot. A sense of loneliness and isolation, rather than a positive desire for glory, was probably responsible for his decision to join the Army. He became an Ensign in the 60th Rifles on 4 July 1858, and of course there was plenty of money available to buy his commission.

Redvers Buller made, on the whole, an unfavourable impression upon those who knew him in the first years of his Army life. They found him a country clodhopper, raw and brash, and a clodhopper who did not acknowledge inferiority, but having once got an idea into his bullet head, argued interminably for it, unmoved by the fact that he was contradicting his seniors. They did not care for his little eyes, with their hint of furious temper, and they may have found something comic in the fact that his speech was rendered slightly indistinct after his front teeth had been knocked out by a kick in the mouth from a horse. His fellow subalterns called him, surely in irony, the Judge, because of his habit of repeating the words of another Buller, who had been a Judge of the King's Bench; 'The greater the truth the greater the libel.'

Nevertheless Redvers Buller made his way in the Army, and became known, partly through the force of his personality, partly through his great physical strength. He saw service for some months in India, then in the China War, and then spent seven years in Canada, first as a Lieutenant and later as a Captain. Some of the anecdotes of his strength belong to this period. The 60th Regiment possessed a pack of hounds, and hunted with them in the snow. 'When we got under trees where the crust of twenty feet deep snow was so soft that the big foxhounds sank up to their middles and could not flounder along,' one of his regimental associates recalled, 'Buller would take a hound under each arm and snowshoe to a harder surface.' On another occasion, when two men carrying a big

30

basket of provisions for a fishing trip were exhausted, Buller put the basket on his shoulders and walked off with it. He took part in the Red River Expedition to subdue the French Canadian Louis Riel, who seized Fort Garry, near Winnipeg, pulled down the Union Jack and set up the flag of a 'Provisional Government' for the country. The expedition was commanded by Wolseley, and Buller, now promoted to Captain and in command of a company in the 1st Battalion, went with him. So far as fighting went the expedition was, as Buller said afterwards, an utter farce. When Wolseley's men reached Winnipeg they were enthusiastically greeted by one half-naked drunken Indian. They reached the back of Fort Garry as Riel walked out of the front, went round to the front themselves, formed line, fired a twenty-one gun salute and gave three cheers for the Queen. Riel rode away at leisure while the troops marched in, with the band playing the regimental quickstep. There was no fighting at all.

As an exercise in the movement of troops through difficult country, however, the expedition was by no means farcical. Wolseley had to take his soldiers twelve hundred miles, the last five hundred and fifty of which were negotiated in specially built boats which successfully passed through a series of lakes and rapids. On this expedition Wolseley was greatly impressed, not only by Buller's immense strength, but by his intrepidity and quickness of thought. He made a difficult night passage which another officer had declined to attempt, was nearly drowned when trying to push a boat off a rock, carried enormous loads on his back, and was wonderfully good with his hands. 'He could mend a boat and have her back in the water with her crew and all her stores on board whilst many would have been still making up their minds what to do.' It was Buller's identification of himself with his men, as well as his uncertain temper (he once pushed the legs of a chair through a glass door at an officer who persisted in watching a game of billiards after being warned that he was not wanted in the billiards room) that made his Riflemen look on him with reverence. They realized, as one of them said, 'that his interests were identical with their own, that there was no barrier of class distinction between them, that he could do everything better than they could', and that behind the

31

ferocity of his manner lay a tender heart. The boy who had been so severely beaten found, now that he had become a man, no difficulty in keeping order without corporal punishment. Like most of the soldiers who were to come under his command, the men in Buller's company adored him.

The pattern of his career was fixed when, in 1873, Wolseley asked for Buller to be his Intelligence Officer in the Ashanti War. Thereafter he was one of the 'Wolseley Ring', and his mental allegiance to Wolseley was complete and sincere. He rose with Wolseley, but he rose by his own merits too. The success of the Ashanti campaign belonged almost wholly to the commander, but Buller received a CB and was appointed Deputy Assistant Adjutant-General at the Horse Guards. In the same year his elder brother died, and he became Squire of Downes and a wealthy man. He might have retired from the Army, but by now he was a soldier dedicated to his career.

After four years at the Horse Guards he was sent out to South Africa, and given command of a unit of Light Horse in the Kaffir War and the Zulu War that followed. In this war he performed the recklessly courageous acts that first made him famous. The war had begun disastrously with the slaughter of some thirteen hundred troops in an undefended camp at Isandhlwana. Thereafter the British were on the defensive until reinforcements arrived from home. Buller was attached to a column commanded by Evelyn Wood. In the course of a diversionary attack on a Zulu stronghold on Inhlobana Mountain Buller and Colonel Russell, who commanded another body of Irregulars, found first that the mountain was impregnable, and then that they were attacked by the Zulu Impi in overwhelming numbers. The engagement prefigured curiously in one or two of its aspects what was to happen at Spion Kop more than twenty years later. There was a misunderstanding between Russell and Buller, who were on different parts of the mountain plateau, as a result of which Buller found his retreat down a difficult mountain path totally uncovered. Another misunderstanding arose when Buller sent off his second-in-command, Barton, with thirty men, with the instructions that they should bury two dead officers and then return to camp by the way they had come. Buller sent a message after Barton, telling him to return by the 'right' of the mountain, Barton misinterpreted what was meant by the right, turned to the left, found himself among the Zulu Impi, and was killed with half of his men. But Buller's personal courage in this engagement was magnificent. He picked up two wounded men and carried them out of the way of the advancing Zulus, brought in a Captain who had lost his horse, and then dragged a wounded Lieutenant out of the way of the Zulus, and covered his retreat. After this engagement he was awarded the Victoria Cross, and became known as 'the Bayard of South Africa'. His group were in the saddle for a hundred consecutive hours, during which they covered over 170 miles. In action he seemed to the Zulus some sort of devil or evil spirit, as he led his men at a swinging canter, his reins in his teeth, a revolver in one hand and a knobkerry in the other, his face streaked with blood. In camp his appearance was extremely unconventional. He would stalk through the horse lines in the early morning wearing shirtsleeves, riding breeches without leggings, slippers and a red scarf, which he used as a night cap. Later in the day he wore a large broad-brimmed soft felt hat with a puggaree of red cloth, a coloured flannel shirt and tweed shooting jacket, corduroy breeches with leather at the knees, and brown leather butcher boots. He rode a pony of fourteen hands that looked barely up to his weight.

His men were dressed almost as oddly, in leather-patched patrol jackets dyed mimosa colour, rough open-necked flannel shirts and baggy brown cord breeches. Buller refused to be bothered with sabres, and his men carried their weapons slung to their bodies and not to the saddle. They carried all sorts of weapons – Martini-Henry and Snider carbines and long Martinis – and they were, according to one who rode with them, 'rough, undisciplined, disrespectful to their officers, fearfully slovenly and the veriest drunkards and winebibbers that ever took carbine in hand'. They were not, however, disrespectful to Buller, and when the troops were paraded before Wood (now a General) and Buller, Wood was loudly cheered but Buller 'came in for such an ovation as he will probably never forget, and which moved him enough to make his voice tremble as he wished all goodbye'.

When he returned to England, Buller found himself a legend. To his soldiers he was a father figure, both loved and feared. One man, when told to ask forgiveness for a minor offence, said that he could not do it because he could not face Buller. He was called to Balmoral with Evelyn Wood, and there received by the Queen. He was the sort of bluff soldier she liked, and she wrote to Disraeli that Colonel Buller was 'a grand soldier, who has shown an amount of bravery and power of indefatigable work *hardly* to be surpassed', adding that, although generally reticent, he 'speaks very *plainly* his mind when asked'. Disraeli invited him to Hughenden, an invitation he refused because the Prime Minster had been unwilling to receive a visit from Lord Chelmsford, the commander who had been replaced by Wolseley. When he went home to Devon flags and mottoes of welcome were displayed at Crediton station, and his carriage was dragged from the station to his own door. Wolseley, never slow to praise his favourites, reported to the Duke of Cambridge that Wood and Buller had been 'the life and soul of this war'.

It was in such wars that Victorian military reputations were made. In 1882, Buller served in Wolseley's campaign against Arabi Pasha. He was on his honeymoon – he married a cousin and a Howard – when a letter came from Wolseley saying that he wanted Buller as his Chief of Intelligence. The Bullers returned to England on the same night and two or three days later he left for Ismailia. He took part in the brilliant attack on Tel-el-Kebir. The reflections he put down in a letter to his wife show the beginnings of a split in his mind about fighting, which was to develop greatly in later years:

> I felt like two people; when I thought of the coming fight my spirits rose and I felt so happy, and then I thought of you and that you might be made miserable, and I felt that it was really wicked to be glad there was going to be a fight. I do believe that it is wicked and very brutal, but I can't help it; there is nothing in this world that so stirs me up as a fight.

Two years later he was out in Egypt again, now an acting Major-General. He gained more glory as second in command of a British expeditionary force sent out under Major-General Graham to pacify

Suakin and relieve the garrison at Tokar. He distinguished himself while in command of the 1st Infantry Brigade by relieving Graham when his 2nd Brigade was in confusion. It was the day of the hollow square formation and Buller was in his element when a volley from the 2nd Brigade struck the left face of his own square, which not surprisingly became unsteady. He brought up a gun in line with the waverers, and was able to relieve the hard-pressed Graham. It was natural that when Wolseley was appointed to command the Gordon Relief Expedition he should ask for Buller as Chief of the Staff. One aspect of Buller's part in the Expedition seems again to cast a long shadow forward to the South African War. When both Sir Herbert Stewart, the leader of the Desert Column, and his dashing second in command Colonel Burnaby were killed, Wolseley sent Buller to take command. Buller's instructions from Wolseley began, 'Above all things don't get wounded. I can't afford to lose you,' but in general he was given a good deal of latitude. He was to clear the enemy out of the Metemmeh neighbourhood, and then co-operate with the river column coming up the Nile. It was a time for boldness but Buller, who behaved always with such courage when not in supreme command, was now strangely hesitant. He would dearly have liked to attack Metemmeh, he said, but 'on the whole I concluded that I ought not to attack but to march out'. Had he been right? Well, he thought so, but he had been 'sorry for it ever since'. After waiting for several days at Abu Klea, during which he received almost daily letters from Wolseley expressing hopes and fears about the Metemmeh attack, Buller at last withdrew. If this withdrawal was necessary, there was no good reason for delaying it for more than a week. There was a reason, but not a good one: the uncertainty that Buller felt when placed in sole command.

Such was Buller's active military career up to the time of the South African War, and looking back at it one is astonished by the way in which his talents were overestimated. He had never held any independent command, except the one forced upon him because of the deaths of Stewart and Burnaby; he had never had the opportunity of evolving any strategical or tactical plan involving an army; there was no indication that he was anything more than a courageous and resourceful subordinate commander on the field of battle, with a surprising capacity for desk work and administration when off it. Buller was shrewdly aware of his own abilities and limitations. Writing to his wife shortly after the Gordon Relief Expedition had begun to move down the Nile, he said that the position of Chief of the Staff suited him very well:

> One, that is, involving all the responsibilities of execution without those of invention and preliminary organization. I never have credited myself with much ability on the inventive side; all mine, if I have any, is on the executive side, and possibly if I have a strong point it is resource, which is a great help in execution.

But this was not the general view of his ability. Gladstone's remark that Joshua 'couldn't hold a candle to Redvers Buller as a leader of men', might be regarded as characteristic rhodomontade, but Wolseley was not overstating the case when he wrote that 'all look to you as the coming man in our army', and after the failure of the Gordon Relief Expedition Viscount Esher noted in his Journal: 'Buller is said to be the best man – take him all round – in the British Army. Not a very pleasant fellow.' It would not have been surprising if, as the years passed, Buller had come to accept the valuation placed upon him by others, but he was too honest to do this. There is nothing to show that he ever regarded himself as a military genius or that he changed the view that he was ideally suited to be a field commander carrying out the orders of a creative strategist.

Such doubts and hesitations, however, were known only to his family, and perhaps to a very few friends. He had been at the Horse Guards now for ten years, apart from his earlier periods of service there: for a few months as Deputy Adjutant-General, then for three years as Quartermaster-General and after that as Adjutant-General in the place of Wolseley. The only break in this almost continuous period of desk work had been the few months in 1886 and 1887 when he was sent to Ireland as a kind of Special Commissioner to hunt down the 'Moonlighters', groups of peasant nationalists who went about disguised at night in Cork and Kerry, stealing cattle and demanding arms. He was fairly successful in checking the Moonlighters but later, when appointed Under-Secretary, he disconcerted the Government by the energy with which he put the case of the miserably poor tenants in Southern Ireland.

'The fact is that the bulk of the landlords do nothing for their tenants but extract as much rent as they can by every means in their power', he wrote to Sir Michael Hicks-Beach, Chief Secretary for Ireland. 'For 120 years British bayonets have backed up landlords in extracting excessive rents, and have supported them in grossly neglecting their tenants.' The remedy he suggested, a Compulsory Purchase Act, with changes in the law in favour of the peasants, was totally unacceptable to the Government, and the indignation which sprang from his comparison of his own paternalistic care for his Devon tenants with the wretched condition of the peasants in Ireland was interpreted as radicalism by some members of the Government. Back at the War Office he reorganized the haphazardly-run Supply and Transport system, which had remained in civilian hands even after the disasters of all supply services during the Crimean War. Buller welded the several incoherent and independent groups responsible for various aspects of supply and transport into one whole, a new formation called the Army Service Corps, which was placed under the control of the Quartermaster-General. The creation in a space of thirteen months of this new Department, with its delicate care for the susceptibilities of the old Commissariat and Transport staffs combined with the division of a structure which allowed for the speedy and complete militarization of the staff of the Corps and its existence as a separate entity, was Buller's principal administrative achievement. The change was revolutionary, and it could not have been effected smoothly in so conservative an organization as the Army but for Buller's prestige as a fighting soldier, and his obstinate determination to get his own way. To have obtained the approval of the Duke of Cambridge was a triumph in itself, and it was widely believed by those who followed Roberts that Buller was practically a dictator at the War Office, and that the Duke was a mere rubber stamp for his decisions. So Nicholson wrote triumphantly to Roberts in 1894, when an Indian Army officer had been promoted against what was thought to be Buller's wish: 'It is satisfactory to find that Buller is not so all-powerful as people fancy, and that his obstinacy and dictatorial behaviour are not altogether acceptable to the authorities.' The face that Buller presented to the world was that of a man boastful and overbearing, whose argumentativeness had hardened to intolerance, and who was often brutally rude to his subordinates. The picture is a long way from being the whole truth.

His correspondence with Roberts, when Roberts, as Commander-in-Chief of the Indian Army, criticized the new Musketry Regulations and Firing Exercises put out by the War Office, is marked by goodwill and even deference. 'We have, I believe, met but once and that on an occasion when you are not likely to have retained a recollection of me as an individual,' Buller wrote in December 1890, in his nervous, elegant hand. 'But I hope you will not take that as a bar to our corresponding, and that, if there is any change you want, or anything in which you think I could help you, you will not hesitate to write to me.' It is true that in this correspondence Buller always had the last word, so that Roberts' suggestions rarely had much practical effect. When he criticized the new Musketry Regulations in detail, he was told that although Buller personally agreed with all he said, the Regulations had had to be got out in a great hurry, and it had seemed better to make amendments afterwards. When he told Buller what type of Horse Artillery gun would be most suitable for Indian use, the Adjutant-General blandly replied that although he had read Roberts' suggestions with great interest, 'as far as I can make out the manufacturing people will describe your postulates as impossible'. When Roberts pressed the virtues of long service soldiers Buller said regretfully that he would like to agree, but could not disabuse himself of the opinion that long service had only been given up because it failed to get recruits. Buller had the power and knew it, but the relations between the two men were unstrainedly friendly, even when Buller was mildly rebuking Roberts for permitting an officer formerly employed in the Indian Intelligence to write a paper expressing strong opinions about the Northern Frontier question.

Such, then, was Redvers Buller: a man of powerful but not quick intelligence, lacking in creative imagination; an excellent organiser and administrator, who had been accustomed now for years to the exercise of almost unquestioned power; a man who had developed a taste for food and wine, so that his waist had thickened considerably while he sat in a War Office chair. It was said by many that he ate and drank far too much, particularly too much champagne. 'He eats too much', Lord Esher wrote tersely in a letter to a friend, and Wolseley, attending one of the Regimental dinners that bored him, told his wife that Buller had asked for her address and that he had given it, 'but I am sure, with all the champagne he had "on board" he was not likely to remember'. Yet Buller had few illusions about his own military stature. When Campbell-Bannerman offered him the position of Commander-in-Chief, he said that it should go to Wolseley, and accepted only when he understood that Wolseley would never be appointed by a Liberal Government. Now that the Government had fallen, his position was a difficult one. Probably he expected that the incoming Unionists would confirm his appointment. In the meantime he told nobody of the honour he had so nearly received.

Chapter Five *The Appointment*

Wolseley's first reaction to the fall of the Liberal Government, and their defeat at the polls, was elation. The Unionists must, he felt, offer him some new post, and if so it could surely not be at less than £4,000 a year. The £30,000 granted him after Tel-el-Kebir had all been lost by a rash investment, and Wolseley's concern about money was erratic but frequent. He now began to make financial plans based on his speedy return to England. They had better, he told his wife, re-establish themselves at the Ranger's House at Greenwich, which had been given him by the Queen after his loss of the grant. The cost of their gardener would be made up by saving on home-grown flowers and vegetables. But a few days later he was cast down when he learned that the Marquis of Lansdowne, who as Viceroy of India had been on extremely friendly terms with Roberts, was to become Secretary of State for War, and that St John Brodrick was likely to be Under-Secretary.

Wolseley already knew and disliked Brodrick. 'Any system of government that can give over the army to such a prig must be rotten to the core,' he said, and speculated gloomily that even if he got the appointment it might be worth only £2,700. So far was he from knowing the real situation that he now believed his own appointment as Commander-in-Chief to have been prevented only by the defeat of the Liberals. Now, with two Roberts-lovers in Lansdowne and Brodrick at the War Office, what hope was there for him? On 3 July he wrote to his wife, 'My dear little woman, make up your mind not to be broken-hearted if this little Indian man be preferred to me... To you I confess I am downhearted.' He arranged a telegraphic code with her by which she would know what was happening. *Hurrah* would mean that his appointment was certain, *Good, Indifferent* and *Bad* conveyed various shades of likelihood, and *Ended* meant that the appointment had gone to somebody else. With this code settled he paid another visit to London, where he was told by everybody that Buller was to receive the appointment. Evelyn Wood hinted to him that Buller was, in some way or another, being dishonest in his handling of the negotiations, but this Wolseley found it hard to believe. At last he confronted Buller in person, and asked him the situation point blank. Buller must have found it hard to know what to say. He told Wolseley the truth, although not quite the whole truth. 'Had Campbell-Bannerman not been turned out, I was *not* to have succeeded HRH nor was Roberts, and I gathered it was Buller.' Buller told him truthfully that he had urged Wolseley's name on Campbell-Bannerman, but unavailingly. Wolseley went back to Ireland in a sadly depressed state. Lansdowne, he had been told, wanted Roberts; Buller was obviously in a strong position; nobody, it seemed, favoured Wolseley. 'I have given up all hope for myself,' he wrote to his wife. 'Alas, alas, my life's vision and ambition is at an end.'

When Roberts learned of Lansdowne's appointment, his hopes too must have risen. So, certainly, did those of Nicholson, now back in India, who wrote to Spenser Wilkinson that it was vitally important that Roberts should be made Commander-in-Chief, Chief of Staff under a Royal Commander-in-Chief, or Master-General of the Ordnance. To relegate Roberts to Ireland and hand over the administration of the Army to 'the Wolseley gang' would be fatal to progress. He proposed a wild scheme for putting Roberts' name forward as prospective Commander-in-Chief by means of a special Parliamentary resolution. Roberts deprecated this, but went so far as to write to his friend Lansdowne, saying that he very much hoped that a Horse Guards appointment could be found for him. The reply, written on 18 July, spelled the end of his hopes.

One of my first thoughts when I was given my present appointment was that it would be delightful to have you at my side, if we could possibly manage it.

But I fear that this is impossible, and that the arrangement made by my predecessor, under which you are to go to Dublin, must stand.

A few days later Buller, as Adjutant-General, sent the formal notification of Roberts' appointment to Ireland. In truth, for all Wolseley's fears and Roberts' hopes, there had never been any chance that he would receive an important Horse Guards appointment. The Queen, who shared the general feeling that Indian Army officers knew nothing of the Home Army, was totally opposed to him, the Duke of Cambridge was not greatly impressed by his talents, and he had, of course, no backing among those in office at the Horse Guards. Even his great hope, Lansdowne, seems not to have supported his claim. Roberts accepted the Irish appointment with more equanimity than was shown by his followers. Nicholson, indeed, seriously wondered whether it was worth his while to continue in the service. When he learned this Roberts wrote to Spenser Wilkinson, with a rare touch of malice: 'He (Nicholson) is sufficiently well off to be independent of the service, and I have often remarked that men in that position seldom remain unless things go exactly as they desire.'

With Roberts out of the way as a rival, Wolseley's jealousy was for the time being replaced by concern to strike a good financial bargain with his successor. In a letter of welcome he regretted that his wife, who had never had good health in Ireland, would not be able to receive the incoming Commander-in-Chief and his wife, and suggested that Roberts might like to buy some of the things he had had to buy himself, such as blinds, felt covering and matting for the rooms. Or perhaps Roberts would like to buy his hunter, Sir Redvers? Roberts said that he would make up his mind when he arrived, and on 1 August the two Field-Marshals met for the first time.

Those who knew Wolseley well agree that the brusquely sarcastic manner characteristic of him in his prime as an active soldier had mellowed into an invariable, and even elaborate, courtesy. He was no longer the Wolseley who when asked as Adjutant-General his opinion of two candidates for office had replied briefly: 'A is very clever but a damned thief; B is very honest but a damned fool.' He had given up sarcasm as he had given up the long moustache he had worn for years, a moustache, which had somehow inflamed his enemies almost more than his words and actions during the years of the fiercest struggles for Army reform. His moustache was now the customary short one of any British officer. Wolseley's politeness to Roberts and his wife, however, hid a strong secret sense of irony. Roberts, he told his wife, had looked at the horses and had said that Sir Redvers was very tall. This was not surprising, since Roberts himself was 'so *very* small' that he would probably have been unable to mount the horse. Altogether, sight of and conversation with him merely confirmed what Wolseley had already known, that Roberts was a man of no account. 'I have always regarded him as a scheming little Indian who has acquired a great reputation he would never have had but for the necessity of setting someone up to counteract my influence in the Army.' As for Lady Roberts she was, as might have been expected, vulgar, so that Mary the housemaid who showed her round was really much more ladylike, but Wolseley was delightedly dismayed to find that she was also revoltingly ugly. 'My eyes, what a woman. I have never seen a more hideous animal in my life.' It would have been interesting to have had Roberts' account of their meeting. One is safe in saying that it would have been less vivid and more generous than Wolseley's. He did not buy Sir Redvers, or any other of the horses and carriages that Wolseley wanted to sell.

The elimination of Roberts did not, however, put Wolseley's mind at rest. He now became aware that, with the return of the Unionists to power, the Queen was again pressing the claims of the Duke of Connaught. The post of Ambassador at Berlin was to fall vacant, and the German Emperor was on a visit to England. The Queen, who had her own sort of dexterity in getting what she wanted, asked if Wolseley would be an acceptable successor to Sir Edward Malet and the Kaiser, always delighted by the idea of surrounding himself with military men, jumped at this prospect. In the meantime

Wolseley, who had been told by Evelyn Wood that Lord Salisbury was being pressed very hard to accept the Duke of Connaught, rashly wrote to the Duke and said that as he heard the Queen wished to make a Royal appointment, he willingly waived any claim of his own. At the same time, he asked the Duke's help in getting either the Berlin post or appointment as Viceroy of India. When, therefore, Lansdowne wrote and asked if he would be interested in going to Berlin, Wolseley sent back a sort of qualified acceptance, saying that since he could not be Commander-in-Chief he would be happy to accept any position in which he might be thought useful. No sooner had he written this letter than it occurred to him that he might be abandoning his own claim, not for the Duke as he intended, but in favour of Buller. That was a thought hardly to be contemplated, and as Wolseley did contemplate it, his conviction that Evelyn Wood was right and that Buller had in some way tricked him, grew. Buller was on the spot, and no doubt he was even now toadying to Lansdowne.

'I suppose Buller will make himself so agreeable by avoiding all differences of opinion with the new minister that it may be thought so complaisant an official will suit the politicians in office better than a man like me.' And what had Buller done at the War Office? Left the Army without a sufficient reserve of small arm ammunition. 'I would not do those sort of things in my old age even to obtain employment.' A letter from his former Military Secretary, Major-General Swaine, told him the state of the market:

Buller appears to be still the favourite. The following reasons are given: 1. Because the Army seems evenly divided between yourself and Lord Roberts and therefore it is better to take neither. 2. Because there will he no C-in-C, but a Chief of the Staff with clipped wings, consequently a Field-Marshal is too big a man for such an office. 3. This point has not been openly advanced, but I have been made to feel it – the two Field-Marshals are too clever and too outspoken, and the Cabinet would prefer a plodder to a genius.

There was, however, one trump card that Swaine thought Wolseley could play. Why should he not show political colours at last, by asking to be put up for the Carlton Club? Wolseley immediately and most unwisely, followed this suggestion, and sent in his application. Unwisely, because nothing could be more embarrassing to any Government than such an obvious implication that jobbery had taken place over what was supposed to be an unpolitical appointment.

By the end of July Wolseley had tentatively accepted the tentatively offered post of Ambassador at Berlin, and had caused potential embarrassment to the Government by his Carlton Club application. The strands in which he had enmeshed himself were now, however, decisively cut. He had been creating phantom opponents for a position which, after the change of Government, was certain to come to him. Neither Salisbury nor Lansdowne had any doubt that Wolseley was the right man to be Commander-in-Chief. Both were resolute that there should not be another Royal appointment, Salisbury disliked and distrusted Buller, and Roberts was never seriously thought of as a possibility. The Carlton Club application was shelved, because it proved conveniently impossible to gather a quorum together, and Lansdowne wrote to Wolseley offering him the choice of the Berlin appointment or of the position of Commander-in-Chief. Salisbury told the Queen afterwards that he had hoped and expected that Wolseley would choose Berlin, but that was a transparently disingenuous remark. Nobody who knew Wolseley could have had any doubt of his answer.

The Queen had been outmanoeuvred, but she fought to the last. The Emperor, she said, was very anxious to have Wolseley and would be greatly disappointed if he did not go to Berlin. She did not share Salisbury's distrust of Buller, whom she thought a thorough gentleman with considerable independence of character and one who, she added, 'has held aloof from the press, which perhaps others have not'. Moreover, Lansdowne had never asked her permission to offer the Commander-in-Chief's position to Wolseley, as he should have done. But for all her protests the Queen must have known that Salisbury and Lansdowne would have their way. Wolseley became involved in some clumsy explanations, as he told

45

Salisbury that his only object in proposing himself for Berlin was to make it easier to pass him over had the Queen wished to appoint the Duke of Connaught, and telegraphed to Lansdowne that he was grateful for the Emperor's flattering wishes and for the Queen's thoughtful consideration, 'but would infinitely prefer to be head of the profession in which I have spent my life and with which I am so well acquainted'. He had done everything possible to lose the position to which his abilities entitled him, but had been rescued by the politicians. The Queen sent Salisbury an angry telegram: 'I dislike the appointment of Lord Wolseley as C-in-C, as he is very imprudent, full of new fancies, and has a clique of his own', but she accepted it. Wolseley's telegram to his wife said: 'Hurrah.'

PART TWO

THE WAR OFFICE, THE GOVERNMENT AND SOUTH AFRICA

Now in the 61st year of the reign of ER,
There was trouble in the land of OOM.

Rhyme in *Punch*.

Chapter One *The Condition of the Army Question*

The condition of the Army had been a matter for anxious debate ever since its out-of-date tactics and utter administrative inefficiency had been demonstrated by the Crimean War. It had been agreed by everybody after the War that the Army must be brought up to date, but every move towards modernization met two stumbling-blocks: the conservatism and ignorance of those whom Wolseley called 'the bow and arrow Generals' and their subordinate officers, and the cheese-paring of successive Governments. The broad-bottomed resistance to change of the Duke of Cambridge has already been made clear, yet it is doubtful whether this was really so damaging to the Army's efficiency as the refusal of both Liberal and Unionist Governments to provide financially for an Army capable of fulfilling their political dreams of an ever-expanding British Empire.

Towards such expansion all politicians, even Gladstone, were irresistibly led by the pressure of Britain's increasing industrial power, which constantly demanded the opening of new markets. It was inevitable that as Africa, India, the whole world of the Orient, opened up as fields for commercial exploitation, other European countries should compete for such virgin prizes. During the period, nearly half a century, between the Crimean and Boer Wars, the idea that British Imperial supremacy might be threatened by France, Russia and Germany, in that order of danger, was never long out of the minds of British Prime Ministers. The strength of the British Army was between 200,000 and 250,000 men, of which something approaching half was kept permanently in India, to administer the country, subdue the population and avert any possible threat of invasion by Russia. It was a matter of principle, accepted by all Governments, that this force must not be substantially reduced. To garrison other parts of the Empire, to fight Colonial Wars, and to engage in wars with other European powers, there was a Regular Army of rather more than that number. But this was, as Wolseley said, very largely an army of make-believe, for the troops in England was not maintained upon a wartime basis, and no such thing existed as a complete Army Corps, organized and trained as such. This English Home Army might have to fight a war against a French Army of 500,000 Regular soldiers, or a German Army nearly three-quarters of a million strong. The reserves available to France and Germany were between four and five million men. The British Army Reserve was a purely theoretical concept. Many thought that it did not exist at all, and the most optimistic estimates did not put it at more than 100,000 men.

When the figures are put so baldly, they seem almost incredible. How could the Government of an expanding Imperialist power contemplate leaving their country and its possessions so obviously open to attack? In part the Governments of Britain placed their faith in the defensive power of the greatest Navy the world had ever seen, but in part their willing self-deception was encouraged by the luck and good judgment that had kept Britain out of any major war after the Crimea. A fragment of the Home Army had proved perfectly capable of handling the Kaffirs, Ashantis and Zulus. Would it not be expensive folly to provide for an enormous Army, which might never be used? This hopeful view accorded with the British sense of national pride. The French and Germans raised their large armies by different forms of compulsory service, but conscription in Britain was felt to be both undesirable and unnecessary. Successive Governments were concerned to control the Army, and in particular to curb the autocratic power enjoyed by the Duke of Cambridge. The anomaly has already been observed by which the most intelligent Army officers during the eighteen-seventies and eighties frequently found themselves upon the side of the civilians whose object was to cut down the size and autonomy of the Army. By working with the civilians they might at least be given freedom to improve methods of training and obtain modern equipment, whereas alignment with the Duke of Cambridge meant a blind-eyed refusal of any kind of change in training or administration.

The most important and most unhappy instance of the effect of civil interference with military affairs was the Stanhope Memorandum. This brief note by the Liberal Secretary of State for War, Edward Stanhope, in 1891, laid down the general objects for which the Army was maintained. At this time the main military concern of the Government, strange as this now seems, was the defence of Britain against possible invasion by France. The expansionist plans of the French, and the aggressive tendencies that were discerned in the military programme of the Third Republic, greatly alarmed the Liberal Government in power. A series of fortifications were constructed for the defence of London. Since it was thought that the French attack would come from the south or south-east, these defensive positions were placed in Essex on a line from Tilbury to Epping, and in the south on a line along the North Downs. A chain of linking fortresses was constructed, principally in Kent and Surrey, and these fortresses were themselves to be mobilization centres, manned by over a hundred thousand volunteer infantry and artillerists and more than two hundred guns. It was in these circumstances that Stanhope wrote his secret Memorandum about the objects and limits of the Army. It was to support the civil power, find men for India, supply garrisons at home and abroad, and 'to mobilize rapidly for home defence two Army Corps of Regular troops and one partly composed of Regulars and partly of Militia...for the defence of London and for the defensible position in advance and for the defence of mercantile ports'. When all this had been done, and not till then, the military authorities might aim 'at being able, in case of necessity, to send abroad two complete Army Corps, with Cavalry Division and Line of Communication'. But the need to use forces of such size was thought 'sufficiently improbable to make it the primary duties of the military authorities to organize our forces sufficiently for the defence of this country'. This fear of invasion was not a scare that faded after a year or two, for in 1897 Spenser Wilkinson was writing in 'The Defence of London' of the connecting works between the Kent and Surrey fortresses, and of the trenches and gun placings that had been planned. Almost all British military thinking during the last twenty years of the nineteenth century was dominated by the essentially political terms of Stanhope's Memorandum, and its terms were invoked by Governments in response to demands for more money or more troops. This was the Army's function, this and no more: to mobilize two Army Corps for defence, and a further one partly of Militia, and to be ready 'in case of necessity' to send two Army Corps abroad.

Right up to the time of the South African War the Stanhope Memorandum was faithfully, and indeed more than faithfully, observed. It was easy, as soon as the numbers of men needed in South Africa was realized, to see the absurdity of the Memorandum. If more than two Army Corps had to be sent abroad, then Britain would be practically denuded of Regular soldiers. For years, however, the politicians refused to contemplate such a possibility. The scathing comment made by the most able Army bureaucrat of his time, Sir Henry Brackenbury, that 'we are attempting to maintain the largest Empire the world has ever seen with armaments and reserves that would be insufficient for a third class Military Power' was even more applicable to the men than to their arms. The shortcomings of the War Office, as we shall see, were many, but the basic responsibility for the inadequate size of the Army and its obsolete equipment rests with the politicians, not with the soldiers.

Chapter Two *Wolseley in Power*

So Wolseley entered into his kingdom. He did so with a gesture characteristically disdainful and impolitic. It had been the custom for many years that the Duke of Cambridge, as Commander-in-Chief and a member of the Royal family, should take the salute at the Trooping of the Colour. Wolseley assumed that this honour would fall to him, but the Queen wished otherwise, and it was settled that the Prince of Wales should take it. The Prince had a most uncertain seat on a horse, and it was said that the animal, which had to bear him, was given several hours' exercise in the early morning to make it perfectly docile. An undignified proceeding, perhaps, but as one observer commented, 'it does seem far better to be on the back of a tired horse than on your own back on the ground'. Wolseley found that he was too much occupied to attend, and his absence was noticed, not favourably.

He entered into his kingdom. Letters of congratulation came in their dozens, including generous notes from Roberts and Buller. Wolseley did not learn for a long time how near Buller had been to becoming Commander-in-Chief; but his own appointment temporarily assuaged all doubts and suspicions. To Roberts he wrote that he felt sure their relations would always be of the most congenial nature, and that Roberts would like the Irish command, which had 'a great deal to recommend it from a military, social and sporting point of view'. When, however, Roberts ventured a week later to suggest that a certain Colonel in the Royal Artillery should be promoted, Wolseley's reply was in effect a crack of the master's

53

whip. Roberts' views would always have great weight with him, he said, but he pointed out that a Promotions Board existed, which received Confidential Reports. Unfortunately 'the Confidential Reports by the old generals of the Indian Army tell us little, as they never seem to report badly on any Colonel or Lieutenant-Colonel. All their geese are swans'.

He was the master now: but the kingdom over which he ruled was not that over which the Duke of Cambridge had held sway for so long. The slow erosion of military control of the army since the first Cardwell reforms had been checked in 1888, when the Duke was made nominally responsible for almost everything connected with the soldier except his pay. It was to this autocratic power that Wolseley wished to succeed, but the tide of reform was too strong for him. There had been a sort of unspoken understanding among politicians of both parties that when the Duke at last retired the post of Commander-in-Chief should either be abolished completely, as a majority of the Hartington Commission had recommended, or at least should be stripped of much authority. In the end a compromise was reached, partly in deference to the Queen's wish that the Duke of Connaught should succeed Wolseley.

It was agreed that the Commander-in-Chief's tenure of office should be no more than five years, and his powers were very sharply limited. He was to be the 'principal adviser of the Secretary of State on all military questions', and was to exercise 'general supervision' over all the military departments: but the Adjutant-General, Quartermaster-General, Inspector-General of Fortifications and Inspector-General of Ordnance were to have their separate spheres of authority, and were to deal with the Secretary of State directly about matters relating to their own departments without consulting, or necessarily informing, the Commander-in-Chief. The effect of this was greatly to increase the power of the Secretary of State in relation to that of the Commander-in-Chief. Wolseley does not seem to have exaggerated when he said, much later, that under such a system the Army was not commanded by a professional soldier, but administered by a civilian Secretary of State. The position of Commander-in-Chief, he said to Lord Salisbury in a minute he wrote when relinquishing office, had become 'merely a high-sounding title, with no real responsibility attached to it', which had 'no useful military purpose'. Either he should be given true power, or the position should be abolished.

Such thoughts, however, were far from Wolseley's mind when he first sat in the office of the Commander-in-Chief, which was separated from that of Lord Lansdowne only by the office of the Under Secretary of State for War, St John Brodrick. Wolseley and Lansdowne saw each other several times a day.

Chapter Three *Wolseley and Lansdowne*

'He is a most gentlemanly prig, of intelligence and education but he could never be more than a highly polished gentleman, with much refinement and education but still a prig all over, incapable of great thought or startling decisions or of very broad views or courageous conduct in public affairs.'

This comment of Wolseley's on Lansdowne has a basis of truth. Many, perhaps most, politicians are idealists in their way. They would like to do the right thing if doing it were easy, but they remember that politics is the art of the possible, and that everything may be lost by pressing for too much too soon. Henry Charles Keith Petty-Fitzmaurice, fifth Marquis of Lansdowne, traced back his decent on his father's side to Norman times, his ancestors having migrated to Ireland in the twelfth century and become Lords of Kerry. His mother was the daughter of Comte de Flahault, an aide-de-camp of Napoleon and of a Scottish heiress. Lansdowne had been a politician, by inclination and by right of birth, from his early manhood. At the age of twenty-three he had been offered, and accepted, the sinecure post of Junior Lord of the Treasury in a Gladstone Government. He had resigned in 1880 from another Liberal Ministry because he disapproved of the Irish Land Bill, and when eight years later he was offered by Salisbury the important position of Viceroy of India, he accepted it. As Viceroy he was courteous and urbane, much liked by his subordinates and completely trusted by Roberts. Lansdowne was a politician more flexible than most in his dealings with other members of the

Cabinet, yet he was not content, as his predecessor Campbell-Bannerman had been, to leave the military men largely to their own devices. He was as genuinely concerned as Wolseley for the efficiency of the Army, but faced with any crucial decision involving considerable expenditure he was likely to agree with those members of the Cabinet who thought that any Army demand was certain to be immoderate, and could safely be reduced. Wolseley might have established a satisfactory relationship with a determined Minister like Cardwell or an indolent one like Campbell-Bannerman, but the courteous moderation of Lansdowne was deeply uncongenial to him. The relations between the two were formally polite, but never trusting or friendly, as had been Lansdowne's relations with Roberts.

As soon as he arrived at the War Office Wolseley set himself to the task of circumventing the Stanhope Memorandum while continuing to pay it lip service. The total force envisaged by Stanhope had never existed, even upon paper, and within three months of Wolseley's taking office Lansdowne had received a long and well-argued Minute asking for an increase of 11 battalions of Horse and Field Artillery and 15 battalions of Infantry, some 16,000 men in all. In proportion to the size of the Army at that time such increases were large, although they still would not have provided the four Army Corps, two for home defence and two for a Colonial or other war overseas for which – as Wolseley interpreted it – the Stanhope Memorandum allowed. The horrified Lansdowne worked out that the immediate extra cost of carrying out the proposals would be £2 million, and that there would be an annual increase in the Estimates of £1 million. His Minute in reply was not merely unencouraging, but positively disapproving. He could not put such a scheme before his colleagues, he said, unless the need for it had been amply demonstrated, and he made it clear that such a demonstration would need to be nothing less than clear proof of immediate national danger. In reply, Wolseley said that the financial difficulties did not lessen the military problem, and used as illustration one of the tart similes that came readily to his pen:

A man may be too poor to pay for coals, and if he is, he is quite right not to order any. But the fact that he is right will not prevent his being frozen if the temperature goes too low – the coals would.

Wolseley got only a small fraction of what he had asked for, but in other matters Lansdowne supported him. The first months of the Wolseley régime saw a fierce renewal in Parliament and the press of the campaign against the short service soldier, and against the system of linked battalions. The spearhead of this attack was H O Arnold-Forster, a civilian with a passionate interest in warfare, who attacked the whole organization of the Army in a series of letters in *The Times* which received editorial approbation. It seems so obvious today that long service could not possibly produce a large or efficient army that it is hard to understand the passions engendered by this controversy, but it is well known that the British Army has always distrusted innovation. Arnold-Forster was perfectly correct in saying that regimental officers detested short service almost without exception, and that the majority of officers in high commands also disliked it. Wolseley might say scornfully that 'the man who wants to get back to long service is a fellow who believes in making water run up hill, and who thinks that by putting his own watch back he can delay the sun's rising', but this was in fact very much the attitude of the hundred and seventy Service Members of Parliament. The task of answering Arnold-Forster's barrage was given to Sir Arthur Haliburton, who had for years been Permanent Under-Secretary to the War Office, and Lansdowne stood firm in support of Wolseley. He supported the Commander-in-Chief's insistence on the Army's need to possess some ground on which practical manoeuvres could take place, with the result that a block of land on Salisbury Plain fifteen miles long by five and a half miles wide was purchased. Up to a point he supported Wolseley also in his demand that the soldier's pay must be improved. This was done by putting an end to the 'grocery stoppage' of threepence a day for rations, but Lansdowne acquiesced in a plan through which this was partly nullified by the cancellation of 'deferred pay', another stoppage which was paid on discharge to men who had twelve years or more service. Wolseley stigmatized the cancellation of deferred pay as cruel, but his angry note to Lansdowne ('You want to add half an inch to the height of a man's collar and you recoup yourself by cutting the same amount from the tail of his coat') had no effect. The net result was that the soldier got his full shilling a day, seven shillings a week. It is not surprising that only the lowest and least intelligent class of man joined the Army.

For two years Wolseley struggled to shape a modern Army, to devise four Army Corps (the limit of what had been specified by Stanhope) which should be capable of defending Britain or of fighting overseas. He had signal successes, in the organization of a mobilization plan which when the South African War came worked perfectly, and in the supply of a constant stream of recruits: his failures, which will appear later, were almost disastrous. So far as Britain possessed an army that was a fighting machine at all, it had been created by Wolseley, but the passionate intelligence and fury for efficiency that had carried him along in the face of Government indifference and Army opposition for so many years, now lost their impetus in a matter of months. In his prime he might have overcome the Government's disinclination to spend money, Lansdowne's nervous caution, and the changes at the War Office which so greatly limited his powers. Perhaps this new system was unworkable, but he made no attempt to work it. The Adjutant-General was first Buller and later Evelyn Wood, and he could rely upon them to keep him informed of what happened in their Departments: but he left the other great officers very much to their own devices. In the life of this man of unquestionable genius there were two tragedies: that at the height of his powers as commander he never encountered an enemy who seriously tested his ability, and that he reached the position of Commander-in-Chief ten years too late.

He had been in office for less than a year when those who came into close contact with him were alarmed by his failing memory. Lord George Hamilton, who sat next to him at dinner, mentioned one of Wolseley's secretaries, Sir Beauchamp Duff. He was astonished when the Commander-in-Chief denied that he had ever had any secretary of that name. General Lyttelton, 'a humble member of the Wolseley gang', as he called himself, came to the War

59

Office to work in the AG7 Department created to handle mobilization arrangements, and was shocked by Wolseley's lapses of memory. Buller, when Lyttelton talked of it with him, said that they must do their best to see Wolseley through.

There were times when he talked and wrote with his old acuity, but his condition became markedly worse after an operation in 1897 for what was said to be glandular poisoning. He began to hate the War Office, and to dislike Lansdowne. 'It is difficult to lead my little man of small mind and undecided views,' he wrote to his wife. 'He does look so like a cross between a French dancing master and a Jewess.' Lady Wolseley was busy converting an old farmhouse at Glynde in Sussex into a new home for them, and he looked forward eagerly to the days when he could escape from the War Office and the round of regimental and club dinners which he had always disliked. He applied his favourite condemnatory word to city life. 'Oh the country! the country!' he wrote. 'Where is the vulgar person who would prefer to live in the city?'

Chapter Four *Chamberlain and Milner*

When, upon the change of Government in 1895, Joseph Chamberlain was appointed Colonial Secretary, he said that he had two qualifications for the position. 'These qualifications are that, in the first place, I believe in the British Empire; and, in the second place, I believe in the British race. I believe that the British race is the greatest of governing races that the world has ever seen...and I believe that there are no limits to its future.' Chamberlain became the spokesman for perhaps three-quarters of his countrymen when he praised the glories and acknowledged the responsibilities of an Imperialism that seemed to be at the zenith of power. Not even his late Liberal friends cared to deny his thesis that it was a Christian duty to enlarge the empire and so 'carry civilisation, British justice, British law...to millions and millions of peoples who, until our advent, have lived in ignorance and in bitter conflict'. They said only that Chamberlain was not the man to put it forward. 'He has forgotten everything, repented of everything, repudiated everything,' said Sir William Harcourt, alluding bitterly to Chamberlain's anti-Imperial and Radical past, but what really angered the Liberals was Chamberlain's skill in confronting them with the necessity of declaring themselves for or against the Empire. Nobody except a small number of extreme Radicals cared to say a word against the development of the greatest Empire the world had ever known, and the Liberals were reduced to deploring the Colonial Secretary's drum-beating and sabre-rattling, to applauding the end while condemning the noisy crudity of the means. Yet even when the 'means' were shown in all their crudeness Chamberlain found no difficulty in defeating the Liberals. Within a few months of his taking office there had occurred the fiasco of the Jameson Raid. The Liberals hardly knew whether to deprecate more the disgrace of the Raid itself, or the inefficiency with which it had been carried out: but they were in no doubt about the magnanimity of the Boers in releasing their prisoners for trial in Britain, or about the complicity of Brummagem Joe.

> If Jameson makes a wicked raid,
>   And strikes a treacherous blow,
> On searching records, I'm afraid
>   You'll find it worked by 'Joe'.
>
> If bullying Kruger is the scheme,
>   At which we're never slow,
> The wretched business, it would seem,
>   Is all arranged by 'Joe'.

wrote the Liberal MP Sir Wilfred Lawson, and to many Liberals it must have seemed that their greatest enemy had destroyed himself. They had sadly misjudged the feeling of the time. Dr Jameson and his friends returned to find themselves national heroes, and the heroism was rather enhanced than blurred when a few of them were sentenced to short terms of imprisonment. Recent documents leave no doubt of Chamberlain's general knowledge of and acquiescence in the idea of the Raid, but at the time a Select Committee triumphantly acquitted him of complicity. The incident strengthened rather than weakened his hand at the Colonial Office.

This municipal reformer from Birmingham was as a politician quite the opposite of Lansdowne. A courageous and skilful strategist, he was prepared to take risks to further the Imperialist dream, and yet was prepared also to be, when necessary, infinitely patient. After the failure of the Raid Chamberlain saw the need for a period of quiescence in South Africa, yet he wanted also to see there as High Commissioner a man with a vision, an energy and a patience resembling his own. The ageing and timid Lord Rosmead, who had been mentally overwhelmed and morally shocked by the Jameson Raid, retired. In his place Chamberlain appointed a man in his early forties, a little-known Civil Servant who had been for the past five years Chairman of the Board of Inland Revenue, Sir Arthur Milner. The choice shows Chamberlain's supreme political skill and perceptiveness. An executive hand has rarely been in more perfect sympathy with a directing brain.

Milner's 'credo' was found among his papers after his death. His vision of an ever-expanding Empire was almost identical with Chamberlain's. The first great principle must be, he said, to 'follow the race'.

> The British stock must follow the race, must comprehend it, wherever it settles in appreciable numbers as an independent community. If the swarms constantly being thrown off by the present hive are lost to the State, the State is irreparably weakened. We cannot afford to part with so much of our best blood...
>
> In another twenty years it is reasonable to hope that...all Britons, alike in the Motherland or overseas, will be Imperialists, that it will be the happier fate of those who come after us to create that State, which it has been our duty to preserve for them the possibility of creating.

Today we view suspiciously such an invocation of the State and the Race, but it would be wrong to identify the ideas of Milner in any way with those of the Nazi theorists of racial purity. Milner had come to his beliefs through a long period of intense and agonizing spiritual struggle. As a young man he had lectured on Socialism, and had projected a book about Lassalle. Later he had worked for the Liberal *Pall Mall Gazette* when it was under the editorship of John Morley, and later still had been an unsuccessful Liberal candidate for Parliament. It was very slowly that this Englishman who had spent the impressionable years of his childhood and youth in Germany had become convinced of the mission of the British race to save the world by ruling it, but once the conviction had been imparted to him he never wavered in support of it. Chamberlain was a practical politician working for national glory, but Milner was a pure, narrow idealist who found it hard to understand how others could fail to see that the benevolent paternal rule he wished to impose upon them was for their own good. Chamberlain was flexible, Milner dogmatic. He had that certainty of his own rightness in principle which is common to saints and revolutionaries.

Milner arrived in Cape Town in May 1897. The situation he found there was, as he had expected, a difficult one. Cecil Rhodes had been discredited after the Jameson Raid, but in the Cape Colony a weakly pro-Rhodes ministry led by Sir Gordon Sprigg hung uncertainly on to office. Half the white people in Cape Colony, Milner reported gloomily to Chamberlain, were at heart fellow citizens with the Free Staters and Transvaalers, although they professed loyalty to Britain. The President of the Orange Free State was an Afrikander Nationalist named Marthinus Steyn, who had been elected in March 1896, in preference to the pro-English J G Fraser. Steyn was known to favour closer relations between the Free State and the Transvaal, whose President was Paul Kruger. The Transvaal was, of course, the heart of discontent against British rule in South Africa. In 1881, after the defeat of a small British force at Majuba Hill the Transvaal had been made an independent Republic in everything, except that Britain exercised what was vaguely called a suzerainty over the rights of the South African Republic to make treaties with any country except the Orange Free State. It is likely that the Transvaal would have remained independent but for the discovery of gold in the eighteen-eighties at Barberton, and then along the Witwatersrand. Thousands of people eager to get rich quickly flocked to Johannesburg which in 1896, ten years after its foundation, had a white population of more than fifty thousand, of whom no more than six thousand were natives of the Transvaal. Of the rest more than 16,000 came from the United Kingdom and another 15,000 from Cape Colony. There were 3,000 odd Russian Jews, more than 2,000 Germans, and a few Australasians, Dutch, Americans and French. There was a native population of a further 50,000 most of whom worked in the mines.

Another Government than Kruger's might have seized the mines and worked them for the national profit. But the Boers were not interested in working the mines, and such an approach was in any case too simple and direct to be Kruger's way. The foreigners, the Uitlanders, were allowed to exploit the mines and to get rich from them, but they were not given any share in the Government of the country. The rapidly growing numbers of Uitlanders represented a threat to the Boers' control over their own country. There were no more than 90,000 Boers. What if, in a few years' time, the Uitlanders should actually form a majority of the population? It seemed to Kruger and his Parliament, or Volksraad, only common sense to deny them the vote, and to wring from them as much money as could be got without causing positive rebellion against the Government.

To this latter end Kruger introduced in 1881 his concessions policy. There was a concession – that is, a monopoly – for the manufacture of spirituous liquor, another for the manufacture of gunpowder and dynamite (which was extensively used in blasting operations), another for the manufacture of railways. Most of these concessions fell quickly into the hands of financial speculators who used them unscrupulously, and the capitalists operating the Rand gold mines were irritated both by the expense and the inefficiency of the concessions. Most of the Uitlanders would have been prepared to put up with these irritants for the sake of making money, but a minority remained which, organized into a body called the South African League, was prepared to try to enforce British supremacy in the Transvaal by any means, including force of arms. It was upon the help of the South African League – that is, upon a rising in Johannesburg – that Jameson had relied to support his ill-fated Raid. When it came to the point the leaders of the League had flinched from open insurrection, but both before and after the raid they maintained a highly vocal agitation about the indignities to which they were subjected. These indignities were real enough to any Government that believed, as did the Unionist Government in the strong Imperial sunlight of the eighteen-nineties, that any United Kingdom subject anywhere should come under the protection of the crown, but it is not likely that the problem of Kruger's Republic would have seemed so urgently important but for the great diamond industry of Kimberley and the goldfields of the

Rand. Such an upright man as Milner would never have been affected by these considerations, yet the thought that British subjects were putting money into the pockets of ignorant Boers must have seemed, both to him and to Chamberlain, a reversal of the natural order.

To Milner's lucid mind there was no doubt about the end, although the means of reaching it might be doubtful. He divided South Africans into those who desired the supremacy of Britain and those who opposed it. Milner fully appreciated the strength and integrity of such a man as W P Schreiner, who succeeded Sprigg as Prime Minister of Cape Colony, and who said: 'I am a South African first, but I think I am English after that,' yet in the end he was bound to regard Schreiner as an enemy when he wished to put the interests of Cape Colony before those of Britain. And although Milner spoke of the need for patience, his ardent Imperialism would not permit him to be patient for long. He warmly applauded the naval demonstration made at Delagoa Bay in July, two months after his arrival, and the despatch of a regiment and two batteries to Natal. Before leaving England he had said that he would let twelve months pass before offering any opinion about affairs in South Africa, but now he told Chamberlain confidently that these two measures had averted war, and that the only way in which to make any impression upon the Transvaal leaders was to take up a strong attitude, and to impress upon the Boers the danger they ran in defying Britain. 'We have put our foot down and we must keep it there.'

The British agent in Pretoria, Conyngham Greene, fired Milner's indignation in weekly letters, which alternated alarms with hosannas. Thus Greene told one week of seething discontent among the Uitlanders and of the 'dire straits' into which the Transvaal Government had got. 'They have been told in London, Paris and Berlin that they will get no help as long as they do not put their own house in order and give the Uitlander a look in. They see by the presence of the Imperial troops on the border that we do not mean to stand any more nonsense.' A little later, though, he wrote of the armaments that the Transvaal was amassing with German connivance, and of the terrorism practised by the Boers upon the Uitlanders, terrorism 'worthy of a Star Chamber or Inquisition of the Middle Ages'. Or again he told Milner of the violence planned against his own person by the Field Cornet of the Krugersdorp district, who was also the editor of an Afrikaans newspaper, or gave news of the £100,000 spent yearly by the Transvaal Government on Secret Service and asked pathetically that he should be allowed to spend £100 in 'rewarding useful people by the gift of some little souvenirs'. The regular letters of Conyngham Greene and the Governor of Natal, Sir Walter Hely-Hutchinson, convinced Milner that his policy of employing a strong hand inside a barely mailed glove was the right one. 'As far as I can see ahead the post of High Commissioner will be a *fighting post*,' he wrote to Chamberlain in October 1897, and four months later he said: 'There is no way out of the political troubles of South Africa except reform in the Transvaal or war.'

Milner, in spite of the glacial impression he made upon many people at first meeting was a man of mercurial temperament, and he often felt depressed that he was surrounded by enemies of Britain, for it was as such that he counted the South African politicians of almost every coloration, from Kruger to Schreiner. Chamberlain found imposed upon him the not uncongenial task of occasionally cheering or checking his lieutenant. He warned Milner not to go too fast and too far, and deprecated a little his enthusiasm for the ambitious Conyngham Greene. When Milner, after less than a year in his post, suggested that Greene should be given a knighthood Chamberlain demurred. 'On the whole I think that he has been made a great deal of and treated with very great consideration, and that he may well wait a bit longer for Honours.' (In fact, Greene had to wait until 1900.) This is interesting because it shows the importance Milner attached to the gossipy reports he received from Greene. These reports, combined with long and often alarming letters from Hely-Hutchinson, played a large part in determining his attitude.

By 'reform in the Transvaal' he meant primarily concessions made by the Volksraad which, within a short space of years, would give the Uitlanders a voice in the government of the country, and so lead to British control. Neither he nor Chamberlain wanted war – what statesman ever wanted war who could achieve the ends of his foreign policy by peaceful means? – but they were determined to obtain British supremacy in South Africa. That this was an essential condition of any negotiations was what the Boers never understood, but an understanding would have been of no help in reaching a settlement, for Kruger would never have given way upon any issue which affected the Republic's power to rule within its own frontiers. The President, a perfect representative of his people in his simplicity and farmer's cunning, his deep devotion to religion and his readiness to use holy texts for worldly purposes, was a type of opponent with whom Milner, a brilliant product of European civilization, was unlikely ever to reach agreement. On one side was the world of committee and conference room, on the other that of the horse dealer chaffering at a fair. Milner and Kruger did not meet until the High Commissioner had been in South Africa for more than two years, but their mutual antipathy had been established long before then.

The assumptions made by Milner and Chamberlain about British supremacy took it for granted that the Transvaal could, if necessary, be brought to heel by overwhelming force. The garrison must be strong enough to contain any Boer attack until troops could be sent out from England, and in August 1897, Milner wrote to Lord Selborne, Chamberlain's Under Secretary, that he was not quite satisfied with the strength of the garrison. 'Our present strength is rather over 8,000 men. To be really secure we ought to have nearer 10,000.' He added, however, that he thought that with the present force 'we could just hold our own, in case of war, till the necessary force for assuming the offensive could be sent out. But it would be a tight fit'.

These views were no doubt those of General Goodenough, at that time commanding in South Africa. They did not, however, coincide with the ideas of the Intelligence Department at the War Office.

Chapter Five *The Warnings of the Intelligence Department*

The Intelligence Department at this time cost the nation a mere £11,000 a year. By the end of 1899, when the South African War began, the amount had risen to something over £18,000. There was a Director of Military Intelligence, Sir John Ardagh, who had an Assistant Adjutant-General and a staff of four clerks. There was a Mobilization Branch of eight, four of them clerks, and an Imperial Defence section with a staff of three. There was a section devoted to maps and printing, and four Foreign Intelligence Sections with a total staff of fourteen. Colonel á Court was one of two officers appointed to 'look after France, Italy, Spain, Portugal, Central and South America and Mexico, and not only to learn all about the military resources of these countries, but to answer questions relating to them in the House of Commons and to write papers, whenever they were needed, on every sort of question connected with them'. The Intelligence Department was under the direct control of Wolseley, but it was not housed with the rest of the War Office in Pall Mall, but was on the far side of the Park, in Queen Anne's Gate.

The Government, rather than the War Office, must be blamed for the fact that the Intelligence Department was so hopelessly understaffed. The Mapping Section had a staff of less than thirty, compared with some two hundred and thirty in the similar French organization, and one hundred and sixty in the Russian. When the numbers are so absurdly inadequate it is the system that must be blamed, rather than individuals. Sir John Ardagh thought that it would have needed £150,000 a year to make a proper topographical survey of the Empire, but that a grant of even £20,000 a year was so unlikely that there was no point in asking for it. One of the most unhappy consequences of this understaffing was the fact that there were, practically speaking, no useful maps of South Africa. In 1896, just after the Jameson Raid, Colonel Grant of the Mapping Section made a map of Northern Natal. He made it in three months, with the aid of two Colonial officers. No application was made to the Treasury for money, partly because it was thought certain that no special grant would be made, and partly because the state of tension existing at the time made it seem desirable that the work should be done as quickly and quietly as possible. No mapping was done south of Ladysmith. 'We had no money, and I think the Intelligence Department considered that at the moment that met the necessities of the case,' Grant said afterwards. In the mapping, as in all other planning for war, the assumption was made that the Boers could not possibly advance far into British territory, so that a map south of Ladysmith seemed almost otiose. Lack of money combined with carelessness to make such maps of South Africa as existed markedly inaccurate, because they were often drawn up with little genuine information. 'We had no power to make surveys ourselves,' Grant said. 'We simply used to get maps that existed, and information or sketches from anybody who could supply it, and then make a map of our own from those.' No more certain guarantee of inaccuracy could be given, and when the war came all the maps of South Africa were found to be practically useless.

Two officers, an occasional attached officer and a military clerk dealt with the defence of all the Colonies, and one of these, an attached officer named Major Altham, was sent out to South Africa in April 1896, formally as Military Secretary to Goodenough, in fact with special instructions from Wolseley to carry out an Intelligence survey. On his return, Altham and Ardagh produced a series of memoranda on the military situation in South Africa. The amount allocated for the whole of this work was £2,000. It is remarkable that with such slender resources the Department was able so nearly to assess the strength of the Boer forces.

In June 1896, Altham said that in the case of any serious Boer attack it would obviously be impossible to hold the line of the Orange River. In October Ardagh made calculations showing that the Boers throughout South Africa might be able to put a maximum of 48,000 men under arms, although he added that 'of these a proportion would be totally untrained to shoot or ride'. (The actual numbers involved were reckoned, after the end of the war, to have been some 12,000 in excess of Ardagh's estimate, but this total included old men and boys.) In April 1897, a short memorandum from Ardagh stressed that the British forces in South Africa were 'manifestly inadequate to protect our interests during the inevitable interval' before the arrival of troops from England, and said that more men were needed both in the Cape Colony and in Natal. At the time when Milner believed that an increase of 2,000 men would make the defences 'really secure', Ardagh was saying that the British forces were preposterously small, and would be insufficient to resist even a modest attack from the Transvaal.

The warnings of the Intelligence Department, which were later to be elaborated into a specific and remarkably accurate account of the armaments purchased by the Boers, were little heeded. Ardagh, silent, polite, skinny-necked, monocled, was not the kind of man to press urgently the points he made in memoranda, nor indeed did his rank permit him to do so. 'The great military officers at the War Office were as a rule Lieutenant-Generals or of higher rank, while I was a Major-General, and rank goes for a good deal in the confabulations of military people,' Ardagh said afterwards. The Intelligence Department was in truth regarded chiefly as an information section. Ardagh's reports went to Wolseley. Lansdowne learned of them not through Wolseley, who used the information in them in his own memoranda to Lansdowne, but through his friendship with Ardagh in India. The reports were also seen by Chamberlain, and an elaborate routine of buck-passing carried on by subordinates took place. Graham, the Under Secretary at the Colonial Office, expressed Chamberlain's 'grave concern' at the possible inadequacy of the British forces, and pointed out that on Lansdowne rested 'the responsibility of deciding what military measures should be taken to safeguard the interests of the Empire in

South Africa'. Knox, the Permanent Under Secretary of State at the War Office, replied that the force required depended upon 'political conditions which are not very clearly defined at present', since it seemed 'impossible to predict' whether the Transvaal Government would take the offensive. If they did, no doubt a force of between 30,000 and 40,000 men would be required. Pending their arrival, was there really anything to be gained by sending out a smaller force for service on the frontier? General Goodenough submitted, as he was asked to do, a defence scheme based upon the existing garrison. He was not asked whether he thought the garrison adequate, and like a good Army officer of the period, offered no opinion on the point. Wolseley made a fresh demand upon Lansdowne for an increase of 16,000 troops, and said that the Auxiliary Forces for home defence were 'armed with a very insufficient number of obsolete guns which are a disgrace to England and would be laughed at by any European army', but he did not specifically mention South Africa. Both soldiers and politicians were disposed to consider much more seriously the prospect of war with France, and Wolseley was concerned with countering, in his own words, 'the largest invading force that France can be expected – under favouring conditions – to put across the Channel'.

In 1898, a war with France was thought to have come very near when the French made a gesture towards seizing the upper Nile valley by sending a force of some hundred men under Major Marchand to occupy Fashoda on the Nile. At Fashoda Marchand hoisted the French flag, and then awaited British reactions. These were swift. General Kitchener, fresh from victory at Omdurman, arrived at Fashoda with five gunboats and enough soldiers to outnumber Marchand. He made no military move, but put up the British and Egyptian flags to the south of the French flag, and left the politicians to fight a diplomatic battle. The exchanges in it were sharp but not bloodthirsty, and after weeks during which war over Fashoda seemed a serious possibility, Marchand retired. In March 1899, an agreement was made which defined the British and French spheres of influence in this part of Africa. War had been averted: but even the possibility of a European war, which would stretch British military resources to breaking-point, made the politicians refuse to accept the idea that any large force could be needed in South Africa.

The position, then, when Milner made his blithe statement about the possible need for 2,000 more men was that Chamberlain, Lansdowne, and (as he afterwards agreed) Wolseley all suspected or knew that the forces in South Africa could not contain a serious Boer attack. The logic of the situation demanded that a considerable increase in the number of British troops in South Africa should be accompanied by an increase in the total size of the British Army, but dislike of increased expenditure and fear of offending the Transvaal blended with the confidence engendered by years of unbroken success in Colonial wars against greatly superior numerical forces to dictate a policy of political inaction. The number of troops in South Africa remained absurdly inadequate for the task that Ardagh and Altham had foreseen might be imposed upon them, that of fighting a nation in arms.

Chapter Six *Milner Returns to England*

General Goodenough had chosen Ladysmith as the place at which the main body of the 4,500 troops he had available for the defence of Natal should be stationed, with outposts pushed out to Colenso, Estcourt and Glencoe. This fateful decision was accepted without question at the War Office although Ladysmith was, as all military experts afterwards agreed, a wretched defensive position, situated as it was in a basin surrounded by hills. Ladysmith was an easy place at which to accumulate stores, since it was a railway junction, but in the case of a serious attack the railway line would be cut, and the force based there might find itself compelled either to defend the place or to abandon its stores. The War Office authorities, however, felt confident that, as one may say with a touch of exaggeration, one British Regular soldier was worth any number of Boer farmers, and the choice of Ladysmith as a base remained unquestioned.

In April 1898, Wolseley put in a vigorous minute pointing out that the troops in Ladysmith had no proper supply of provisions, and asking that two months' supplies should be collected there. He also asked for money to buy mules and wagons, and pressed for the despatch of a regiment of cavalry and three batteries of Field Artillery to Cape Colony. This minute remained unanswered. In September, Altham produced another memorandum on 'Frontier Defence in South Africa in a War against the Dutch Republics'. He pointed out the enormous quantities of arms which had been bought by the Transvaal Government, so that their forces were fully armed with quick-firing guns, machine guns and rifles, and that they had a reserve of 30,000 rifles with which to arm sympathizers from the Cape. He emphasized the importance of discovering the exact attitude of the Orange Free State in case of war, since much the easiest route of advance for British forces would be through the Free State by way of Bloemfontein. Like Wolseley he urged that mules and wagons should be bought and cavalry remounts purchased, pointing out that if purchases had to be made suddenly the Government would have to pay exorbitant prices. Lansdowne paid little attention to this memorandum, which at the time must have seemed to him of small importance. After two years at the War Office he was confronted squarely with the problem that, in one form or another, faced every Secretary of State for War in Queen Victoria's reign, that of inducing the Government to provide money for the Army.

The particular stumbling block at this time was the Chancellor of the Exchequer, Sir Michael Hicks-Beach. In February the critical reception given by Hicks-Beach, Chamberlain and even Salisbury himself, to proposals by Lansdowne which involved the expenditure of another £1$^{1}/_{2}$ millions a year caused him to offer his resignation. Salisbury wrote a soothing letter, pointing out that Lansdowne's suggestions had been accepted, and saying that he should not be offended 'because we did not accompany our submission with a hymn of praise'. The resignation was withdrawn, but the additions that Lansdowne had obtained, of ten more battalions and fifteen batteries, were a mere fragment of what would be needed if Britain should be engaged in a great general war. Yet, having obtained so much, Lansdowne felt it totally unreasonable that more should be demanded. He turned a deaf ear to Wolseley, and ignored the suggestions for providing transport and buying remounts. Milner often suggested to Chamberlain that the Boers were bluffing, but in practical and immediate terms the bluff, or the self-deception, was on Britain's side. The Boers had tens of thousands of men, and all the arms they needed. Opposing them were 8,000 troops, insufficiently supplied with arms, stores and transport.

Of more concern to Milner, however, as time went by, was the failure of people in Britain to appreciate what he called the 'all-overshadowing nightmare' in which he lived. There was, as he saw it, disloyalty and almost open treachery everywhere around him. Sprigg, who was regarded by the Afrikanders as thoroughly pro-British, seemed to Milner a mere waverer. His hopes, stimulated by Conyngham Greene, that Kruger might be defeated in an election for the Presidency by the moderate reformer Schalk Burger, who was supported by the Johannesburg mining magnates, were shattered when Kruger obtained almost four times as many votes as Burger, and had a two to one majority even in Johannesburg. And when Binns, the British Prime Minister of Natal, sent Kruger a telegram of congratulation on his re-election, Milner really despaired. Clearly the Transvaal under Kruger was not going to carry out any reforms and the right policy, Milner wrote to Chamberlain, was to 'work up to a crisis...by steadily and inflexibly pressing for the redress of substantial wrongs and injustices'. It was because the crisis took so long in working up, because people at home felt such a faint interest in South African affairs, that Milner felt it necessary to come home to plead his case. He sailed for England at the beginning of November 1898, and did not return until February.

The Acting High Commissioner in his absence should have been General Goodenough, but Goodenough became ill and in October suddenly died. Milner wrote to Chamberlain that the question of Goodenough's successor was of first importance. It would be really disastrous if the War Office should 'use the opportunity to provide for some worn-out Lieutenant-General for whom they were anxious to find a billet' rather than sending 'a man of energy and resource and of some political sense'. On his way home in the *Scot*, Milner passed the *Hawarden Castle*, which carried the new Commander-in-Chief and Acting High Commissioner, Sir William Butler, on his way to the Cape. If Milner had known the political views of his temporary successor it is likely that he would have asked the captain of the *Scot* to return to Cape Town. In the long tale of tragic misunderstandings and miscalculations that makes up the story of Britain's relations with South Africa during the decade, the appointment of Butler introduces a passage of pure comedy. This voluble and charming Irishman was totally opposed to every aspect of Milner's policy.

Sir William Butler was sixty years old. He had accompanied Wolseley on the Ashanti expedition, and so was a member of the 'Wolseley gang'. He had been with Wolseley also in Natal in 1875, when Wolseley acted as temporary Governor of the Colony, and there Butler made many friends both in Natal and in the Orange Free State. He had fought in the Zulu War, had been mentioned in despatches for his conduct at Tel-el-Kebir, and was one of the few officers to distinguish himself on the Gordon Relief Expedition. Butler, Wolseley said, had the gift of imagination, 'that quality so much above the other gifts required for excellence in military leaders'. He was a lively and amusing writer, as he had shown in several volumes of reminiscence, which read like adventure stories. He had the qualities of energy and resource that Milner had desired, and in addition possessed an extensive knowledge of South Africa. It was this last qualification, no doubt, which prompted Wolseley to choose him, yet in truth no appointment could have been more maladroit. Butler was an Irishman, and an ardent Catholic who had seen in his childhood the effects of the great Irish potato famine, and had felt bitterly ever since about English rule in Ireland. Later he had become a friend of Parnell, and a strong supporter of Home Rule. Moreover, he had already come into violent collision with the civil side of the War Office when, in 1888, he had prepared a report on the Army Ordnance Department which had so much infuriated Edward Stanhope, then Secretary of State for War, that he had given instructions for all printed copies of it to be called in and destroyed. After the Jameson Raid Butler had attempted to discover the Raid's origins, and his inquiries had left him in no doubt that Rhodes was the villain of the piece, and that the Raid had been prompted by 'financial intrigue and sordid speculation and unblushing falsehood'. He was thus disposed by nature to have a fellow-feeling for all rebels, and to distrust all financial combines. He had in addition a dislike of Jews that was shared by many Army officers in high commands.

Butler was vegetating quietly in command of the South Eastern District of England when he received a cipher telegram asking if he would accept the command at the Cape. He came up to London, went to the War Office, and also saw Chamberlain, who afterwards complained that he had not been consulted about the appointment. But was he not negligent in failing to make sure that the man sent out to the Cape would be a faithful executant of his policy? Chamberlain talked to Butler for some half an hour, and mentioned the Dutch Republics only once. 'If they should force us to attack them', he said, 'then the blow would have to be a crushing one.' Butler did not comment, but 'continued to look steadily at the eager, white, sharp, anxious, tight-drawn face which was leaning towards and over the office table', rather uncomfortably aware meanwhile that the eyes of the third person in the room, a permanent official, were just as steadily fixed on *him*. It is somehow typical of Butler's régime at the Cape that his first duties on arrival should have been to sign the extradition papers of a company secretary wanted for fraud, who had travelled out with him on the *Hawarden Castle* and had been the life and soul of the company, and to confirm the death sentence passed upon a Kaffir. This he refused to do.

Milner had left a letter to await Butler's arrival, in which he had said that South African affairs were fairly calm, and had optimistically suggested that nothing causing serious embarrassment was likely to arise. Within a couple of weeks, however, Butler had rebuked the editors of English papers in the Cape for their 'outrageous language of insult and annoyance', and in his first public speech had said that South Africa, in his opinion, did not need a surgical operation. He had discovered also that all political questions in the country were being 'worked by a colossal syndicate for the spread of systematic misrepresentation', operated from Johannesburg, which he called Jewburg. The city contained, he said, 'probably the most corrupt, immoral and untruthful assemblage of beings at present in the world'. He had been sitting at Milner's desk for less than three weeks when an incident occurred in Johannesburg which offered an ideal opportunity for 'working up to a crisis'. A Uitlander named Edgar quarrelled with another Uitlander and knocked him down. The injured man's friends called the police, the 'Zarps', who were of course Afrikanders. The Zarps broke into Edgar's house without a warrant and one of them, after being struck by Edgar with an iron-tipped stick, shot him dead. When the policeman, Jones, was tried he was acquitted.

Such an incident was just what the South African League had been waiting for. An Edgar Committee was formed, meetings were held, and a petition addressed to the Queen. The British Vice-consul said that he would gladly send it on to the proper quarter. The petition, however, had been published in the *Cape Times* and Butler, seeing in this an attempt by the South African League to force his hand, refused to forward the petition to England, saying that he would see them damned first before he did so. Angry meetings of the League were held in the Cape and at Port Elizabeth, at which resolutions were passed demanding Imperial intervention. Butler, unperturbed, told the organizers of these resolutions that they did not justify the cost of cabling them to London, but that he would send them by the mail steamer. He wrote home to Chamberlain that the situation in South Africa was not really difficult at all. A little good will was needed, no more than that. 'What we want is honest men. If you could induce a few of that class to emigrate here, we might have hope in the future; but I fear that neither Houndsditch nor even the Stock Exchange will help us much in that line.' Milner, in London, saw his policy being torn to pieces, and was driven almost frantic. 'I am going to pay dearly for this holiday,' he wrote. When he returned in February, the two men met for the first time. Butler showed Milner a copy of a telegram and despatch he had sent, putting the blame for the Edgar agitation wholly upon the South African League, and saying that the Transvaal Government had been quite right to prohibit public meetings, which were bound to lead to disorder. He was disappointed to see that the High Commissioner read these documents with undisguised impatience, and rose to leave saying, 'I envy you only the books in your library'.

Chapter Seven *'My Name is High Commissioner Butler'*

Milner returned well pleased with the results of his visit to England. He had found 'the "no-war" party still in favour in the highest quarters', and so was unable to push his point of view as hard as he would have liked, but he had been heartened by his talks both with members of the Government and with prominent Liberals like Rosebery and Asquith. The politicians on their side were deeply impressed both by Milner's intellect and by the earnestness with which he advanced the views that he knew to be right.

After his return to South Africa, Milner felt less strongly about Butler for a time. The Edgar case, although it made his blood boil, was unfortunately not extreme enough to justify any tremendous measures, and like other people he found Butler an agreeable character. 'As far as Butler goes I think the ludicrous episode of his High Commissionership had better now be buried in oblivion,' he wrote to Selborne. 'He seems to me *sub-conscious* of having blundered, and I don't expect to have any trouble with him.' Selborne sent back a few lines of doggerel, which began:

> My name is High Commissioner Butler.
> The world has never seen a subtler.
> I had not landed at Cape Town a day
> When I saw that Milner had gone astray

Butler, meanwhile, was making a lengthy tour of Natal and the other frontiers, with the idea of preparing a new defence scheme, as he had been asked to do by the War Office. In Ladysmith he inspected the force stationed there. This force had recently been augmented by a brigade division of eighteen modern field guns. A demonstration had been planned soon after the arrival of these guns, and some of the local Boer farmers had been invited to watch it. The guns were drawn up 3,000 yards away from a ridge called Wagon Hill, and twenty goats were tethered on the hill. Shrapnel fire from the guns began, and was continued for twenty minutes. Hosts and visitors then went to inspect the dead goats. But not one of them was dead. On the contrary, their numbers had been increased from twenty to twenty-two, two kids having been born during the shooting. Butler came back from this trip with a plan of defence in his mind. He did not, however, communicate it to the War Office, apparently because he feared that it would not be well received, nor did he tell Milner of it.

The High Commissioner was now working hard to obtain some decisive intervention by the British Government, not only in relation to the position of the Uitlanders but also with regard to the treatment of the Indian and Coloured peoples in the Transvaal. A second petition was drafted by the Transvaal branch of the South African League. More than 20,000 signatures were obtained, and this second petition was sent to London. Milner's telegrams and cables became stronger and more militant in tone, and at last the Government yielded to his wishes and published a long telegram which he had written in response to a request from Selborne that he should send a statement of his views in a form suitable for publication. In this telegram Milner based his case firmly upon the denial of voting and other rights to the Uitlanders:

The spectacle of thousands of British subjects kept permanently in the position of helots, constantly chafing under undoubted grievances, and calling vainly to Her Majesty's Government for redress, does steadily undermine the influence and reputation of Great Britain.

The case for intervention, he said, was overwhelming, and he asked for 'some striking proof of the intention, if it is the intention,

81

of Her Majesty's Government not to be ousted from South Africa'. This 'helots' telegram caused all the excitement and perturbation Milner could have wished. Leopold Amery, then a correspondent on *The Times*, thought it 'one of the most masterly State documents ever penned'. Chamberlain, who seems to have felt that Milner was getting a little out of hand, thought that its publication would make 'either an ultimatum *or* Sir A Milner's recall necessary'. The Milner-Chamberlain policy divided the Cabinet, for several Ministers felt uncomfortable about the idea of appearing to impose their will upon a small independent country. These feelings were clearly expressed by Arthur Balfour, when he said that if he were a Boer, 'nothing but necessity would induce me to adopt a constitution which would turn my country into an English Republic'. Balfour had a nice feeling for the forms that should be observed. Britain, he said, had 'a *right* to ask for these and for other like concessions', but he did not think that they should do more than ask, and no doubt they would be refused.

The telegram did not, however, lead either to an ultimatum or to Milner's recall. It led to the Bloemfontein Conference, at which Milner and Kruger met for the first and only time.

Chapter Eight *The Bloemfontein Conference*

The idea of a conference at which all the problems that divided Britain and the Transvaal should be discussed originated with the Cape Colony politicians, who saw the two countries drifting towards war. Steyn also supported the idea and Milner felt obliged to accept it, although the eagerness for the conference expressed by Steyn, Schreiner and other politicians seemed to him merely evidence that they were trying to protect Kruger. It was, he thought, 'a very clever move' which had had the effect of 'relaxing for the moment, unfortunately as I think, the screw upon the enemy'. In a letter to Selborne he expressed his feelings very openly:

> I don't want war, but I admit I begin to think it may be the only way out. *But, if so, we must seem to be forced into it...* I think I ought to be *very stiff* about Uitlander grievances and put my demands on this subject high... My view is, that absolute downright determination plus a large temporary increase of force will ensure a climb down. It is 20 to 1.

The sentence in italics was omitted by the editor of the *Milner Papers* many years later. No doubt he felt that it said too much too clearly. If there was to be a fight, Milner added in his letter to Selborne, better have it now than in five or ten years' time.

In the meantime, what of the General? Milner naturally asked his advice about the military position, but Butler was not helpful. Could any pressure be exerted on the Transvaal by moving the troops in

Natal forward to the frontier, Milner asked? Butler laughed at the idea, and said that the existing force could only hold certain positions in Natal and Cape Colony that he had fixed upon in his mind but refused to reveal to the High Commissioner. To bring pressure on the Dutch Republics would need, he thought, at least 40,000 men, and it can hardly have consoled Milner to be told that the real trouble did not lie with the Dutch but with 'the occult influences at work, backed by enormous means and quite without conscience', who were trying 'to produce war in South Africa for selfish ends'. It is not surprising that after his interviews with the General Milner looked ill and worried. He was sleeping badly and was, as he put it in his Diary, 'feeling my heart'.

He went to Bloemfontein unwillingly, and with the clear intention of forcing concessions from Kruger that would make the eventual supremacy of Britain in the Transvaal only a matter of time. It is more difficult to say what Kruger expected of the Conference. It would be absurd to suggest that Kruger wanted war, yet true to say that he put great faith both in the righteousness of his cause and the strength of his armaments. The burghers had defeated a British force at Majuba, and had gained their independence thereafter. If the British were again taught the strength of the Boers, would not the lesson be a salutary one? With such thoughts in mind, Kruger came to the Conference not at all as a suppliant. He was prepared to make concessions, but conceived of them in terms of a deal in which he would obtain something in return.

It is said that, at a reception before the Conference given by President Steyn, Milner ignored the outstretched hand of Kruger. The story may be apocryphal, but it reflects the coldness of the chief participants (who had to communicate through an interpreter) towards each other. Milner tried throughout the six days of the Conference to confine the discussion as nearly as possible to the wrongs of the Uitlanders. Kruger produced an elaborate scheme offering the franchise to Uitlanders on a sliding scale according to their years of residence, but he hedged this round with a whole range of conditions which would have meant that very few of them were enfranchised for several years. And he asked directly what Milner had to give. He must tell his burghers, he said, 'that something has been given in to me, if I give in to something'. Such an approach, which for Kruger was as natural as breathing, was deeply antipathetic to Milner. Since his cause was just, how could he have anything to give? He replied contemptuously that he did not intend to deal with the franchise as 'a sort of Kaffir bargain'. Milner despaired of Kruger, but he paid considerable attention to the Transvaal State Attorney, Jan Christian Smuts, upon whom Kruger was said to rely.

To Milner the young Smuts, who was obviously brilliantly clever and had a high and rare reputation for honesty, must have seemed a man more susceptible than the President to persuasion by Milnerian reason. Such a thought indicates the limits of Milner's imagination. In relation to the really decisive demand, the speedy enfranchisement of Uitlanders so that they might have the chance of becoming a majority in the Volksraad, Smuts was adamant as Kruger himself. 'Milner is as sweet as honey,' he wrote to his wife, 'but there is something in his very intelligent eyes that tells me that he is a very dangerous man.' In truth there was no point at which the narrow vision of Milner matched the even narrower vision of the Boer leaders. If the High Commissioner's premises are granted, his impatience with the obscurantism, ignorance and low cunning of the Boers was reasonable. If the premises of the Boer leaders are granted, Kruger's agonized cry on the last day of the Conference, 'It is my country that you want... I am not ready to hand over my country to strangers', has genuine pathos. In the forces opposed at the Conference one can see, according to one's lights, a progressive Imperialism struggling against a backward and bigoted community of farmers, or a capitalism greedy for gold determined to extinguish a flame of nationalist freedom. But the cold words with which Milner ended the Conference: 'This Conference is absolutely at an end, and there is no obligation on either side arising out of it,' were not misunderstood.

In the four months that followed before the war began there were to be proposals and counter-proposals, the British Government were to waver and almost retreat and then advance again, the Boers were to offer or appear to offer concessions, and to agree to a joint enquiry which they knew the British would find unacceptable. But these varying winds did not ruffle Milner as he pushed towards his goal of supremacy, with its risk (but no more than a twenty to one risk) of war. His letters and telegrams stiffened the possibly sagging backs of Ministers. A month after the Conference had ended he was telling Chamberlain that the Bloemfontein proposals had been 'Something like a *minimum*...and perhaps even too moderate'. A week later he was almost rebuking the Colonial Secretary for his incaution in enthusing over one of the suggested compromise schemes, and noting in his Diary: 'Great change for the worse in attitude of Home Government.' Chamberlain, who had called the proposed compromise 'a great victory', was made to see that he had been mistaken. In August Selborne was firmly asked to see that things should be brought to a head, and told that 'people here, who are on our side, made up their minds for war, calmly realizing what it meant'. There are times, after the Conference and before the outbreak of war, when Milner's role seems to be enlarged: he is no longer merely the executive hand, but the directing brain as well.

PART THREE

PREPARING FOR WAR

'I was astonished beyond measure to hear of our utter unpreparedness... How could this have been permitted? And who is responsible for it?'

LORD ROBERTS
to SIR HENRY BRACKENBURY,
December 1899.

Chapter One *The Last of General Butler*

There remained the problem of Butler. At the end of his letter to Chamberlain giving details of the breakdown of the Conference, Milner added a paragraph, which shows his determination to force this issue to its end:

> One word in conclusion. The General. He is too awful. He has, I believe, made his military preparations all right, but beyond that I cannot get him to make the least move or take the slightest interest. There are a hundred things, outside his absolute duty, which he ought to be thinking of, especially the rapid raising of volunteers (there is plenty of good material about) in case of emergency. He simply declines to go into it. He will just wait for his WO orders, but till he has commands to mobilize, he will not budge an inch or take the slightest interest. His sympathy is wholly with the other side. *At the same time there is nothing to lay hold of.* He never interferes with my business and is perfectly polite. But he is absolutely no use, unless indeed we mean to knuckle down, in which case he had better be made High Commissioner.

Butler was also out of favour with the War Office. It has been said that he did not tell them his plans. He had been asked to prepare a plan for frontier defence soon after his arrival, and in February Evelyn Wood had again asked for his views, putting to him specific points about the positions that should be occupied in Natal. These letters Butler left unanswered. On 8 June, he received a peremptory telegram asking him to send a summary of his plans in cipher. On 14 June, the very day on which Milner was writing to Chamberlain about him, Butler sent his plan in detail. With regard to Natal it was based, like Goodenough's, on concentration at Ladysmith. He proposed to push the main body of troops forward to Glencoe Junction, retaining a reserve at Ladysmith and forming entrenched posts between Newcastle and Estcourt. These dispositions have something dreamlike about them, when one considers the small force in Natal, but the over-confidence they express was shared by all British military opinion. Butler did at least stress the fact that in Cape Colony the forces available would be much too weak to hold all the bridges, and he emphasized that all the dispositions depended upon the attitude taken up by the Orange Free State. Running through his whole report was the implication that any conflict would take on the character of a civil war, in which most of the inhabitants of Cape Colony would be actively or passively anti-British. He brushed aside the question of enlisting Volunteers in a sentence. 'They would only come under my command at the very last moment, and their co-operation to any large extent might even then be doubtful.'

The longer Butler stayed in South Africa the more convinced he became that the whole idea of war had been created by the Jewish capitalists of Johannesburg working, as he told Milner, under the direction of Cecil Rhodes. He was concerned to do nothing that might, in a military sense, play into Rhodes' hands and thought it his duty to go even further and to apprise the authorities at home of the true situation. He had lent Schreiner a copy of Trevelyan's *History of the American Revolution,* and the Cape Premier's comments seemed to him so cogent in relation to prospects in South Africa that he sent the letter to the Queen. He wrote to the War Office, quoting Carlyle and Ruskin and stressing the responsibility of the Jews. 'Carlyle writing fifty years ago could only see one honest man in the crowd: "It is the drill-sergeant". Let us stick to that and leave the Jews and their gold alone.' A few days after the end of the Conference Butler stigmatized a suggestion of Milner's that a second version of the Jameson Raid should be attempted, from Rhodesia towards Pretoria, as 'too silly for official language to deal with calmly'. According to Milner, this plan was to be carried out only in the event of war. Butler, however, believed that they were discussing it as a deliberately provocative move, and said that he would carry it out if he received official instructions in writing, but that without such instructions he would not be responsible for precipitating a conflict. 'It can never be said, Sir William Butler,' Milner replied ironically, 'that *you* precipitated a conflict with the Dutch.'

On 22 June, Butler received a cable cipher message from the War Office telling him to buy transport mules for the troops in South Africa, and asking questions about the provision of mules and wagons in large quantities. The last sentence of the cable rashly asked whether he had any comments to offer. He promptly replied that he strongly deprecated the despatch of reinforcements, and that a war between the white races would be the greatest calamity that ever befell South Africa. This was too much for Lansdowne, who sent back a sharp rebuke:

> You cannot understand too clearly that, whatever your private opinions, it is your duty to be guided in all questions of policy by those who are fully aware of our views, and whom you will, of course, loyally support.

For Butler it was the end of the road. The High Commissioner, the Colonial Secretary and the Secretary of State for War were all against him, and it was now simply a question of choosing a convenient moment for his departure. On 20 June, Chamberlain had asked Milner to bear with the General a little longer, saying that his recall would cause a commotion and that if large reinforcements were sent out he would immediately be superseded. But Milner was not content to leave it at that. On 24 June, when Butler showed him a copy of his critical remarks about reinforcements, Milner noted in his Diary: 'Butler or I will have to go.' Early in July the General received a private letter from the War Office telling him that if the reports that he sympathized with the Boers were true, he would be well advised to resign. Butler, among whose virtues subtlety was not included, went to Milner and asked whether he had been in any way a hindrance or embarrassment'. Milner immediately said that he had been, and Butler went back to his office and wrote out a letter of resignation. On 8 August, this was accepted, and a fortnight later he left South Africa.

It has been said that the Butler episode was one of pure comedy, but there remains the question how far he was right in his general assessment of the situation. There is no doubt that Kruger and his Volksraad prepared for war, and were ready to fight rather than make considerable concessions to the Uitlanders. So far Butler was wrong. He was wrong, too, in attributing to Rhodes and the capitalists of Johannesburg and Kimberley an influence they no longer possessed. No doubt Rhodes and his friends were anxious to obtain untrammelled control of the Transvaal goldfields, but there is no proof that this was the prime concern of the British Government. Yet perhaps he was right in thinking that war was not inevitable and that an agreement, temporary like all agreements, could have been reached. The conflict between Milner and Butler shows very clearly the extent to which the character of Milner was responsible for the war. Another High Commissioner, more patient and less eager for immediate Imperial glory, might have come to an agreement at Bloemfontein or later, when the Volksraad made what were, by its own standards, great concessions. Perhaps some of the concessions were illusory, but others could have been made the basis for getting what Milner wanted in the course of years. He was not prepared to wait so long. Chamberlain, reading his brilliant, lucid reports, and seeing behind them Milner's rage for Empire, his deep conviction of the mission of the British people, was moved to actions and gestures that he might not have undertaken if another man had been at the Cape.

No doubt the psychological basis of Milner's attitude lay in the rigidity of a personality that demanded to dominate. The novelist Olive Schreiner, the sister of the Cape Premier, wrote to Milner three months before the war began: 'We would all have loved you if you would have let us,' but such a love Milner could not freely give or accept, however much he may have desired it. His benevolence was real, but it could be bestowed only when he was in a position of power. He had a genius for handling subordinates, but no talent for negotiating with equals. The ideal human situation for him was that which prevailed in South Africa after the war, when he was able to exercise sympathetic and kindly control over those who were proud to be known as Milner's young men.

Chapter Two *How Many and How Soon?*

It was not until the Conference had decisively failed that the Government contemplated the necessity of preparing for war. The difference between Milner and Chamberlain was that the Colonial Secretary, like so many later statesmen, wanted to obtain his ends by all means short of war. The Jameson Raid had been forgiven but not forgotten, and another fiasco of the same kind would have been deeply damaging to Chamberlain's prestige. The Colonial Secretary was therefore anxious not to offend the Transvaal by making the military demonstration in force which Milner wanted. Even after the Conference he still hoped for peace, and indeed it is not likely that he would have been able to carry the Cabinet with him in making any gesture that could be interpreted as provocative. Salisbury and Balfour were opposed to the use of force, primarily on the ground that an attack by Britain on the Transvaal would have an unfavourable effect on British relations with France, Russia and (especially) Germany. Sir Michael Hicks-Beach was opposed to the expenditure involved. The Cabinet rejected decisively a suggestion made by Wolseley after the failure of the Conference that an Army Corps should be mobilized complete on Salisbury Plain under the General whom it was proposed to place in charge, and they rejected also his proposal to accumulate transport and commissariat supplies in Natal and to send out supply officers who would purchase mules. They agreed, however, that a commander should be appointed for the Expeditionary Force that would be sent out in case of war. The choice fell on Buller.

It could hardly have fallen elsewhere. The exploits of twenty years ago had made Buller a legend in the minds of the general public, and he was feared and loved also in the War Office. His views were expressed with such force that it seemed almost impious to question them, and generally the questioner was met with such a dismissive blast of contempt that he would not enter the ring a second time. Buller was particularly impatient of civilians who interfered in military matters, and he had such a violent antipathy to Sir Arthur Haliburton, who was for a long time the Permanent Under-Secretary of State for War, that relations between the Adjutant-General's department and the civil side of the War Office were always in a state of crisis. Buller had, Haliburton said, a rough exterior and an explosive interior, but although there were many to echo this opinion or to say, like Viscount Esher, that he was not a very agreeable fellow, nobody doubted his military capacity. When he left the War Office in 1897 to take up the Aldershot command he was, Colonel (later General) French said, a pattern for everybody to copy. During training 'he knew every single thing that was going on, but we never heard his voice at all. He never interfered, but we saw he understood everything, and he pointed out the mistakes that had been made'. Nor would it be right to think of Buller as an uncultured or stupid man. There is no reason to dispute the essential truth of the portrait drawn by his friend Edmund Gosse of a genial, irascible country squire with a passion for hunting and for growing apples: a man concerned as his father had been to do good in his parish, an administrator of local charities and chairman of the School Board; and a man with a wide general culture, who enjoyed the work of Ruskin, Arnold and Meredith and was friendly with Millais and Leighton. Buller was not a fool, nor did he lack sensibility. It was a misfortune that other people thought he possessed military genius.

In the second week of June, Buller was told by Lansdowne that in the event of war in South Africa he would hold the chief command. His response was unenthusiastic. He said that he had never held an independent command, and that he thought it would be better if he were Chief of Staff to Wolseley. Lansdowne replied that everybody had recommended Buller, and that the consensus of opinion was remarkable.

'Well, no man should decline to try what he is worth,' Buller answered. 'I will do my best.'

Lansdowne may have attributed these words to false modesty, but he would have been wrong to do so. After leaving the Secretary of State for War, Buller went into Wolseley's office and General Lyttelton, who was in the office, was startled to hear him say that he did not want the command, was sick of South Africa, and if he was forced to go out there would return to Britain as soon as he could.

Having appointed a Commander-in-Chief, the Government rested content. No steps were taken to prepare for mobilization or to despatch troops. Wolseley and Buller peppered Lansdowne with memoranda. Wolseley urged again in July that an Army Corps should be mobilized, and also that some 10,000 men, an Infantry Division and a Cavalry Brigade, should be sent out to South Africa. Buller pointed out the vital importance of discovering whether the Orange Free State would be friend, enemy or neutral. Lansdowne temporized. His belief in the virtue of inaction must have been strengthened by a meeting that took place in his room later in July, attended by Wolseley and Buller. Wolseley asked whether Buller thought that, in the event of an ultimatum being addressed to Kruger, the present positions in Cape Colony and in Natal were safe. Buller rashly replied that as long as clever men like Butler and Sir W Penn Symons (who had just gone out to command the troops in Natal) were satisfied, he saw no need to send out troops before the despatch of the Army Corps that would be needed in the case of war. This casual remark reinforced Lansdowne's natural inclination not to press his colleagues in the cabinet for money in excess of the year's Army Estimates, and during the whole summer the Government flinched away from serious preparations for war. 'I am working hard,' Wolseley wrote to his wife, 'but it is difficult to lead my little man of small mind and undecided views'. In August, 2,000 men were sent out, 'to strengthen our own position, to reassure the colonist, and, above all, to strengthen our diplomacy', as Lansdowne complacently put it. Wolseley pointed out that such a demonstration would take in nobody, and repeated his demand for another 10,000 men to be sent out. Lansdowne told him that the political situation had materially improved, and that Chamberlain saw no occasion for reinforcements.

In the end Milner pushed the Government into action. Greene told him, and he passed on to Chamberlain, stories of drilling going on every night and shooting competitions being held every day, in Pretoria and outside Johannesburg. Observation parties of burghers had been stationed along the Natal border. Seventy French quick-firing guns and sixteen large Krupp guns had been ordered. Milner still insisted, as late as the middle of August, that the Transvaal would 'collapse if we don't weaken, or rather if we go on steadily turning the screw', but he expressed grave alarm about the military position, and castigated the 'imbecility' of the War Office in not sending out more reinforcements. He could not know that the reluctance to send them lay not with the War Office but with the Government.

The Government's curiously circuitous approach to the War Office no doubt reflected Lansdowne's determination to keep power in his own hands. Wolseley was not kept informed of the political or diplomatic situation, but early in September Salisbury asked Buller for his ideas about the way things were going. Buller put down his complaints in a private letter, pointing out that the line of advance had not been settled, that no transport had been arranged, that it would take sixteen to twenty weeks for an Army Corps to reach South Africa from the time that an order was given, and that it was foolish to issue an ultimatum without having the means of enforcing it. His conclusion could hardly be criticized: 'The situation is one in which the diplomatic authorities should consult with the military authorities.' He sent a copy of this letter to Wolseley, saying that the time must surely have come when the Commander of the expedition should be a partner in the negotiations. Wolseley wrote a savage minute to Lansdowne:

We have lost time, a misfortune in war, and in preparing for war, which is deplorable... We have committed one of the very greatest blunders in war, namely, we have given our enemy the initiative. He is in a position to take the offensive, and by striking the first blow to ensure the great advantage of winning the first 'round'. Let us hope he may have no skilled soldiers to advise him upon this point.

In June, Altham had produced what proved to be a remarkably accurate estimate of the armaments of the Transvaal and the Orange Free State. He also stressed the practical certainty of the Free State being hostile in the case of war with the Transvaal. Wolseley did not show this memorandum to Lansdowne, but the Secretary of State saw it through his friendship with Ardagh. Faced with the demands of Milner, and the insistence of Wolseley and Buller, the Government gave way. They agreed that a force of some 10,000 men should be sent to Natal, although to Wolseley's annoyance they decided that most of them could come from India. 'I always remember that the battalion which lost us Majuba was an old one from India,' he said. But in this the Government had its way, on the ground that the men from India would arrive more quickly. Sir George White, formerly Commander-in-Chief in India, and latterly Quartermaster-General at the War Office (a proof that it was possible for those outside the charmed Ring to reach this Mecca) was appointed to command the force. Not for another fortnight, however, was sanction given to spend money on supplies and transport. On 22 September, a grant of £860,000 was made, and purchasing was begun. On 7 October, mobilization was ordered in England. On the 9th the Transvaal sent an ultimatum, demanding that the troops on its borders should be instantly withdrawn, that all reinforcements should be sent back to the coast, and that troops on the sea should not be landed in South Africa. This ultimatum was of course rejected. On 11 October, the Transvaal forces invaded Natal.

So Milner's twenty to one shot had come home: but he had the consolation that the British ultimatum in preparation had not been sent and that, to a superficial glance at least, Britain had been 'forced into it' as he had wished. The war, upon the whole, came to him as a relief from tension. To Chamberlain also it was in some ways a relief; for the ultimatum had been difficult to devise. As he had said in one telegram to Milner, it was hard to know just what to ask for. 'It seems difficult to treat as *casus belli* refusal by state to which we have given complete internal independence to grant a particular form of franchise by aliens.' Chamberlain felt complete confidence in the military outcome. 'To me, as a civilian, it seems incredible that the Boers should be able to make a successful offensive attack on any British force.' Wolseley, who had shared Milner's belief that Kruger would not fight, was delighted to smell gunpowder even from a distance:

> I rejoice beyond measure to think the war must now come. Come it would most certainly some time or other, and now is the best time for us... Buller will I am sure end the war with complete success for England, and that is what I most think of and crave most, my own mere personal longings must not be mentioned in the same breath. But oh, how I envy him!

Smiling and calm, he attended a performance of *King John* on the night that war was declared. He assured his guests that the campaign would be a short one.

Chapter Three *Buller's Departure*

Buller did not behave like a man to be envied. His sympathies, like those of many Army officers, were with the Boers rather than with the Uitlanders, and he thought that 'the Boers would not bring it (a war) on unless we did'. He was justifiably annoyed by the delay in deciding a line of advance until the end of September, when the Cabinet had agreed that an advance through the Orange Free State by way of Bloemfontein might be considered. This route was decided upon, but after the decision had been made there was no discussion of the plan of campaign. Wolseley gave no detailed instructions to White, nor did he give any to Buller, thinking that the position to be held by any Commander in the field must be left to that Commander's discretion. No doubt this was reasonable, but the truth is that there was no preliminary discussion because there was no General Staff to draw up data and assess possibilities. There was nothing beyond the Intelligence Department's reports to discuss, and Buller was simply given *carte blanche* to conduct the war in any way he wished. When, as we shall see, he broke away from the intended line of advance and went to Natal, Wolseley thought he was wrong. 'He went there on his own hook entirely, and at his own instigation... I thought it was wrong, but I never told him so. I did not think it was my business to do so; it would have been improper for me to do so.'

Buller's feelings alternated between extreme gloom and unfounded optimism. He disliked Lansdowne, and when Buller disliked a man it meant that social communication between them was practically at an end. When, later, he complained that he had not been able to obtain information at the War Office, Lansdowne was caustic:

> I say, having served in the War Office with Sir Redvers Buller and knowing his relations with the War Office staff, that there was not a room in the War Office that Sir Redvers Buller could not have walked into whenever he pleased, with the certainty that whatever assistance he called for in that room would be given to him without demur. I have known Sir Redvers Buller for some time and it never occurred to me that he was a particularly diffident person, or very easily intimidated, especially by civilians.

Buller was to complain also, after the war, that he had had no voice in the selection of his staff, but according to Wolseley's Military Secretary, Sir Coleridge Grove, this was not correct. Buller, Grove said, was frequently consulted, and his wishes were always acceded to. A few days before his departure for South Africa, he saw the complete list in Grove's room. He took the paper to a standing desk at one of the windows, read it through carefully and then returned it, saying, 'Well, if I can't win with that staff I ought to be kicked.' On a visit to the Queen at Balmoral he told her that the war was not likely to be a long business, and that he did not think there would be much hard fighting. He feared that by the time he arrived in Cape Town the whole thing might be over. The Queen liked him as she had never liked Wolseley, and she noted in her Journal that he had 'much that was interesting to say in his blunt, straightforward way'.

There were those who had already detected the crack of indecision in Buller which was to widen rapidly under the pressure of South African events. Lyttelton, who had taken part in a Staff Ride in Sussex under Buller's supervision, had been surprised by his lack of enterprise, and in the great Salisbury manoeuvres of 1898 he had, to everybody's astonishment, been outgeneralled every day by the Duke of Connaught. More than 50,000 men had been under arms in these manoeuvres, which were the first of their kind ever to have been held in Britain. Wolseley referred in his report on them to the failure of enterprise and independence shown both in the commands and among individual soldiers. Summing up on the final day he said that a frontal attack on a fortified position could not succeed unless the attacking force was double the number of the defenders and pointed out that Buller, who had been making such an attack, had only equal numbers, and that his men had marched several miles before fighting. Buller, who was standing nearby, ejaculated: 'I have been making a fool of myself all day.' The news of Kitchener's victory at Omdurman came through during the manoeuvres, and the guns on the Plain fired a salute. Ian Hamilton, who was present at the manoeuvres, attended a luncheon party at a country house 'where all the Generals met, and Buller with a very red face gobbled up all sorts of good things'. Hamilton made the observation that 'the rising of this new star in the East had eclipsed that red-faced Martian', an imprudent remark which was not well received. An aspect of the manoeuvres which had particularly impressed Buller was the plan by which Lipton's provided a mobile canteen which supplied grocery, vegetables and chocolate. He was to adapt this novel idea for use in South Africa.

At twelve minutes past two on the afternoon of 14 October, he left Waterloo Station by a special train, accompanied by his personal staff. An attempt to conceal the exact time of his departure had failed, and a big crowd collected outside the station to cheer his portly figure as it moved along the platform in bowler hat and blue overcoat. The Prince of Wales, the Duke of Cambridge, Lansdowne, Wolseley and Evelyn Wood had assembled among many others to say goodbye and to wish him luck. They joined Buller and his wife in his saloon, which was lined with yellow silk. His wife kissed him, the Prince of Wales shook hands, they all left the saloon. The assistant superintendent waved his flag to put the train in motion. The crowd sang 'Rule, Britannia'.

'I think it's about time all this was over,' said one of the aides-de-camp as the train left the station, but it was watched for all along the route, and was cheered by country people. An enormous crowd, headed by the Mayor, had gathered at Southampton, and Buller refused an invitation to a civic luncheon. The Mayor, however, followed him on to the *Dunottar Castle* to say goodbye. He approved the arrangements made for him, which included the conversion of the ladies' dressing-room into his office. Just before the ship's five gangways were removed, he was seen walking with the ship's captain, Captain Rigby, towards the bridge.

As the ship moved away there was much emotion, as the sound arose of ladies' voices first, and men's later, singing 'God Save the Queen'. 'Sir Redvers Buller is emphatically a strong man,' *The Times* said. 'His emotion was manifest. Everybody shared it.'

Chapter Four *The Unready Army: Numbers and Equipment*

Wolseley's arrangements for mobilization, and for the calling out of the Reserve, emerged triumphantly successful when they were put to the test. He had boasted that the War Office could mobilize two Army Corps more quickly than the Navy could provide ships for them, and the despatch of an Army Corps and a Cavalry Division to South Africa, and the calling up of the Army Reserve were carried out with perfect smoothness. More than 98 per cent of what Wolseley's opponents had always said was a non-existent Reserve rejoined the colours and the Commander-in-Chief, after paying a visit to Southampton to watch the first detachments embark on 20 October, reported to the Queen: 'I never saw five finer Batns., *not one* man under the influence of drink.' In little over a fortnight from the date that mobilization was ordered, more than 20,000 men had sailed, with no worse mishap than that one ship's propeller fouled a hawser, so that it had temporarily to return to port. He urged the mobilization of a second Army Corps ('Lord Wolseley knows the Queen will be glad to hear from him that over two Army Corps could be mobilized *quite easily* in a fortnight'), but the Government would not agree to this. The Field Force sent out consisted of more than 47,000 men, some 31,000 of them infantry, with nearly 6,000 cavalry and mounted infantry. It was hoped and believed by the Government that this force, together with the men already sent out under White's command, would be ample to defeat the Boers.

Although the mobilization was so successful, the despatch of an Army Corps to South Africa left Britain in a bad position in relation to home defence, which, it will be remembered, was a prime concern of both Government and War Office. Supposing that, during the course of the South African campaign, the country should become involved in war through a Russian invasion of Afghanistan, or through another Fashoda, what military resources could be found to meet it? Although the minimum acceptable height for a soldier had been reduced by half an inch in 1897, to 5 ft. $3^1/2$ inches for infantry of the line and 5 ft. 6 inches for gunners, and was reduced further still before the outbreak of war, the supply of recruits had never been sufficient to meet the Army's needs. Many of the recruits were, in any case, untrained boys who could not be sent overseas to fight, and their places had to be taken by reservists. In the 1st Battalion of the East Lancashire Regiment it was found that, out of a total strength of 947 soldiers, only 370 were fit for overseas duty. This was exceptional, but a figure of 25 per cent of men suitable only for home or garrison duty was commonplace. The Army at home, Wolseley said a little while after the start of the war, was in a helpless and hopeless condition. He meant the remark as a blow at the Government, but the responsibility for the condition of the Army rested also upon the Commander-in-Chief and the other powers at the War Office.

Wolseley was a professional soldier, with the limitations implied in the phrase. He was jealous for the reputation of the Regular Army, and sceptical of the ability of any auxiliary forces. The most important of these in Britain was the Militia, the old 'Constitutional Force' of England, which had a theoretical strength of more than 125,000 men. It might have been possible to create out of them an effective body for the defence of Britain, but the War Office showed little interest in doing this. Men who enrolled in the Militia undertook to train for twenty-eight days a year, a period obviously inadequate for any standard of military efficiency to be reached, yet long enough to be extremely irritating to employers of artisans and clerks. The bulk of the Militia, therefore, were agricultural or other labourers, many of them Irish and illiterate. A considerable percentage of them went into the Regular Army, a smaller but still

105

quite large number deserted, and only some 20 per cent completed their six years of training and entered the Militia Reserve. The generally low standard of Militia officers reflected the lack of interest taken in the force by the War Office, but it was also a consequence of the Regulation by which the Lord Lieutenant of the County to which the Militia battalion was attached had the right to select officers. The Lord Lieutenant was given a month to make his nomination, and only if he failed to exercise his right was the appointment passed on to the Regimental officer commanding the district.

More interest had been taken in the Yeomanry, which represented the mounted force of the Militia. Wolseley, as has been mentioned, was anxious to modernize the Yeomanry and to enforce upon them some degree of organization, but he met with great resistance, not only from the Duke of Cambridge. The Yeomanry had always existed as a series of small private armies based upon particular localities, and paid for largely by the officers and commanding officers of each unit. Many of them resented attempts made to induce them to take musketry courses and to destroy their independence by, for example, the provision of transport for mobilization.

The third auxiliary force were the Volunteers, who had come into prominence after the Crimean War, when the inefficiency of the British Regular Army had been fully revealed. In Stanhope's plan for the defence of Britain it had been designed that the Volunteers should occupy some of the fortresses around London. The utility of this plan was limited by the unlikelihood of an invasion force giving them the nine days which the Government felt that they would need to settle into their defensive positions. In fact the defence plans were never carried out, and although the Bloomsbury Rifles, for example, camped at Fort Wallington on Portsdown Hill, they did so to use the cooking facilities of the fort and not to carry out manoeuvres or military training. The Volunteers were the predecessors of the Territorials. The minimum amount of training required of them was negligible, a few drills and a little class firing, but in some units far more was done. The efficiency of the force depended largely on the quality of the officers, and these varied from intelligent amateur strategists to men who were totally incompetent for any form of command, but could not be removed because they had spent large sums of money on their Units, and in many cases owned the drill halls in which they met. Training was carried out at weekends, and there was a loose liaison with the War Office by which Regular barracks were sometimes borrowed. The Volunteers had practically no Field Artillery, and any machine guns they possessed had been bought privately by enthusiastic officers.

The position at the beginning of the war, then, was that the Militia were inadequately trained and had far less than their proper complement of officers, the Yeomanry were split into tiny fragmentary forces and were under military law only when being trained and exercised, and the Volunteers were patchy groups, some being well trained and good shots and others practically untrained. No coherent arrangements existed for sending these forces overseas, or providing transport for them. The intention of the War Office when the war began was to use the Militia for employment on the lines of communication if that proved really necessary, and not to use the Yeomanry or the Volunteers at all. Few of the military and civilian critics of the War Office establishment questioned this procedure. Their ammunition was reserved for the failure of the Government and the War Office to provide adequate forces for home defence. In the event, the first Militia battalion was sent out to South Africa at the beginning of 1900, and in order to obtain enough officers the Inspector-General of Recruiting, Major-General Borrett, appointed what he called 'educated young gentlemen' whose names were suggested to him by Lansdowne, Wolseley and other officials at the War Office. These educated young gentlemen went out, as Borrett said afterwards, knowing nothing. 'I could not train them,' he said. 'I had nothing to do with training. My business was to find the men and the officers.' It was not, he agreed, an ideal system, but he thought it was better than nothing.

The obscurantism of the authorities was most clearly shown in relation to the Volunteers. In August Colonel Sir Howard Vincent, a Unionist MP who was Commandant of the Queen's Westminster Rifles and had been Commissioner of the Metropolitan Police, offered to raise a battalion of unmarried men between twenty and thirty years old for active service, and another battalion for garrison duty at home. He sent this offer through the Under Secretary of State for War, and received no other answer than that it had reached the War Office through the wrong channel. When war broke out he tried to discover the right channel, and found that his offer should have been made through the GOC Home District. He renewed it, therefore, through the GOC and received no answer at all. Most men would have given up at this point but Colonel Vincent, who was receiving hundreds of letters from men eager to go to the war, persisted. He wrote again to the War Office, and asked a question in the House. He was told that the Secretary of State fully appreciated his patriotic spirit, but that under the Volunteer Act of 1863, Volunteers could be mobilized only in the case of invasion, and that they certainly could not be sent abroad. Three weeks later Vincent wrote again, complaining that volunteers were being accepted from Cape Colony, Natal, Canada, New Zealand and Australia. Surely they might be sent from Britain too? He received a chilly answer, to the effect that it would be a great mistake to enlist volunteers until their services were required, and 'there is at present no probability of this'.

Vincent had been dealing with the civilian side of the War Office. Three days later, on 29 November, he received a placatory letter from Wolseley, saying that there were many first-rate men and excellent officers among the Volunteers:

> But there is not that evenness of efficiency in any Volunteer battalion that would bring it up to the level of an ordinary line regiment. However, the day may come when we shall be only too glad to employ Volunteer corps on active service, and I shall rejoice to see it.

The day came sooner than Wolseley had wished or expected. During the third week of December came the Black Week, as it was called, when British forces were defeated at Stormberg, Magersfontein and Colenso. Quite suddenly the War Office and the Government capitulated. On 15 December the Lord Mayor of London drove down to the War Office and saw Wolseley, who agreed verbally to the raising of the City Imperial Volunteers. Within four weeks the first detachment of CIVs had embarked for South Africa.

Wolseley's desire to keep the auxiliary forces out of South Africa so that glory should go to the Regular Army was extended to the forces offered by the Colonies. He saw that it would be necessary to accept help from them, but was determined that it should be as little and as inconspicuous as possible. The Australians were told on 3 October, that seven hundred and fifty men in all might be sent. (Before the war ended, Australia, New Zealand and Canada had each sent several thousand.) They might be Infantry, Mounted Infantry or Cavalry, but – it was a phrase that became notorious – 'in view of numbers already available, Infantry most, Cavalry least, serviceable'. The mistake was a gross one. Within two or three weeks of the beginning of the war it was realized that a large proportion of the army must be mounted if it was to fight effectively in the great spaces of South Africa against an enemy consisting almost entirely of mounted men. But in any case, the Colonists were men accustomed to riding every day on horseback, and to finding their own way for a hundred miles without guidance. They were natural mounted infantry, and in fact the Australians ignored the suggestion in the telegram, and sent horses with their men. Wolseley lamely explained later that he had meant to exclude Cavalry, but not to exclude Mounted Infantry. He had had, he said, the Yeomanry in mind, who were 'very good mounted troops, but of no use as Cavalry'. But the true reason was that two or three thousand infantry were unlikely to play a conspicuous part in the fighting, whereas that number of mounted troops might well take some of the shine off the achievements of the Hussars and Lancers. Now, at the end of his career, Wolseley was at the mercy of the worm of pride, which made him long for a victory achieved by British arms in which the Home Army, the Army of the War Office professionals, should play the supreme, unquestioned part.

The British Army in 1899, then, was in numbers equipped to fight a minor but not a major war. There was a whole separate army of 70,000 men in India, an army with whose finance and administration Pall Mall had little to do. There were in the Home

Army two Army Corps of Regular troops, and the third Army Corps partly composed of Regulars and partly of Militia, called for by that guiding light, the Stanhope Memorandum. But if these Army Corps, which included the Reserve, were used for offensive expeditions abroad, nothing but the unorganized Militia, Yeomanry and Volunteers would be left for the defence of Britain against possible attack by the several European powers unequivocally hostile to this country. The truth is, as Roberts said afterwards, that none of the experts had ever contemplated the employment of more than, at the most, an Army Corps in relation to a foreign expedition. When, as finally proved necessary, more than 250,000 men were sent to South Africa, the strain on Britain's manpower resources was very considerable.

So much for numbers. The position with regard to arms and equipment was much more serious.

These, it will be remembered, were no direct concern of Wolseley's. The Heads of Department at the War Office made their reports direct to Lansdowne. Early in 1899, however, Wolseley became alarmed by reports about the lack of reserves, and obtained the appointment of Sir Henry Brackenbury as Director-General of the Ordnance. The ordnance factories had for several years been under the direction of the Financial Secretary at the War Office, but Brackenbury urged successfully that they should be transferred to him. Once in control, he instituted an enquiry into the whole arms and stores position. It was Brackenbury who in 1888 had prepared a memorandum on 'French Invasion' and during his first months in office he was fully occupied, on Lansdowne's instructions, with preparation of a large scheme for the rearmament of the country's coastal fortresses, most of which were armed with obsolete muzzle-loading guns which would have been practically useless against ships with modern armour. It was not, therefore, until the summer that he was able to work in earnest on his inquiry into arms and equipment.

Every large organization needs to have within it one intelligent bureaucrat in a high position, and Brackenbury filled this role in the British Army at the end of the nineteenth century. Unsuccessful as a fighting soldier, this pasty-faced black-moustached, not very agreeable man was a brilliant administrator and organizer. During the eighties, as head of the Intelligence Department, he had been Wolseley's chief adviser on administrative reform. The Duke of Cambridge, naturally enough, disliked him. When Lord Edward Gleichen told the Duke at dinner one night that he was working in the Intelligence Department, the Duke put his hand on the young officer's knee. 'So you are under Brackenbury,' he said. 'A dangerous man, my dear Gleichen, a very dangerous man.' Brackenbury made his report on 15 December 1899. At this time the war had been in progress for a little more than two months, and there was general recognition that the fighting powers of the Boers had been underestimated. Viewed in the light of the prolonged effort that the country would have to make, the deficiencies revealed in Brackenbury's report were appalling.

Some of them, indeed, would have seemed incredible if they had not been curtly documented. When the war began there were ten batteries of Horse Artillery 12 pounder guns on the Home and Colonial Establishment. In reserve there was only one battery, which had been converted to an experimental quick-firing system. There were 50 batteries of Field Artillery, with no more than nine in reserve. Five of these nine had already, at the time of Brackenbury's report, been sent to South Africa. There were three batteries of howitzers, and in reserve only a single 5-inch howitzer, one carriage and two ammunition wagons. The gun ammunition reserve of 200 rounds a gun had been exhausted in the first weeks of the war, and Brackenbury had had to borrow ammunition from the Navy and from the Indian Government. The establishment of machine guns was short by 25 per cent of the authorized number of 1,224, and machine guns that had been provided for fortresses at home had to be sent to South Africa. The reserves of harness and cavalry saddlery were similarly swallowed up in the first two or three weeks of fighting. There were 1,700 sets of mule harness in reserve to meet the tens of thousands needed. The infantry accoutrements were hopelessly inadequate, only 10,000 sets being held in reserve to meet the wear and tear of 364,000. Many of the Army Service Corps vehicles were obsolete, and almost all were unsuited to South African conditions. There was a reserve of 5,000 single tents and 100 hospital marquees, when many times this number was needed. The reserve of accessories like pegs, ropes and mallets was not sufficient to supply a fiftieth of the South African demand. There was no reserve at all of hospital equipment.

The position with regard to general stores and clothing was even worse. All of the boots had to be changed, because the thick clump soles of the boots that were used for home service separated in South African conditions, and the foreign service boots had to be hand sewn. The clothing in reserve was all red or blue: there was no khaki clothing. Forty thousand khaki drill suits were ordered, but after the troops had embarked it was decided that the drill was too thin, and should be replaced by khaki serge. Then the frock of the khaki serge suit had to be changed, because the factories said it was too difficult to make. Brackenbury had, in fact, to change the whole clothing equipment of the Army, replacing cloth pantaloons by cord, knee boots by ankle boots and puttees and blue helmets by white. More, and worse, than this, the system of the Ordnance Factories, while they were under the control of the civil side of the War Office, had been gradually divorced from any real knowledge of military requirements. Thus the Enfield factory, which made the Army's rifles, had been for two years without a Superintendent, and the gun factory had lacked a Superintendent for several months. There was nobody in charge with the power to make any shifts of production that might be necessary. The civilians who ran the factories were naturally not anxious to disturb the Accountant-General with demands for money to be spent on capital equipment. Much of the machinery was obsolete or inefficient, and the factories were quite unable to meet the demands made on them by the war. The forces in the field were found to need a quantity of 3 million pieces of small arms ammunition weekly, and at the time of Brackenbury's report only $2^{1}/_{2}$ millions could be supplied by the Ordnance Factories and the trade combined, even with night time and Sunday working.

A day or two before Brackenbury put in his official Minute he saw Roberts, who was on a brief visit to England, and told him of the shortages. Roberts was horrified:

I can't get our conversation of yesterday out of my head. I was astonished beyond measure to hear of our utter unpreparedness, and it makes me tremble to think of what might happen if France or Russia had any idea of the wretched state we are in as regards stores, munitions of war, etc. How could this have been permitted? And who is responsible for it?

It is a reasonable question. The answer is not a simple one, but the main responsibility certainly lay with the Government, with the civilian side of the War Office, and, if an individual is to be singled out, with Lansdowne. But the whole system was geared for delay rather than for action. Great bundles of papers went the round of the departments, increasing in size as they travelled, and ending generally on the desk of the Adjutant-General or the Quartermaster-General. Often decisions could not be reached because officers on leave had taken away papers, which contained vital information. These officer's bags, or pouches, travelled with them all over the country, sometimes being lost or mislaid for weeks at a time.

Lansdowne's responsibility rests in his failure to co-ordinate the reports he received from Heads of Departments, his inability to imbue them with any spirit of urgency and his reluctance to press for money. When Brackenbury discovered, as early as February 1899, that all the clothing was unsuitable, he put in a demand for £335,000 to provide for it. This, however, was kept back because, as Frank Marzials, the Accountant-General, explained, a gentleman in his office was checking Brackenbury's calculations. This gentleman did not hurry over his work because he knew that the question could not be considered until July or September. A matter of urgency? Marzials did not think it was, and in any case everybody knew that the Chancellor of the Exchequer would not grant a supplementary estimate for a sum of that nature at that time of the year. One may wonder what could be a matter of urgency if the question of supplying clothing was not, but in practice the matter of clothing reserves was left until, within a few months, it merged into the immediate matter of supplying clothing for the coming war.

The civilians stonewalled over small sums as well as large ones. In July, Brackenbury applied for a grant of less than £18,000, which was required to make carts and wagons suitable for use in South Africa. To do this it was necessary to fit them with powerful screw brakes and to convert them to ox or mule draught. This request was four times refused or ignored, until on 22 September, less than three weeks before the outbreak of war, it was finally sanctioned. Brackenbury, determined that the responsibility for this should be placed clearly on Lansdowne, described the whole course of negotiations in a Minute, and handed a copy of the Minute to the Secretary of State, 'as I did not want to be doing this behind his back'. He fully shared the contemptuous dislike Wolseley felt for what both considered the pusillanimity of Lansdowne. 'Such a small-minded man it would be difficult to imagine,' Wolseley wrote to his wife, and it seemed to him that one of the parents of such a mean, cheese-paring little figure must have been a Jew. The habitual politeness of Wolseley, and Lansdowne's desire to be pleasant to everybody, kept their meetings free from surface disagreement, but by the time that war came the relations between Lansdowne and his principal advisers were very strained.

The system of costing each item separately in advance was partly responsible for the delays at the factories. Demands received in one day at the Woolwich, Weedon and Pimlico factories involved the detailed pricing of 138 separate items. The total cost, calculated to a farthing, had then to be estimated by the Director-General of Ordnance, who had to put it before the Mobilization Board, and finally to apply to the Permanent Under-Secretary of State for War for approval. At Brackenbury's insistence this arrangement was altered by Lansdowne, who agreed that he should act independently, 'in cases of extreme urgency'. Brackenbury interpreted this freely, and ordered what he wished, simply reporting what he had done afterwards. Whereas in September he had been unable to spend the few thousand required to convert the carts and wagons, by the end of the year he was sending in such brief weekly reports as: 'DGO reported to the Board the following expenditure. The orders given by him during the week ended 9th December 1899, amounted to £491,411.'

The system by which the chief War Office officials reported direct to Lansdowne was very largely responsible for the Army's unreadiness. The Intelligence and Mobilization sections, which were responsible to Wolseley, worked efficiently, and Brackenbury obtained results because of his determination to fight and fight again for what he wanted, but the other departmental heads were made of less stern stuff. The Adjutant-General, Evelyn Wood, who was by now extremely deaf, seems to have given up very early the struggle to exercise independence, and to have accepted his subordinate role. The Inspector-General of Fortifications, Sir Richard Harrison, had realized that the reserves of his department were inadequate, but unlike Brackenbury he had not tried to do anything about it. 'We look upon the market as our reserves,' he said. But suppose that the reserves were things that could not be bought upon the market? That, Harrison acknowledged to the Commission that questioned him after the war, was a real difficulty. They had had, for example, a reserve of some $3^1/2$ miles of railway, and he agreed that it was not enough. In South Africa several hundred miles had been needed. But how could they get more? It was 'a simple question of money', and the money had not been granted. Then there was the matter of pontoons. They had pontoons which would bridge a gap of 80 yards, but the Orange River was 300 yards across. Evidently, therefore, the pontoons were not of much use. Something more was needed, and Harrison had been thinking about this problem for a long time. How long? For twenty years, he admitted, ever since he had been in South Africa at the time of Majuba, in 1881. And what had he done about it? What Sir Richard Harrison had done was to say often in lectures that the pontoon establishment would not be adequate in case of war. He had not thought it worth while to press for more money, because he knew that he would never get it. Besides, he was content to rely on the market.

So also was Major-General Truman, the Inspector-General of Remounts. The War Office, basing themselves upon the use of only one Army Corps in South Africa, estimated that no more than 25,000 horses could possibly be needed for the campaign. Truman, who bought an average of 2,500 horses yearly in peacetime, thought that this number could easily be bought in the United Kingdom. He therefore made no inquiries about buying in other countries and when, within a few weeks of the beginning of the war, it became apparent that horses and mules would be needed in tens of thousands, the officers of the Remount Department were sent to

Canada and the United States, to South America, Austria and Australia. Their needs were urgent. They often had to pay high prices, and just as often the animals they bought were poor creatures, or were unsuitable for South African conditions. The great bus horses of the London Omnibus Company proved excellent for use with the Horse Artillery, but most of the animals sent from other countries were much inferior to the wiry little Boer horses, many of them hardly more than ponies. More than 500,000 horses and 150,000 mules and donkeys were eventually used in the two and a half years of the war, and casualties from injuries or exhaustion were as high as 60 per cent among the horses. Neither Wolseley nor Lansdowne can be acquitted of blame in relation to this vast miscalculation. Wolseley urged that horses and mules should be bought before the war began, but he never made even provisional arrangements for purchases in large numbers. Remounts, it is true, were in the department of the Quartermaster-General, first Sir George White and then Sir Charles Mansfield Clarke, and they had the excuse that when they tried to buy some mules for South Africa before the war, the contract was cancelled by order of the Secretary of State.

When all the deficiencies in guns and equipment of the unready army are added together, their effect on the British conduct of the war was not decisive. There was for a time a shortage of artillery, and the artillery was generally inferior to that put into the field by the Boers, but this shortage never affected the issue of a battle. The converted carts and wagons went out late, but not so late that they were greatly missed. The Government, horrified by Brackenbury's Minute, immediately set up an inter-Departmental Committee under the chairmanship of Sir Francis Mowatt, the Permanent Under-Secretary of the Treasury. Money, which it had been so hard to obtain in the years before the war, was spent to the tune of £19 million for clothing and ordnance stores. The deficiencies, except those in relation to horses, did not greatly affect the length and nature of the war.

Chapter Five *The Unready Army: Officers and Men*

In 1899 the training of British officers had changed a good deal from the heyday of the Duke of Cambridge, when practical military training for a junior officer was thought unnecessary, providing a proper standard of smartness was achieved on the parade ground, but the Army remained very much a career for the sons of officers and gentlemen. The reformers who abolished purchase in 1871 entertained the hope that officers would henceforth be selected by competitive examination, and that the Army would thus attract its share of the most intelligent young men in the nation. This was not what happened. There was an examination for entry to Sandhurst, but boys of the right class were rarely excluded. There were tutors who had a strange, almost magical, knowledge of the questions that would be asked, and coached their students in answering them. If the worst came to the worst and a boy got a mark of 18 out of 500 in Latin, a special dispensation was likely to provide for him if he was one of the right sort.

There were people in the Army, including Roberts and Wolseley's Military Secretary, Sir Coleridge Grove, who thought that Sandhurst should be abolished and that the Army should try to recruit honours graduates from Universities, but they were in a tiny minority, and their ideas were regarded as wildly impractical. There was a great resistance throughout the Army to the idea of promotion by selection, and it was not only the Indian Army officers who put in unvaryingly favourable reports on officers eligible for promotion. The system, as Evelyn Wood put it, was 'seniority, tempered by rejection in very bad cases, but they had to be very bad'. When promotion was likely to be refused to an officer eligible on grounds of seniority, his commanding officer would almost always speak for him, stressing very often his success in good society or his skill at polo. If it was still thought that promotion should still be refused, a paper had to be sent by the Commander-in-Chief to the Secretary of State, and he had to be convinced that he would be able to answer the questions that would probably be asked in Parliament. The composition of the officer class was ordered also by the fact that a private income was practically indispensable. A young subaltern's pay was £100 a year, and this did not cover his expenses. There was a general understanding that a man coming into a line regiment should have a private income of at least £150 a year, and that one entering a cavalry regiment should have £500 a year. There were exceptions, of course. Lord Dundonald, one of the South African commanders, records the remark of an old friend of his who was appointed to be Riding Master to the 2nd Life Guards. 'I can't realize it yet. I never thought Charles Burt, the butcher's assistant, would ever have his legs under a gentleman's mahogany.' But Captain Burt was a rarity, and social intercourse between the classes was strongly disapproved. Charles á Court, going from Eton to Sandhurst, found there some dreadful outsiders, three or four of whom were found to have gone so far as to dine with the commandant's cook. 'We decided to punish them in our own way. We took them down to the Lake and threw them in, and if they were not drowned it was not our fault.' Officially the commandant gave them 'a deuce of a rowing', unofficially he told them that he was glad they had done it.

Only a small minority of young officers took their duties seriously. Most were content to play games, take part in ceremonial parades, and go on the Staff rides that Wolseley had instituted on the German pattern. Those who were eager to learn the craft of war found it difficult to do so. Sandhurst was the great training ground, and at Sandhurst there were in theory courses in military engineering, topography, administration and law, as well as in tactics, and in French and German. In practice, according to Evelyn Wood, 'Sandhurst was never inspected in anything except the bayonet exercise, which was something appropriate to the Alhambra or the Empire Theatre, but is no use for war. Sandhurst has done that, and has done marching past (what Frederick the Great did at Potsdam), and has never been inspected in one of the things that make for war'. Nevertheless, young men of promise came out of Sandhurst. They commonly went on to higher military training at the Staff College.

Lord Edward Gleichen, who went to the Staff College in 1890, found himself learning again in the first year what he had been taught at Sandhurst. A great deal of field sketching was done. 'Many hours did we spend on five hour sketches of the country round, with due attention to contours, great accuracy of hachuring and careful colouring.' For military strategy and history they used studies based on the Franco-German War. Their professor was one of Wolseley's admirers, Colonel Maurice. His lectures, Gleichen thought, were almost profound, but they suffered from his unfortunate habit of saying French when he meant German and east when he meant west. They also did some fieldwork, studied tactics, and carried out elementary schemes illustrating minor tactics. In the second year they did more outdoor work on horseback (the newfangled bicycle was despised), made more sketches, made road reports and drew up purely theoretical schemes of attack and defence. They devised schemes for railways, but as they had no instruction from railway engineers, these were the products of ignorance. There was plenty of time for cricket and hunting. The commandant at this time was an Irish dandy named Colonel Clery. He wore side-whiskers dyed blue, and dressed in a scarlet coat and wide trousers (he was unable to wear riding breeches because of his varicose veins), with buckskin ankle boots and gold spurs. Clery's strong brogue made it difficult for the students to understand what he was saying, but this was less important than it may appear, since he knew hardly one of them by sight. By 1899 Clery, now a Major-General and Sir Francis Cornelius Clery, had been succeeded at the Staff College by Colonel Hildyard, and the course there had become more practical and up-to-date. It included several courses in foreign languages. Wolseley had tried unsuccessfully twenty years earlier to inaugurate these, and to impress their importance upon young officers. Hildyard's attempts to increase the range of studies and to widen the curriculum, however, were limited by lack of money.

The generals of the British Army in 1899 were not lacking in ideas, both theoretical and practical: the trouble was that, as it proved, they were all out of date. Their theories were all taken from the example set by the Franco-Prussian War. The short service system found its origin in the success of the Prussian system of three years compulsory national service; the Prussian discoveries in relation to the maximum effective firing power of artillery, made in the 1866 war against Austro-Hungary and confirmed by the war against France, were carefully marked and taken to heart; above all, their development of a General Staff, the 'brain of the army', whose sole business it was to plan campaigns in advance, was envied by all other European nations. The Hartington Commission had recommended that there should be a Chief of Staff at the War Office in place of the Commander-in-Chief, and had their suggestions been adopted, some of the mistakes made in the South African war would undoubtedly have been avoided. But in practice the worst was made of both worlds, the old one in which the Commander-in-Chief had reigned supreme, and the new one in which he was to be replaced by a Chief of the Staff. Intellectually Wolseley knew that a General Staff was necessary, but in practice he was delighted to be Commander-in-Chief. The final result was to leave the War Office without any planning organization at all. There was no department whose job it was to plan campaigns and make recommendations about them. The Intelligence Department did what it could, but, understaffed and manned by comparatively junior officers, it could not do very much. Buller had no plan of campaign settled when he went to South Africa, but only a vague agreement about his line of advance. White received no instructions about the part he and his troops were to play. These Generals complained afterwards, but there is no indication that they found such haphazardness anything but natural at the time.

Nor were the critics of the Wolseleyites more prescient. Roberts deprecated the excessive admiration of all things Prussian, and thought that in Britain neither a Chief of the Staff responsible for planning military operations nor a General Staff was really required. In 1891, he wrote to Spenser Wilkinson, commenting upon Wilkinson's study of the German General Staff, *The Brain of an Army*, which greatly influenced military thought in Britain:

> My opinion is that the Army Headquarters Staff should do the precise work of the Grand General Staff of the German Army, and that there is no need to upset our present system.

The senior officers of the British Army read Wilkinson's book, and were full of admiration for the achievements of the German General Staff as he described them, but few of them realized the systematic planning that such a system involved. Their admiration of the Prussian system was no more than word deep. Their reputations had been made on fields of battle where individual courage was the paramount quality, and where organization was confined to the provision of supplies and transport. Few of them had any idea of how to use a staff, although some were much quicker than others to learn, and very few of their staff officers knew their duties, or understood that they should act as a team. For instance, the man appointed as Buller's Chief of Staff was Lieutenant-General Sir Archibald Hunter, who went straight from India, where he was serving, to Durban. He joined Sir George White in Ladysmith as a temporary measure, was retained by White when Ladysmith was besieged, and never did join Buller. The loss of his Chief of the Staff was accepted by Buller with perfect equanimity. He did not ask for a replacement, but simply appointed a member of his own staff.

In any case, the British Generals would not have thought it necessary to make elaborate arrangements for staff work in relation to a war in South Africa. A war against a European power might carry unknown perils, but South Africa was a country they knew, a country in which British courage, skill and power of improvisation had won many notable victories. Almost all of the men originally chosen for command in South Africa had experience of the country. Buller's name was a legend there, a legend feared and respected by the Boers. Forestier-Walker, who had replaced Butler at the Cape, and Symons, who commanded the troops in Natal before White's arrival, had taken part in the Zulu War. Many of the other Generals were chosen partly for their knowledge of the country. Nor did the War Office lack men with experience of African conditions. Wolseley had been at one time Administrator of the Transvaal. Evelyn Wood had had imposed upon him the distasteful task of negotiating the terms of peace with the Boers after the defeat at Majuba. Nothing could have seemed more right and natural than that the men who knew South Africa and had won fame there should have been placed in command, yet in practice nothing could have been more disastrous. It was not merely that many of these men were in their late fifties, and old for active campaigns: their great fault was that they had learned nothing and forgotten nothing since the days fifteen or twenty years earlier when they had fought against the Zulus or the Basutos, or in Egypt and the Sudan. They read of modern fire power, they knew theoretically the importance of entrenching, they were aware that the bicycle existed, but their dreams were still set upon the cavalry charge, the close order advance, the impermeable British square. Buller understood from the beginning of the war that the Boers' resistance might be the more tenacious because they lived for the most part in little self-contained communities linked very loosely to a central organization. As he put it later in an expressive image:

There are living organisms which can be divided into a multitude of fragments without destroying the individual life of each fragment. As a whole, the organism has ceased to be, but as a multitude of parts its vitality is unimpaired; and if its life is to be wholly extinguished, every fragment must be separately destroyed. With such organisms these communities have much in common.

Knowing all this, Buller was still overbearing, arrogant, and unprepared to take the Boers seriously as opponents. His basic shyness was hidden behind a blustering exterior. Always concerned for the welfare of his men, and deeply considerate of them, he was often brutally rude to the officers on his staff. Perhaps no combination of qualities could have led more certainly to failure.

The quality of the men was conditioned primarily by the fact that the soldier was, as Wolseley said, 'the worst paid labourer in England', so that he came always from the lowest class of unskilled, often illiterate, men, far below the national average of intelligence and physique. Good food improved his physique, but little attempt was made to develop his intelligence. The hand of the Duke of Cambridge rested upon the whole of the Home Army, and the superiority of the Indian Army soldiers so far as initiative was concerned could be attributed directly to their comparative freedom from the Duke's authority. Wolseley's *Soldiers' Pocket Book* was eventually adopted by the War Office, but this simply-written and practical guide to action was useless to illiterate or semi-illiterate men. To Wolseley, far more than to any other man, was owed such changes as had been made from the parade ground evolutions delighted in by the Duke of Cambridge to something more nearly approaching the duties a soldier had to perform in the field, but the ceremonies in which the Duke delighted were retained to the end of his reign. With them went an immense wastage in every Regiment of men who were carrying out civilian jobs, because the Government insisted that such work must be done by Army recruits. Some time after the South African War had ended Evelyn Wood, in command of the Second Army Corps, found that of the forty-eight duty sergeants in one battalion, exactly half had jobs other than those involved in teaching soldiers how to fight. There were fifty-two young soldiers in the battalion who had done nothing for months but clean windows and carry coal, and another sixty-two in hospital as nurses. It was not a great exaggeration to say, as Leopold Amery did in his History of the War, that 'as a school of military training, the Army was nothing more or less than a gigantic Dotheboys Hall'.

The military training of the soldier was confined to three weeks field training during the year, with a certain amount of route marching added to it. There was a great deal of drill instruction, which was devoted chiefly to teaching him to move precisely and exactly to the order of command, so that a line of men might be wheeled through an angle 'with all the precision of a clock dial'. The quality of the musketry training may be gathered from this description:

> It consisted of firing a limited number of rounds at a stationary bull's eye target, at fixed known ranges, progressing from 100 to 1,000 yards, the distances gradually increasing, instead of decreasing, as they normally do in war. Once a year there was 'field firing', when a battalion would spend a glorious morning blazing away at a number of screens set up in conspicuous positions which no sane enemy would ever think of occupying.

It was a matter of general knowledge that France and Germany were far ahead of Britain in range construction and experimental firing.

The army uniform up to 1880 was also of a highly impractical kind. When Sir William Robertson joined the 16th Queen's Lancers in 1877 the undress uniform comprised skin-tight overalls, an equally tight 'shell jacket' cut off short above the hips, and a forage cap the size of a breakfast saucer, which was kept in place immediately above the right ear by a chin strap, which had to be worn under the lower lip and must on no account be kept under the chin except on mounted parades. The development of a khaki uniform, already used by the Indian Army for field service, was carried through by Wolseley working, with uncharacteristic tact, through the agency of the Duke of Connaught, in the early eighteen-eighties. The red and blue, however, lingered for home service use, and in 1896, Wolseley enlisted the aid of the Prince of Wales in an attempt to induce the officers to adapt their dress to the needs of active service. A good deal of gold lace was trimmed away, but much remained. The destruction of the parade ground mentality was beyond Wolseley's failing capacities by the time he reached power. No longer did he start work each day at six and continue almost without interruption into the late evening, but escaped as often as he could to his wife's company in their converted farmhouse at Glynde. There were times when his old anger at inefficiency revived, like the occasion when he inspected the Brigade of Guards in Hyde Park, called the mounted officers and adjutants forward, said to them, 'This is the worst inspection I have ever seen, and the drill is beneath contempt', and rode off the ground: but for the most part he struggled no more against embattled Army conservatism, but occupied himself with perfecting mobilization arrangements and with the endless struggle to get money out of the Government. Shooting practice was still done at fixed targets, the soldiers still received pitifully little practical military training, and they were taught neither to take cover nor to dig entrenchments. They were as little equipped as were most of their officers to fight a serious war.

PART FOUR

BULLER'S CAMPAIGN

'I remarked to Sir Redvers Buller, who was a very kind-hearted man, in talking to him of the fighting, (during the Gordon Relief Expedition) that much seemed very wrong in the world, for here were the Arabs practising fearful acts of cruelty and enforcing slavery on the black people, and here was this same black people whom we wished to liberate, for the most part fighting against us with fanatical hatred, and it seemed impossible to get into their minds that we were friends. Sir Redvers Buller agreed with me, but said that perhaps it was better not to think too much of these matters, but simply to do our duty.'

THE EARL OF DUNDONALD: *My Army Life.*

Redvers Buller has gone away
In charge of a job to Table Bay;
In what direction Redvers goes
Is a matter that only Buller knows.
Whatever you think, whatever you feel,
Give a chance to the Man at the Wheel.
If he's right, he'll pull us through;
If he's wrong he's better than you.
In any event you might well do worse
Than shut your mouth and open your purse.

ANONYMOUS.

Chapter One *White in Ladysmith*

Sir George White was at this time sixty-four years of age. His whole active military life had been spent with the Indian Army, from the time of the Indian Mutiny onwards. He had been awarded the Victoria Cross for his feat in outflanking the Afghan forces with a small troop of the 92nd Highlanders, during the Afghan War of 1879–80, and later he had been an instrument of Roberts' 'forward policy', which was designed to extend the North West Frontier to the borders of Afghanistan. Roberts regarded White as the most dashing and able of his subordinates, and he was chosen to be Commander-in-Chief on Roberts' retirement over the heads of a number of his seniors. Shortly before returning to England he had broken his leg, and it had mended badly. In talking to Irish doctors of the skill they had shown in getting him on to his feet again, White said that he felt that he ought to express gratitude to them for such a 'leg-asy'. He had spent two rather uneasy years as Quartermaster-General at the War Office, and now was pleased by the prospect of seeing active service again. When doubts were expressed about the leg he said that he was fit enough for anything except running away.

Like almost all of the senior officers, White did not believe that there would be serious fighting. 'The big financiers remain confident in the preservation of peace and they watch the pulse of such affairs more closely and with better information than any other body,' he wrote to Roberts from the War Office in September, a day or two before setting out for South Africa. When he arrived he was at once faced with the problem of whether or not he should retain the extreme forward positions that had been taken up in Natal. Symons was at Glencoe with half the troops, and the rest of the force was at Ladysmith. This seemed to some of White's officers, like Colonel Rawlinson (later Lord Rawlinson of Trent) to be ridiculous. Rawlinson thought that the whole of Natal north of the Tugela should be given up, and that White should retire behind the river and hold the river line until the Army Corps arrived. Ian Hamilton, who was also with White, was much disturbed by the strategical position, which he thought, as he said in a letter to Spenser Wilkinson, 'terribly faulty'. He believed that White should withdraw at least as far as Ladysmith. 'A great deal of the old contempt for the Boer is still existing,' he wrote. 'Symons is very boastful and bad in this way.' But the Governor of Natal, Hely-Hutchinson, was horrified by the idea that any Natal territory, and in particular territory that contained valuable coal mines, should be voluntarily given up. He thought that the moral effect of a British retirement would give encouragement to the Boers, and would also greatly affect the natives. Besides, was not Penn Symons, out at Glencoe, perfectly happy about the position? Hely-Hutchinson thought highly of Symons, who had, he said, lots of energy and was as keen as mustard. Rawlinson's view was different. He noted in his journal that Symons and his fellow officers talked as if the war was already over. 'They...speak of a British brigade being able to take on five times their number in Boers, which is silly rot.'

White may have thought that the position was militarily unsound, but he must have been aware that a decision to retire behind the Tugela would be regarded unfavourably not only by Hely-Hutchinson, but also by Milner and, back in London, by Chamberlain. And there was another problem involved. Ladysmith had been used as a supply depot and sixty days' provisions for the troops, with many other supplies, were stored there. If White retired, would he be able to take these supplies with him? There was later much argument about this. White thought that it would have been necessary to abandon his supplies. Ian Hamilton, who was with him, believed that they could have been got away. Roberts, although he agreed that White's dispositions were poor, thought that the political pressure of Hely-Hutchinson and the confidence of

Symons were largely responsible for them. He placed the principal blame upon the original selection of Ladysmith as a main base for stores, when there were no adequate forces to defend it. This was in effect an attack on Wolseley, who said in reply that Ladysmith was such an obviously bad position that nobody in his military senses would have thought of holding it. White, he said, should have burned his supplies and fallen back behind the river at Colenso. White, however, never seriously contemplated such a move. He left the forces where they were, even though he learned that Symons had neglected to consider guarding the water supply for his troops, and hoped for the best.

Symons had always refused to believe that Boer farmers would attack British regular soldiers. He was proved wrong early in the morning of 20 October, when the Boers, having positioned themselves during the previous night on two hills that commanded the village of Dundee and cut off its water supply, began to use their artillery on the British camp. Symons, although surprised, was not dismayed. He ordered a frontal attack on Talana, one of the hills, and ignored the Boers on the other hill, Impati. His men responded gallantly, but the attack was not a success. The British artillery silenced the Boer guns, but not their riflemen. Symons, leading the attack in person, was mortally wounded. The British reached the crest of Talana and the Boers fled. The battle ended, therefore, with a British 'victory', but it was a Pyrrhic one, for the Boers had suffered only 150 casualties, the British more than 500.

On the following day a more successful engagement took place at Elandslaagte, on the line of communication between Ladysmith and Dundee. General French made a dawn attack on the Boer force here with five squadrons of the Imperial Light Horse, a Regiment which had been raised in South Africa by the Uitlanders, and one squadron of the 5th Lancers. The qualifying tests of horsemanship and shooting for the Imperial Light Horse were severe ones, and although the men were armed at this time only with out of date Martini-Metford rifles, they were a formidable force. French was quickly reinforced by White with a force of infantry under the command of Ian Hamilton. They were successful in overcoming a determined Boer resistance, and in capturing two guns, and of course they reopened the line of communications, which had been temporarily cut. But White then became nervous of a further attack by a fresh Boer force, although in fact none was contemplated. He decided not to follow up his victory, but to retire from Elandslaagte to Ladysmith. When General Yule, who had replaced Symons in command of the troops at Dundee, asked for help, White replied that none could be sent. Yule, left to his own resources, decided that he would have to abandon the supplies at Dundee, and also to leave the dying Symons to the care of the Boers. The sixty-mile march back to Ladysmith took four days, and was carried out under very unpleasant conditions. There was nothing to eat but bully beef and biscuits, and nothing to drink but muddy water. At several points the road was blocked by rain. 'We were stopped and kept three hours standing in the mud and pouring rain, the men not having either blankets or overcoats,' a Major in the Irish Fusiliers noted in his diary. 'The whole night long it rained, and the whole night we crawled along, perhaps doing on an average about half a mile an hour. Altogether, it was the most poisonously miserable night that any man could or will ever experience.' The men got back to Ladysmith feeling distinctly depressed.

From these encounters something could already have been learned of the characteristics of the Boer and British fighting men. The Boers did not really fight at all as the British understood it. A few weeks later Clery was to complain: 'The worst of the Boers is that their tactics are never according to rule. You attack them in a position, and when you get there they have galloped off and are coming in on your rear.' The Boers' idea of fighting was to entrench themselves in kopjes and there to rely on the skill of their marksmen and the accuracy of their artillery. They moved in groups, but fought very much as individuals. They were, at this stage of the war, far better rifle shots than the British soldiers who had been taught volley firing at fixed targets. They had no liking for hand to hand fighting, and many of them dreaded the bayonet. To charge them was to invite heavy casualties with little hope of reward, for they would fire at the advancing infantry while it was safe to do so, and then ride away. They felt no shame in running away and did not in any way acknowledge defeat by doing so, for they fought really as a guerrilla army. Among the cover of these rocks and kopjes they were more than a match for the British infantry. It was possible to deduce that White, or any other British general, would need an abundance of cavalry or mounted infantry who could match the mobility of the Boers, and that he would in any case want far more men than White had available to engage them with any hope of success. The very light casualties of Ian Hamilton's men at Elandslaagte, when they had advanced in open order instead of in the customary close order formation should have taught a lesson, and so should the way in which the Boers fired as individuals, instead of in the volleys favoured by British range practice.

As the Boers approached Ladysmith it became distressingly apparent also that the biggest of their guns had a much longer range than anything the British possessed. The most advanced British military thinkers, seeking as always to learn from German experience, had taken particular note of the fact that in the Franco-Prussian War the Germans had been told to fire at not more than 1,800 yards, because that was a range of maximum effectiveness. The Artillery Drill Book of 1896 laid it down that the most distant effective artillery range was 3,500 yards, and that 2,500 yards should be thought of as medium range. The Boers, however, had field guns with a range of 6,800 yards, howitzers with a range of 7,000 yards, and three heavy fortress guns which fired 64 pound shells as far as 11,000 yards. It had been said that these fortress guns could not possibly be made mobile, but the Boers manhandled them into position outside Ladysmith, and these 'Long Toms' caused consternation when they first fired into the town. It might be true, as was said afterwards, that firing at such a distance was very inaccurate, but the moral effect on the inhabitants of Ladysmith, and even on the troops, was considerable. White had no guns that would fire more than 5,500 yards, and although he sent hurriedly for a Naval Brigade from Durban, who brought with them two 4.7 inch guns that would fire up to 8,000 yards, he was still outmatched for distance. By the time the Naval Brigade arrived, in any case, he was shut up in Ladysmith for good.

The lessons from the first two engagements already mentioned had not been even dimly understood by White. In his view both

Talana and Elandslaagte had been notable victories for British arms. It needed, as he thought, only one decisive blow to dispose of this Boer force for good. He sent up a balloon to inspect their positions, and decided upon a dawn attack. This attack was designed to roll up the left flank of the whole Transvaal force which was advancing from the north and destroy it, while ignoring the Orange Free State force which was advancing southwards towards Colenso. There was to be a frontal infantry assault upon the Boer forces entrenched upon Long Hill and Pepworth Hill, outside Ladysmith. At the same time a flank attack was to be made by an infantry brigade drawn from the King's Royal Rifles, the Liverpools, the Leicesters, and the Dublin Fusiliers. This all-important flank attack was under the command of Colonel Grimwood. French, with the cavalry, was to cover Grimwood's right and then advance northwards, pursuing the fleeing Boers. To cut off their retreat completely and finally a column of some thousand men was to be sent right behind the Boer lines, where they would occupy a defile known as Nicholson's Nek. This column was under the command of Colonel Carleton of the Irish Fusiliers, and it was made up partly of this regiment and partly of men from the Gloucesters. The column had with it the 10th Mountain Battery.

This bold plan involved night marches for both Grimwood and Carleton. Grimwood's march was a fairly simple operation, but Carleton had to march right through the Boer lines at night. There were no useful maps, but Carleton's staff officer, Major Adye, was well acquainted with the ground, and he was assisted by local residents, one of whom had a farm near to Nicholson's Nek. The scheme depended for its success on faultless timing, and it could have been conceived only by a very bold man, or by a timid one who felt it necessary to make an attacking gesture. Night marches had been almost unknown in the British Army before Wolseley popularized them with his night attack on Tel-el-Kebir. For success they required a precision and competence in staff work which White's force failed altogether to achieve. Half of Grimwood's brigade took up position properly but the rest of it, including the artillery, left the column during the march and ended up behind Flag Hill, near to Ian Hamilton's force. Grimwood's staff officers were so staggeringly incompetent that they failed to discover that they lacked half their infantry and all their artillery until this was revealed by the light of dawn. At the same time a confusion about the reading of orders caused French to advance his cavalry, not so that it would cover Grimwood's flank as had been intended, but to a point two miles in his rear. In the dawn the hapless Grimwood found his force not only short of half its infantry and all of its artillery, but also without cavalry support.

One further feature of the situation became apparent as soon as battle was joined. White, seeing the Boers encamped upon Pepworth Hill and Long Hill, had assumed that they would stay there. He had not bothered to send out scouts to discover their exact positions. In fact they were still on Pepworth, but had retreated from Long Hill in the night, whether as a tactical move on the part of their commander, General Joubert, through information from the spies who infested Ladysmith, or simply because of their habit of sleeping in their laagers, is not certainly known. They now occupied a semicircular position extending round the entire British force, and there was no question of Grimwood rolling up their flank. Far from this happening, his own unsupported flank would be rolled up if he occupied Long Hill. What was he to do? He wheeled east, concentrated on resisting the violent rifle and artillery fire to which he was exposed, sent for a battery of artillery, and told White the situation. French, advancing in the belief that the time had come for him to pursue the fleeing Boers, found himself subjected to withering rifle fire. He hurriedly retreated again, fell on to the defensive, and reported his troubles to White. Only the artillery attack on Pepworth, helped as it was by the unexpected addition of Grimwood's artillery, was going well. The Boer batteries on the hill were silenced.

White now had the choice of several courses, none of them particularly pleasant. He could make a direct attack on Pepworth and try to break through to Carleton, whose column could be heard distantly in action. He could swing Hamilton's force and the whole of the artillery across to support Grimwood. Or he could retire altogether, and leave Carleton to make his own way back to Ladysmith. What was happening to Carleton? An officers' patrol which tried to get through to him had to return, and heliographic messages failed to elicit any reply. In practice White made no attempt to change the shape of the battle, but simply supported his forces where they seemed to be under pressure, moving up men in support of French and keeping Hamilton's brigade in reserve. The reluctance of British Generals to commit a major part of their forces in any single engagement was characteristic of the war at this time. So the battle continued, an affair of artillery and rifle fire, exactly the kind of fighting the Boers preferred.

In Ladysmith there was something approaching panic. The inhabitants of the town, if one should call the single street of stores and tin-roofed bungalows by that name, had shared White's perfect confidence in the outcome of that morning's battle. Although martial law had been declared, and the military camp on the barren plain nearly two miles north-west of the town was occupied, life continued undisturbed. The arrival of large supplies every day by rail seemed a guarantee of security. Life in Ladysmith was thought by those who came out from England unpleasant, almost barbarous. It was known to be an unhealthy spot, where enteric fever was rife, but the real curse of the place was dust, a thin gritty red dust that blinded the eyes, filled the nose, turned a white shirt brown in half an hour, crept into food and clothing. 'It lies in a layer mixed with flies on the top of your rations,' wrote the war correspondent Henry Nevinson. 'The white ants eat away the flaps of the tents, and the men wake up covered with dust, like children in a hayfield. Even mules die of it in convulsions.' Yet the stiff upper lip characteristic of British colonists was maintained. Ladies exchanged visits, garden parties were held, there was an elaborate pretence of civilized life. The invasion of Northern Natal was as nearly as possible ignored. On this day the war really intruded for the first time upon the town. Shells from 'Long Tom', the first of the Boer guns to be brought into position outside the town, began to land near the railway station at daybreak. The damage they did was comparatively slight, and within a matter of days the townspeople became accustomed to them, but these first shells caused great alarm, as much because of the affront involved in the idea that British people could be shelled by Boers as for any other reason. The alarm was increased by the accounts that came in from the battlefield, and by the arrival of stray mules and gunners who reported that some obscure but alarming fate had overtaken Carleton's column. An attack on the town by raiding Boers was expected. At 11.30 in the morning White, who had been bringing across men from Hamilton's brigade to support Grimwood and French, decided to end an attack, which had achieved nothing.

There is some difference of opinion about the success of the withdrawal. According to White and some of his officers, it was made in perfect order. But by the accounts of other eyewitnesses Grimwood's battalions, which had remained relatively unscathed while they stayed under cover, suffered heavily as soon as they exposed themselves in retreating across the plain to Ladysmith, and their retreat was saved from becoming a rout only by the covering action of the field artillery. French's cavalry, unprotected by artillery, were left to save themselves by speed alone, and retired in utter disorder. This account of events is supported by a member of one Boer commando:

Turning round, we saw the entire British force that had come out against us on the plain that morning in full retreat to Ladysmith. Great clouds of dust billowed over the veldt as the troops withdrew, and the manner of their going had every appearance of a rout.

Christian de Wet, at that time a Field-Cornet, muttered 'Loose your horsemen, loose your horsemen', but Joubert made no attempt to pursue the British. It is possible that, with the generosity that prevailed in what has been called the last of the gentlemen's wars, he was reluctant to pursue a fleeing enemy, but more likely that he lacked the quickness of mind to seize this opportunity. The British were permitted to retire into Ladysmith without being unduly harassed. The Naval Brigade sent for by White from Durban had arrived at about 9.30 in the morning, and cheered the troops and the inhabitants by temporarily silencing Long Tom. With his men safely back in Ladysmith, White made no further attempt to get through to

Carleton's column. It was not until the evening that he learned, through a message from Joubert, of their fate.

Carleton's column should have set out at 10 o'clock on Sunday night. In fact they did not leave until an hour later, chiefly because of delay in loading up the ammunition mules, which the untrained men did not know how to handle. There were nearly two hundred mules, which carried the reserve ammunition and pulled the mountain battery, there was a Maxim gun, two heliographs, and several kegs of water. The column thus equipped was to march silently, and without smoking or returning enemy fire, some seven miles in complete darkness. They would then be behind the Boer lines, but they would also have no direct link at all with the main British force. This hazardous enterprise was almost like a parody of the night attacks practised by Wolseley.

Nevertheless the column, thanks to the skill of its guides, passed through the Boer lines. After three hours' marching they were only two miles from Nicholson's Nek and there were two hours left before dawn. But now Carleton became worried by the thought that he might be caught at dawn in the narrow defile. He decided to turn to his left and establish himself upon the slopes of a hill called Tchrengula, or the Hog's Back. The ascent was at first gentle, then obstructed by boulders, finally almost precipitous. At last, what was almost inevitable happened. Some of the mules lost their footing. There was suddenly what one of the officers described as a roar like that of an approaching train, and in the darkness a number of animals could be seen bounding down the rocky slope. Further down, they came upon the ammunition mules, and in the darkness these panicked too, turning and rushing down with their muleteers. The whole confused mass of men and animals poured upon the body of the Gloucesters, who were just turning off to begin the ascent of the hill. There were shots, shouts, and a few scattered shots in reply from Boer outposts a mile away. Then the panic died away, the officers reformed the men, and they moved up the hill again. It was not until they had all reached the summit that Carleton discovered just what had happened. The mountain battery had gone, except for two gun mules carrying parts of two pieces which were useless by themselves. Only seventeen of the ammunition mules had arrived, so that there was practically no reserve ammunition. The water kegs and the heliographs were lost, and eighty-odd gunners and forty of the Gloucesters had disappeared. It was these men who straggled back to Ladysmith in the morning to tell their unhappy tale.

Carleton might now have been excused for feeling alarm. But his period of timidity had passed, to be replaced by overconfidence. He never doubted that the main attack would succeed, and thought it his duty to support it. He sent back a Kaffir (who never reached White) to tell him what had happened, and proceeded to entrench himself after a fashion upon the slopes of Tchrengula. Major Adye, who was chiefly responsible for the expedition, ignored the advice of the local guides, who told him that the most likely point of attack would be from the north. Without making any attempt at reconnoitring the ground Carleton and Adye decided to defend the eastern and western sides of the hill. The eastern crest faced Pepworth, from which the main attack was expected, and the Royal Irish Fusiliers held this position, while the Gloucesters held the western slopes. A small group of Gloucesters were sent forward to a rise which commanded the re-entrants to the position. Sangars (that is, breastworks of stones) were piled up. The men had not learned to entrench themselves, nor in fact had they any entrenching tools with them.

Dawn revealed to the surprised Boers the English force installed upon Tchrengula, the soldiers building sangars, a knot of officers grouped together, and other men pulling a tarpaulin over a tree for shade. There was desultory firing and then Christian de Wet, who was in command of a group of some two or three hundred burghers, joined with a group of the Johannesburg police or 'Zarps' in storming the northern side of the hill. They were attacking the advanced group of the Gloucesters, and under cover of this attack subsidiary forces attacked this party of the Gloucesters from the flanks. In total numbers the British force was much superior, yet from the beginning of the fight they were forced on to the defensive. They were hampered partly by lack of ammunition, which caused an order to be given that the Maxim gun should not be used at long range, and partly by the practice of volley firing, which led Adye to order that the men must not fire at individuals, but their prime defect was that of totally incompetent leadership. From the beginning the attack came from the north, and it was obvious that if the advanced companies of the Gloucesters were left unsupported they would be overwhelmed, and that the Boers would then command the whole position, yet almost nothing was done to strengthen them, or to bring more troops into the engagement. Carleton and Adye were so convinced that the long range exchange of shots with distant Boers in which the main body was involved was the prelude to the real attack that they paid little attention to what was going on elsewhere. At 11.30 the advance party of the Gloucesters was almost completely enveloped, and they then received an order that they might retire and join the main body. In doing so they suffered heavily from a damaging crossfire. Part of one company failed to get the order to retire, and were made prisoners. The rest, after their retirement, received an order from Carleton, who was still unaware of what was happening, to advance and recapture their position. They were far too weak to do this and it was occupied by the Boers, who now commanded the sangars put up by the British. At about this time Carleton received a heliograph from White. It said: 'Retire on Ladysmith as opportunity offers.' He could neither answer the message nor carry out the instruction.

The Boer command of the sangars was the beginning of the end. Heavy rifle fire drove most of one company of the Irish Fusiliers out of their position, a company of Gloucesters on the west side of the hill were forced to retreat, and another company retreated with them through a misunderstood signal. Through another mistake – they could see no firing, and thought that Carleton had deserted them upon the hill – another little company of Gloucesters surrendered. Their white flag was seen by a company still fighting. This company sent a message to Carleton who, seeing the Boers advancing upon him shouting, waving their hats and trailing their rifles, ordered the bugler to sound the cease fire. A white rag was then held up on a rifle, but the surrender was by no means complete, for some of the Fusiliers were fighting on while Carleton and Adye were walking forward to meet the Boer Commandant and hand him their swords. Thirty-seven officers and 917 men surrendered to the

Boers, who treated them with the greatest courtesy. Some hundred and forty of them were wounded, and less than fifty men had been killed. The Boer losses were trivial. In White's attack from Ladysmith the British dead and wounded were perhaps 300, and the Boer about the same.

So ended Mournful Monday, the most ignominious defeat that British arms had suffered for many years. After it, there was something like panic in the town. Many people, terrified where before they had been supremely confident, fled southwards, crowding the trains. The Hindoos and Kaffirs, said the Australian war correspondent Donald Macdonald, were prominent in this railway rush:

> There were three trains – the carriages filled with white women and children, the open trucks packed thickly with Kaffirs and Hindoos. White men stood back in despair or shame from this shrieking horde, steaming in the hot thunderous Natal night, for they felt their manhood would have been smirched by flight in such company. The native police rounded up the blacks like sheep, and packed them as sheep are rarely packed, prodding them on with their knobkerries.

This was on Tuesday night, but on Wednesday, which was observed as an armistice, the scare grew rather than subsided. It was not only the Kaffirs and Hindoos who were anxious to get away. Many of the white population, fearing death or captivity at the hands of the Boers, left Ladysmith, taking with them no more than the luggage they could carry in a trunk. Half the houses were left empty, and many of the shops were closed. The banks shut, first handing over their money to the military authorities. A good many officers sent their wives and families down to Maritzburg, and there were painful farewells at the railway station. Hundreds of farmers, who had trekked into the town from the north, hoping for security, slept in their wagons in the slush of Ladysmith's streets. On 2 November, the Boer circle round the town closed, and railway and telegraphic communications were cut. French and his staff left on the last train, but White refused to agree to the suggestion that the whole of his cavalry should be sent south of the Tugela. They stayed in Ladysmith, where they served no purpose than that of eventually providing food. He refused also to release Hunter, saying that his presence was indispensable for the defence of Ladysmith. A couple of days later White asked Joubert to permit the departure south of hospital trains with wounded and non-combatants. Joubert refused, but agreed to the formation of a camp five miles out of the town, at Intombi Spruit, for sick, wounded, and non-combatants. At a public meeting on the steps of the Ionic Public Hall, now a hospital, the remaining civilians indignantly rejected the idea of going to Intombi Spruit, with the Boers creeping up on and perhaps surrounding them. Joubert's proposal was accepted only for the sick and wounded, and the inhabitants set about making places to live that were safe from shellfire. Many of them dug out caves in the soft banks of the Klip River, which ran close under the hills to the south of the town, and lived in these caves, which afforded almost perfect protection against shrapnel. Other families constructed shelters by closing up the ends of bridges and culverts with stones and sandbags.

In the meantime defensive dispositions were being made in this scattered town on a plain enclosed in an amphitheatre of rocky hills. The Boers had closed the circle round the town, but the British forces were not greatly inferior in numbers, and their object was to prevent this loosely embracing circle from becoming a noose. To Nevinson, who found men of the Manchesters building small sangars of stones and sandbags along the ridge of the long hill to the south-west called Caesar's Camp, it seemed that the work was being carelessly and listlessly done. 'We're surrounded – that's what we are,' the men kept saying to him. 'Thought we was goin' to have Christmas puddin' in Pretoria. Not much Christmas puddin' we'll ever smell again.' But the defence arrangements were comprehensive, however unwillingly they may have been carried out. The little town itself was quite indefensible as a position, and what White and his staff had to decide was the extent of the perimeter they could safely fortify and defend. The further out they could push the perimeter, the more difficult would it be for the Boers to shell the town effectively, but if the defences were stretched too far it would be easy for the Boers to break through. To defend the great two-mile wide plateau of Bulwana to the south-east, and Lombard's Kop and Gun Hill nearby would have kept the Boers at their distance, but it seemed to White and his advisers that he was not strong enough for this. The perimeter eventually fortified was some fourteen miles round, bounded by a line of kopjes to the north and north-east, following the line of the Klip River on the east, and bounded on the west by a range of hills up to the plateau of Caesar's Camp. Some fortifications had already been built on the north-eastern side, and now these were quickly improved, and stone fortifications connected by covered ways built round much of the rest of the area. On the west the defences consisted mainly of stone forts, each of which commanded a considerable field of fire. The perimeter was divided into four separate commands, and a proportion of artillery given to each. A very comprehensive system of telephone communication was established between the various posts, and also between these posts and headquarters. It was not likely that these defences would be capable of resisting a really serious attack in force, but within the limits of their resources and position White, Hunter, Hamilton, Rawlinson and the rest could feel that they had done a good job.

The effect of the battle of Ladysmith was out of proportion to its significance. It was regarded on both sides as much more than a mere reverse. To the Boers, both of the Transvaal and the Free State, it acted as a tonic, convincing doubters that they would do well to take up arms, and giving new zest to those who from the start had hoped for victory. If a few hundred Boers could compel the surrender of a thousand British Regular soldiers, how could the Boers fail to win the war? Waverers in the Free State and in the northern part of Cape Colony took up arms, and in Cape Town itself the Afrikanders, unready for action, seethed with excitement. The air was full of plots, as it had been a few months before in Johannesburg. As the anxious Milner said, it reeked of treason. On White also the battle had a tremendous psychological effect. He felt, and rightly, that he bore most of the responsibility for the loss of Carleton's column. Most of his staff had been against going out to fight on 29 October, and he wrote to his wife: 'I think after this venture the men will lose confidence in me, and that I ought to be superseded.' He added that he did not think he could go on soldiering. He was not superseded, but after the battle he stayed in his house, and rarely went out among the men. He was never again willingly to face the Boers in the field, and his depression communicated itself at first to the soldiers, 'who had never conceived of the possibility of a British battalion surrendering to farmers', as Rawlinson puts it. That the professionals should be so decisively defeated by amateurs seemed inconceivable. Only the more flexibly minded and younger officers were capable of learning the necessary lessons, and learning them quickly. Hunter was the life and soul of the defence, and Rawlinson and Hamilton also realized that on his home ground the Boer was a formidable enemy, mobile and intelligent. None of them, perhaps fully understood that the investment of White's force increased immensely the task of winning the war.

In England the affair of Nicholson's Nek (as the surrender on Tchrengula was always called) could not be concealed, but it was cushioned with soothing words, and the full shock of White's investment was obscured by misleading newspaper reports, which implied that he had had the idea of a retirement to Ladysmith in mind all the time as a good tactical move. Wolseley had no doubt that it was a major error. At lunch with Lord Esher at Brooks' he said that White should have blown up his magazines, destroyed his food, and retired to the Tugela. 'As it is he is caught in a trap, and it will take an army to get him out.' He wrote in anger and sorrow to his wife:

Since our disaster at Majuba, indeed for the last half-century or so we have had no such disaster as that of yesterday. If they had fought it out and been shot I should have nothing but grief to feel, but now I am humiliated and feel ashamed of the officers who surrendered... Poor little Lansdowne is cast down hopelessly, and the fact that he would not take my advice and send out 10,000 troops to Natal a long time ago must prey upon his mind. My culpability is also serious, for it was I who selected

White – *faute de mieux*. I only knew him by reputation, and he was always crammed down my throat as a great General.

Since White had been a pillar of the Indian Army, Wolseley felt no compunction in disclaiming responsibility for him. But although he announced publicly that the war would be a much more serious business than anybody had thought, he could not help thinking that with Buller's arrival things would be different.

Chapter Two *Buller in Cape Town*

The weather during the sixteen days that the *Dunottar Castle* took to reach Cape Town was often tempestuous. Buller was little inclined to talk about the campaign with his staff. He was even less disposed to talk to the war correspondents on board, since he regarded them as the natural enemies of any military man. It was almost a point of honour with him not to talk to newspaper men, and he did not make an exception for the young correspondent of the *Morning Post*, Winston Churchill. He had written several years earlier, after one encounter, 'The rascal tried three times to interview me, but I knew too much for him, and he had to send off his report without even so much as getting a question into me,' and now the correspondents had to be content with attempts to catch him in the great square box called a multigraph, 'which takes the continuous pictures for the biograph', as one of them put it. The multigraph was set up so as to command a view of the hurricane deck, where Buller walked with his staff before dinner. 'You can catch me if you can, but I won't pose for you,' he said. The biograph operator, W K Dickson, 'caught' him several times – striding along the deck to the barber to get his hair cut, trying playfully to shove the Captain in the way of the multigraph, appearing in uniform just before they got to Cape Town, his face brilliantly illuminated by the rays of the sun. He showed his usual ease in getting on with working people. 'Just think how easily he talked to me all the time he was having his hair cut,' the barber said afterwards. 'And when a man came in for a pipe, and I told him to come later, the General said, "Why, give him his pipe, I am in no hurry" – and I did.'

His staff officers had less success in making him talk. Colonel á Court tried to get some information about the tactics that they would employ. He was told simply that they would knock the Boers off the kopjes with their guns. á Court, although he felt that he was ignorant of many things a staff officer should know, was deterred by the General's manner from asking further questions. But there was no lack of trust in or enthusiasm for Buller. When the *Dunottar Castle* passed a ship carrying some Australians to the Cape, the Colonials waved their broad-brimmed hats and cheered frantically when they heard who was on board. There was a fancy dress ball, and two days of ship's games in which Buller took part. On the day before reaching Cape Town they met the *Australasian*, of the Aberdeen White Star line. A long blackboard was hung on her ratlines, and on it they read, as the ship moved past: THREE BATTLES. BOERS DEFEATED. SYMONS KILLED. 'In a few minutes the *Australasian* was hull down in the distance, but her quick transit had made an incredible difference,' a war correspondent wrote. 'We looked on the sea with enlightened eyes.' They were further enlightened when they reached Table Bay on a dripping wet evening. An officer came on board and told Buller and his staff the news of Nicholson's Nek. When they went ashore on the following morning, received by a guard of honour of the local militia, Buller knew that the plan he had brought out from London had received a severe blow.

Milner awaited his coming in the modest Government House, 'half a country house and half a country inn', with its single sentry patrolling outside the door. His thoughts cannot have been cheerful. He was convinced that there was danger of a rising in Cape Colony, yet it was obvious that few troops could be spared to guard against this possibility. Forestier-Walker was more compliant than Butler, but he inspired no confidence in Milner, who saw that he was unlikely to proceed energetically with plans for raising local troops of volunteers. What could be expected from Buller? The High Commissioner had heard from London that he had appeared alarmingly influenced by Butler. When Buller arrived, driving up with Forestier-Walker through streets bright with waving flags and black with cheering people, he said nothing to raise Milner's spirits. The High Commissioner showed him a map of the districts in Cape Colony, which, as he believed, were ready to rise in rebellion when opportunity offered. Buller gloomily remarked that he was expected to conquer not only the two Republics, but the whole of South Africa.

During the next day or two nothing but bad news came from the fronts, or rather from the various points at which the Boers had attacked. The railway bridges over the Orange River had, at Milner's insistence, been left undestroyed. The High Commissioner had been determined to do nothing that might provoke a rising in Cape Colony, and with this in mind he had requested also that the bridges should remain unguarded by troops. They were naturally seized by the Boers. On 1 November, they crossed the bridge at Norval's Pont, taking prisoners the six policemen who guarded it, and on the same day they captured the bridges at Bethulie, where they crossed in some force. Mafeking and Kimberley were both cut off, and Cecil Rhodes in Kimberley was particularly clamorous in asking for immediate relief. In Natal the small garrison at Colenso had fallen back on Estcourt, so that White was now cut off completely. The Boers were not sufficiently well organized, nor had they sufficient tactical sense, to bypass White as they might have done and sweep down upon Durban, but had they wished to do so there was nothing to stop them. Buller suggested to White that he should stop attacking the Boers and entrench himself behind the Tugela, but White replied that he was strongly entrenched at Ladysmith, and could not get his supplies away. Kimberley, Buller wrote to Wolseley, was 'howling to be relieved'.

The necessity of choice pressed agonizingly on him. When he had been four days in Cape Town he wrote a long letter to his brother Tremayne, which must be one of the most curious documents ever penned by a British General before going into action. The letter, which accompanied some papers sent to his brother presumably for use in the event of his death, is much less concerned with the future than with the past. It is an attempted justification of his own position in relation to Lansdowne, an alibi constructed in advance to excuse defeat. The letter begins:

> I am in the tightest place I have ever been in, and the worst of it is that it is I think none of my creating. I don't know if I shall ever get out of it all right, and I think if I shall fail that it is fair my family should know afterwards what at any rate I had to say in my own defence.
>
> First I must premise that I did not get on with Lansdowne at the WO. His views were that a C-in-C was a mere title and that a Military Board to advise a S of S was a better arrangement. I was distinctly opposed to this arrangement and held that no Army could be efficient which was not moulded by one master mind.
>
> I need not go into particulars. We did not agree. He found it difficult to work with me, and I with him, though I can truly say that I have never worked harder for any one. In the end he told me what no one had ever said before, that I was disagreeable to work with. Such being our relations he sent for me in June and told me, as I thought in a most ungracious manner, that if there was a war in SA I was selected as the Commander. I thanked him, said that it would be a critical operation, suggested a minimum force, asked if any definite line of operations had been selected, or any definite plan made. I gathered none was existent.
>
> I afterwards saw Lord Wolseley, who had many schemes, but said he could get nothing definite out of Lansdowne.

Buller then recites several of the complaints about Lansdowne, which have already been mentioned. He says that when he came up from Aldershot he urged the revival of something resembling his old Adjutant-General's meetings:

> This daily meeting was directed. This came to be called the C-in-C's meeting. The first was held July 13. I confess I had anticipated being invited to attend these meetings, or to comment on their decisions. Nothing of the sort was done. I

never saw their decisions. I am writing plain facts, and I admit that I have bitterly reproached myself for not having insisted on being present. It was a grave mistake. My only excuse is, and I admit that in view of the gravity of the case it is insufficient, that when AG I had instituted meetings identical with these, and used to put all work through them with the best results. When Lord L came to the WO he expressed his strong disapproval of the continuance of these meetings, which then were called at the instance of any Head of Department who wished to consult with his colleagues, and he substituted his Army Board which was only allowed to assemble to consider papers referred to it by himself. In fact he abolished concert. I always said a war would break down his system. It did, but I felt reluctant to press home, what many of my own friends, both Military and Civil, described as a victory for my policy by demanding to attend. My excuse must stand for what it is worth. I think I was wrong.

The arguments between them culminated in Buller's private Minute sent to Lord Salisbury. He tells how this angered Lansdowne:

At my interview with Lord L after the Cabinet of the 7.9. he was very angry at my action in going behind his back, and he especially took exception to my having, as he said, suggested to the Cabinet that I knew nothing of what was going on, which he said was not true as all the WO information was open to me, and that I was not justified in saying that I did not know the force in Cape Colony. I said that it was the fact as I had stated that I had not been permitted to see at any time any of the correspondence that was passing between Mr Chamberlain and Sir A Milner and that I had no knowledge of the actual situation at the Cape nor any means of knowing it.

So he recited his wrongs, ending his letter with the sentence: 'I reached the Cape on the 30.10, the condition of affairs there then is now a matter of history.' It was with history, he must have felt, that he had put himself right in this letter. But now, what was to be done for Rhodes howling at Kimberley and for White penned in Ladysmith? At the time he wrote to his brother, he still meant to stick to the original plan of driving for Bloemfontein. 'I shall be sorry if Kimberley and Ladysmith go, but I cannot help them better.' Within a couple of days, however, he had decided to split up the Army Corps as it arrived, sending Lord Methuen (whom Milner had wanted to see as Commander-in-Chief) to relieve Kimberley, and himself taking charge of the main force, which would go to the relief of Ladysmith. He regarded this splitting of the Army Corps as a temporary measure. He thought that Methuen would relieve Kimberley and that he would join hands with White at Ladysmith, in a matter of days rather than weeks, and that they could then turn to attack Bloemfontein.

This, again, was a fateful decision. Three dispositions of his force were possible for Buller. The first was to ignore the two besieged towns and strike straight for Bloemfontein, the second to ignore Kimberley and use his whole Army Corps in attacking Ladysmith, and the third to split the Army Corps as he actually did. Roberts thought that, upon the whole, what he did was inevitable and right. Wolseley thought it was wrong, and that the original line of advance was the right one:

> When Sir Redvers Buller went to Natal himself, he went there on his own hook entirely, and at his own instigation, and I do not know that I even knew, until he had started or was about to start, that he was going.

In fact Buller sent a telegram to Lansdowne on 20 November, saying that he proposed to leave for Natal on the 22nd, and no doubt Wolseley knew this.

Buller's departure on the 22nd, accompanied by his Military Secretary, Colonel Stopford, and a few aides-de-camp, came as a surprise to the rest of his staff, and also to Milner, who was completely taken aback by his departure. 'I seldom knew what was in his mind, and when he left Natal I did not know until he had gone, nor did many others', wrote one of his staff officers. By leaving Cape Town he solved some problems, but created others. In

Natal he was on the field of action, and would be able to see exactly what was going on. On the other hand, it was impossible for him to act effectively from Natal as Commander-in-Chief on a front hundreds of miles away. He tried ineffectively to exercise control at long distance, sending messages to the Generals he had left in Cape Town. Colonel Wynne, who had stayed behind, wrote the orders to the Generals who commanded in Cape Colony. 'It was not a satisfactory state of things,' one of the sufferers said mildly, and the wonder is that it caused so few serious errors.

During the three weeks in Cape Town, however, Buller and his staff performed prodigies of improvisation in sending off the Army Corps to the fronts on their arrival, and in arranging supply and transport. We have seen that the War Office had only three-and-half miles of light railway available, and the railway staff which had come out to organize an area as large as central Europe consisted of the director of railways, Colonel Girouard, one batman, one horse and one groom. Within a few months this staff had grown to several hundred officers and 5,000 men. The lack of horses and mules has already been mentioned. Yet the troops were sent off to the Kimberley, Cape Colony and Natal fronts very quickly after disembarkation. As Amery says ironically in *The Times History* the Army Corps was 'in every respect capable of achieving a successful march to Pretoria – if only it had been a match for the Boers in the field'. During these three weeks, also, Buller gave permission for the raising of several groups of Colonial troops. Colonel á Court raised the South African Light Horse from exiled Uitlanders, 'the only conditions being that a man should be able to ride and shoot, and should be physically fit'. There were other forces of infantry and mounted infantry, and a corps of Scouts. It was suggested afterwards that Buller might have done more in the way of raising irregular troops at this time, but he was undoubtedly affected by Milner's belief that the enlistment and arming of volunteers was likely to provide arms for the enemy, since the High Commissioner thought that pro-Boers would enlist among the irregulars. Buller was also disturbed by the great difference in rates of pay between the Colonials, who received 5s. a day, and the British regulars who received 1s. He thought, not without reason, that the enlistment of a large number of irregulars would cause discontent.

Buller and Milner did not get on well. To Buller the High Commissioner seemed unduly timid, to Milner the Commander-in-Chief appeared distinctly brash. In response to Milner's continual complaints about the position in Cape Colony, Buller proposed that martial law should be declared, and that the principal Boer spies and agents should be arrested and sent on a transport to Lourenco Marques, with instructions to the Captain that he should make the journey last at least a month. The time for the arrests was fixed, but Milner's position in relation to the Schreiner Government was a delicate one. Schreiner emphasized frequently that any provocative move might tip the balance of neutrality which he was trying to preserve, and cause open revolt in Cape Colony. At the last moment Milner decided that the arrests had better not take place, and that it would be unwise to proclaim martial law. Milner, on his side, was annoyed by Buller's impatience, and disturbed by his fits of depression. On one occasion the General told him, as he had told Lyttelton, that he meant to get back to England as soon as possible. Milner thought that Buller 'showed grasp', but he liked those about him to be optimistic, and to have a sense of Britain's mission in South Africa. Buller seemed to him lacking on both counts, and he was not sorry to see the General leave Cape Town.

Chapter Three *Buller Behind the Lines*

Buller's movements after leaving Cape Town were not marked by the sense of urgency that might have been expected in one who was marching to the relief of an invested force. He sent Clery up to Frere to superintend the troops who were being collected there, and himself remained in Maritzburg for a week, superintending the supply, transport and hospital arrangements. No British General has ever been so solicitous for the welfare of his soldiers as was Buller during this campaign. He consulted with the medical officers about hospitals at every point, and cut through the great mass of forms used by the over-organized medical service. 'The General simply said, "You want so many bearers, get them",' said Sir Frederick Treves, who was with the Natal force as a consulting surgeon. Buller also conceived the idea of having a large Field Hospital at the head of the column, pitched up as far as it could possibly go, so that unwounded men could be brought into it immediately. This experiment proved to be an unqualified success, as did his gesture of permitting nurses to go up with the Field Hospital. Unfortunately the equipment of a Field Hospital, as sent out by the War Office, was based upon tabulated forms which were meant to cover any possible contingency in every climate. They therefore dragged around tons of material, which would have been handy in the Arctic but was quite useless in South Africa. Further, much of the material and many of the instruments were obsolete. 'We were carrying about with us instruments which I should have thought would be found only in museums,' Treves said. The surgical instruments were of poor quality, the system of disinfection imperfect, and some of the medicines had been in their bottles for twenty years. None of this was Buller's fault. Treves regarded the relationship that existed between the General and his medical officers as almost ideal.

Equally admirable was the care that he took in organizing supplies and transport. Treves said that he 'could not say too much for the way in which the supplies were managed – it was splendid'. Remembering those experiments during the manoeuvres, Buller established a kind of precursor of the Naafi in the rear of his lines, where everything from scent to chocolate could be bought by the soldiers. Colonel Morgan, the Director of Supplies in Natal, started this Field Canteen system on credit, buying the goods from merchants in Durban. He soon found that he was making sufficient profit to pay cash for everything. The profits made by the canteen were given to the next of kin of men killed in action or dying of wounds in the field, and the profit made by the Natal Army under Buller amounted to nearly £14,000, which was duly distributed. Buller made an attempt, also, to see that every soldier got a hot meal once a day, even at the front. The supply arrangements were similarly elaborate, as they had to be in view of the fact that officers carried with them personal paraphernalia from gramophones to polo sticks, that Clery took with him a French cook and that Buller's own establishment included a well-equipped kitchen and a bathroom. Buller won the love of his soldiers, a love that was to endure through the vicissitudes of his career, by this concern for their well-being, and his organizing skill was remarkably shown in these Natal preparations, which were necessarily carried out with an almost wholly improvised staff, because the local staff were shut up in Ladysmith and he had left his own staff behind in Cape Town.

The corollary of this careful preparation was that Buller's movements were extraordinarily slow. His army crawled rather than marched on its stomach, and it was eleven days before, satisfied that he had done everything possible at Maritzburg, he went up to Frere. He had no doubt of his ability to get through to Ladysmith, but was already aware that he lacked mounted men. 'Whatever happens I shall, to restore order and protect communications, require a large force of mounted men,' he told Lansdowne, adding that he intended to mount infantry and let them ride in trousers like the Boers. The gloom that overcast him in Cape Town, however, had now disappeared and he no longer felt, as he had done there, 'like a man who had got up late in the morning and was going to be late for everything all day'. Even Amery, one of his severest critics, was impressed at Maritzburg by his calm, imperturbable self-confidence. He had no doubt at all, as he told the Governor General of Natal, that he would be in Ladysmith before Christmas. 'Buller', Hely-Hutchinson wrote to Milner on 2 December, 'is a man who inspires much confidence.'

Chapter Four *Inside and Outside Ladysmith*

Once the soldiers and civilians shut up inside Ladysmith had become used to the idea that they were besieged and would be shelled every day, life settled down to a routine in which the chief enemy was found to be not Boers but boredom. The shelling at first had a considerable effect on morale, because Long Tom was fired from such a distance that no gun on the British side could answer him, but it was comparatively harmless. One of the war correspondents, G W Steevens, described his morning assault:

> Behind the half-country of light red soil they had piled up round him you could see his ugly phiz thrust up and look hungrily round. A jet of flame and a spreading toadstool of thick white smoke told us he had fired. On the flash four-point-seven banged his punctilious reply. You waited until you saw the black smoke jump behind the red mound, and then Tom was due in a second or two. A red flash – a jump of red-brown dust and smoke – a rending-crash: he had arrived. Then sang slowly through the air his fragments, like wounded birds. You could hear them coming, and they came with dignified slowness: there was plenty of time to get out of the way.

All of the big guns were fancifully named by the besieged garrison – Long Tom, Puffing Billy, Fiddling Jimmy, Silent Susan – but none of them did much harm. Some of the shells they sent over were half-charged with coal dust, many failed to burst at all. A few soldiers were killed on the outer defences, but a fortnight's shelling caused casualties in Ladysmith itself of one white civilian, two natives, a horse, two mules, and a wagon. Some half a dozen houses were also damaged. The naval guns replied to the shelling, with equally little effect.

No sieges can ever have been conducted in so gentlemanly a spirit as those in this war. There was no shooting and no fighting on the Sabbath, and often the Boers took a holiday from shooting after any particularly busy day. Firing rarely began before breakfast or continued after tea, and there were regular half-hour intervals for meals. These Boer tactics seemed to those inside Ladysmith to be inexplicable, but they were in truth to be explained partly by the caution of General Joubert, their commander, and partly by the fact that the Boers had no taste for this kind of fighting. Their genius was for guerrilla warfare, not for fighting as a coherent army. They made minor attacks, but did not make any serious attempt at this time to storm Ladysmith. They hoped and expected that after a few days the British would surrender. 'They forget that, though the sieges of ancient history lasted ten years, nowadays we really can't afford the time,' wrote Nevinson. 'The Boers, we hope, have scarcely ten days, yet they loiter along as though eternity was theirs.' These words were written on 13 November.

Far more troublesome than the shelling was the sickness which affected many of the soldiers. There was no shortage of food. One mess menu on St Andrew's Night, at the end of November, was: Scotch Broth; Salmon; Haggis; Saddle of Mutton; Turkey and ham; asparagus; stewed fruit; haddock toast. But at this time little attempt was made to see that there was an issue of fresh vegetables, and little trouble was taken with the drinking water. In consequence dysentery was widespread, and casualties from enteric fever became progressively heavier. The Boers, who also suffered from dysentery, sent to the British ambulance camp for chlorodyne. The British, not to be outdone in courtesy by these besiegers who observed trade union hours, gave them in addition a little brandy.

'Gentlemen,' White said to his staff, 'We have two things to do – to kill time and to kill Boers – both equally difficult.' Difficult indeed it was to kill time. The troops were snugly protected, some in the river bank caves, others behind schanzes and reverse slopes, so that the Boers had little to aim at. There was no great danger, but there was not much to do. Some of the Imperial Light Horse played cricket, keeping a man to watch for the firing of Long Tom. On one occasion the watchman shouted his warning, and the batsman pretended to play a shell. To his astonishment a shell did indeed land on the pitch, three feet away from him. He was knocked down by the impact of it, but otherwise unhurt. Some of the war correspondents and the more literate soldiers held regular Shakespeare reading parties, and others started local papers, a four page sheet called the *Ladysmith Lyre* and a more ambitious periodical called the *Ladysmith Bombshell*.

> A pipe of Boer tobacco 'neath the blue,
> A tin of meat, a bottle, and a few
> Choice magazines like Harmsworth's or the Strand –
> I sometimes think war has its blessings too.

wrote one of the *Lyre's* pseudonymous poets, but for the most part the men found that there were few blessings in a state of siege. They consoled themselves by the thought that they were keeping the main body of the Boer Army occupied. But supposing (it was a thought that must have occurred to almost everybody in Ladysmith at one time or another) that this was not the case? Supposing that, as it was put by Captain Lambton, who had brought up the naval guns, they were being stuck up by a man and a boy? White sent up his balloons, one for genuine observation, the other flown as a distraction, but although the balloon reported the presence of the laagers of ten commandos, White's estimate of the force opposing him was necessarily vague. What he did know was that he had been beaten by the Boers in battle, and he did not mean to engage them offensively again. Only with difficulty was he led to agree to a dashing night raid made by Hunter early in December, when the raiders stuffed a charge of gun cotton down Long Tom's throat, and fired it, thus temporarily putting this and one or two other guns out of action. Hunter, Rawlinson, and some of the other officers longed for action, but they did not get it.

At the time of the investment of Ladysmith, just after the surrender at Nicholson's Nek, there was a force of a little more than 2,000 men, of whom only 300 were mounted, at Colenso. This sketchy collection of regular soldiers, local police and volunteers, offered the only organized resistance to the Boers in Natal, outside Ladysmith. The Boers either failed to realize this, or else Joubert was so much concerned with the investment of Ladysmith that he did not care to engage in any other action. He pushed back the British from Colenso to Estcourt, but he did no more, and at this typical small South African town, a collection of some three hundred detached single storey stone or corrugated iron houses lying in a cup among the hills, the reinforcements sent up by Buller congregated. As their numbers swelled, it became plain that they were greatly hampered by an almost total lack of maps, and also by the poor equipment of the few horses available. Because there were no maps it was difficult to launch any serious attack. Nobody knew just where the Boers were, nor in what numbers. As *The Times History* says, 'A dense, paralysing mist of uncertainty enveloped all things beyond a narrow radius from the village'. One day the alarm gun at Estcourt was fired. Orders were given to strike camp, the tents sunk to the ground like deflated balloons, and were left packed and ready to move. News had been brought in by cyclist scouts that the Boers were advancing along the Colenso road. The garrison were hurriedly spread out along the rim of hills surrounding Estcourt and then, as the hours passed, it became plain that the expected attack was no more than a patrol. The Mounted Infantry exchanged shots with them, and came back. The tents were pitched again, now in pouring rain. Colonel Long of the Royal Artillery, who had recently taken over command, said he would be damned if he would leave Estcourt. The troops stayed where they were, but such alarm and vacillations did not help their morale.

It became very obvious that the scratch force of Mounted Infantry (the cavalry of course were in Ladysmith) was overworked. Lord Dundonald, who had been disappointed not to have been given an appointment in South Africa and had gone out to the country without one, was asked by Buller to organize the mounted troops in Southern Natal. He found that the recently enrolled Thorneycroft's

Mounted Infantry were equipped with saddles which ranged from an ancient cavalry pattern to a light hunting saddle. Many of the horses had sore backs, and both men and horses were being worked to a standstill on reconnaissance and patrol duty.

The chief diversion was the daily departure of the armoured train up the line towards Colenso, a journey which was watched by the soldiers 'much as people go down to see the boats at Dover pier'. The train was not a true armoured vehicle, but an ordinary engine with roofless trucks which had been reinforced by boilerplates with loopholes cut in them for rifles. It was used for reconnaissance some way into Boer territory, as a sort of patrol or scouting medium, and disaster was, as all the war correspondents said, bound to come to it. On 15 November, the day after the alarm had sounded, this prophecy was fulfilled. Long, who was full of enthusiasm for action, had decided to send out the train, armed with a 7 pound naval gun, as an offensive weapon. A company each of the Dublin Fusiliers and the Durban Light Infantry went with it, together with a few sailors to fire the gun and some platelayers to repair the line if necessary. They were accompanied by Winston Churchill. The train puffed through past Frere to Chieveley, and was then ordered by Long to return to Frere. On the way back it fell into a well-prepared Boer ambush. Stones laid on the track took the leading trucks off the line, and three field guns and a Maxim supplemented Mauser fire upon the unfortunate men in the trucks. Thanks to the heroic efforts of Churchill and other volunteers the engine and tender were able to get clear and return to Estcourt. The Boers took 70 prisoners, including Churchill and Captain Aylmer Haldane, the officer in command. It was the last of the armoured train.

As British reinforcements arrived, it was inevitable that the Boers should be pushed back over the Tugela, unless they could destroy the force at Estcourt. Joubert, dividing his army, made an attempt to cut the British line of communication south of Estcourt. The Boer laager was discovered and General Hildyard, who was now in command, gave permission for a night attack on it. The attack was confused and uncoordinated and the outcome of the engagement, known as Willow Grange, was indecisive, but after it the Boers retired behind the line of the Tugela to Colenso. Louis Botha, almost alone among their leaders, was in favour of ignoring the British forces and marching on Maritzburg but this strategy, which would have taken real advantage of their mobility, was much too daring for Joubert and the others. They were prepared to wait for Ladysmith to fall, just as White within it was prepared to wait to be relieved. The British made no attempt to molest the Boer retreat. They moved up to Frere, which henceforth was to be the Army base. General Clery came up to inspect it on 28 November, but this 'queer-looking bloke with a puzzle beard and blue whiskers' did not actually take over the command for another week. Dundonald, who was now in sole command of the small mounted force, made a reconnaissance which established that the Boers were present in large numbers on the north side of the Tugela. Otherwise there was little contact with them. Intermittent, and not very successful, attempts were made to get into heliographic communication with Ladysmith. Much time was spent in training the irregular troops to use their rifles, and to look after their horses. Men, guns, and trainloads of supplies poured into Frere every day.

Chapter Five *Before Battle*

'Ten days ago Frere was a little dark-green plantation hiding a few iron-roofed houses, and set in the midst of a heaving sea of downs. Then a camp came, and today there is a patch, nearly two miles square, of brown, trodden, and dusted grass with brown tracks radiating from it into the grassy distances,' wrote a war correspondent. The Boers before leaving destroyed the iron railway bridge across the river very skilfully, lifting the bridge bodily from its masonry piers so that it lay in the river bed, with the framework and girders contorted like an tangle of forest creepers. With less reason they looted the houses, tearing the leaves from books, burning photographs, pulling up flowers, stuffing clocks upside down into flowerpots, breaking the glass of pictures and windows: the small revenges of a primitive people against the civilization they were fighting. Clery established his headquarters in the windowless and doorless house of the railway stationmaster. Hildyard and his staff were in a roomy cottage half a mile up the line. Among his staff was Major Prince Christian Victor, a grandson of the Queen, whose disposition caused a great deal of trouble. The Queen, Lansdowne told Buller, would like Prince Christian Victor to be employed, but did not want him to run exceptional risks. 'I tumble to situation,' Buller replied, and had the Prince sent back to Durban. This prompted an indignant note to Buller from Bigge, saying that irrespective of any previous instructions, 'Queen and his parents want him treated like any other officer'. To this Bigge appended a private note: 'He wants to fight and I should let him regardless of consequences.' Buller's reply was conciliatory. 'It was too silly about Prince Christian Victor. I have put it right. Tell Queen and the Princess.' It was thus that the Prince found himself on Hildyard's staff.

The most considerable British army of modern times accumulated at Frere. By early December some twenty thousand men were assembled in the vicinity, their tents spreading over the green swelling downs. In the distance the great serrated range of the Drakensberg could be seen, smoky blue in the evening light. Much nearer, just a mile beyond Frere Station, lay the wreck of the armoured train, the trucks ripped through and through by shells, and beside them the mound covering the dead, who had been buried by the Boers. Men of the Border Regiment put a stone border round the grave and chiselled words on a tombstone. When the work was finished a service was held, attended by Prince Christian Victor, Hildyard, and some two thousand men. Adventurous spirits could push beyond the outposts and see the defensive works the Boers were constructing along the northern bank of the river. Otherwise the men bathed and washed their clothes in the khaki-coloured river, and changed the colours of their horses into khaki with a mixture of permanganate of potash and water.

The spirit at Frere, everybody agreed, was quite different from that at Estcourt, and the change was directly associated with the arrival of Buller. Looking tremendously fit, and bursting with cheerfulness, he came into camp at 4 o'clock one morning. 'I have never seen troops re-tempered like this by one man since I saw the extraordinary change which came over the American army on the sudden arrival of General Miles before Santiago,' wrote the experienced correspondent of the *Manchester Guardian*, J B Atkins. Buller was immediately active. He received reports, made the round of the camps, went down to the new trestle railway bridge and walked across it, and asked a great many questions about how long it would take the engineers to put a temporary bridge over the Tugela at Colenso. Later in the day he went out with Clery and Dundonald to study the Boer position from the ridge beyond Chieveley, and advanced almost within rifle range of the Boers. Not a shot was fired at his party. He studied the position for an hour, and then went back to camp.

It was not, however, what Buller did but what he was that inspired his men. The very sight of this big red-faced man on his great bay horse gave them confidence. He spoke with an utter authority that convinced them of his ability to lead them to victory, and they discerned in his merry, twinkling, pig-like eyes a sympathy with and understanding of them that made them feel he was one of themselves. Even his bursts of rage, when the little eyes would change from merriness to ferocity, were something that they understood, and in any case it was well known that this rage was vented most often on the officers surrounding him. His gluttony and heavy drinking they found sympathetic, for would not most of them have been gluttons and drunkards if they had had the chance? As one of his private soldiers put it later: 'Now, no one loves his dinner better than Buller, but if the canteen is not up, Buller won't eat his dinner, and when they hears that Buller can't eat his dinner they hurries up the canteen, and then Buller eats his dinner. We fight like hell for Buller.'

The position when he arrived at Frere seemed to encourage optimism. Methuen had fought the Boers at Belmont and at Enslin and was pushing on to the relief of Kimberley. In Cape Colony General Gatacre was moving his troops up, and French was moving forward his patrols from Naauwpoort Junction. In Natal the threat to Durban had disappeared, and to reach Ladysmith it was necessary only to get across the Tugela and push aside the Boer forces. Clery, in a heliographic message to White before Buller's arrival, said that demoralized Boers had retreated north of the Tugela, and that Kimberley was probably practically relieved. This was over-optimistic, but it did seem in these early days of December that probably within a couple of weeks Buller, having relieved Ladysmith, would be able to revert to the original plan of campaign by striking westward at Bloemfontein or even, if Methuen and Gatacre were sufficiently successful, to move on Pretoria itself.

The force that Buller had available consisted of four infantry brigades, commanded by General Barton, Major-General Hart, Major-General Hildyard and General Lyttelton, a mounted brigade made up of the Royal Dragoons and the 13th Hussars, the recently raised South African Light Horse, and the irregular units like Thorneycroft's and Bethune's Mounted Infantry. There were five field batteries under the command of Colonel Long, who had commanded the artillery at Omdurman, and had sent the armoured train out on its final journey. There was also, partly to counter the long range Boer guns, a naval contingent with two 4.7 and several 12 pounder naval guns, which was under the command of Captain Jones of *HMS Forte*. The brigade commanders varied greatly in ability. Lyttelton was certainly one of the two or three most intelligent commanders on the British side, and Hildyard was competent enough. Barton had already revealed, during the Willow Grange engagement, the timidity and indecision that characterized many British commanders throughout the war, while Hart was a veteran who regarded the deployment of men during an advance as un-British and unsoldierly, and pinned his faith to close order attack and volley firing. The most interesting of the subordinate commanders was the gay and vigorous Lord Dundonald, like Wolseley an early believer in the value of machine guns, and an inventor of considerable ingenuity. Among his inventions was a specially light gun-carriage built of hickory and steel, which needed only one troop horse to draw it, a light ambulance cart which might be drawn by one camel, a light van for use as an office on army manoeuvres, and a man-carrying watertight bag for crossing rivers, in which he had had himself safely pulled across the Thames. None of these ideas was fully accepted by the War Office, although the 'Dundonald carriage', as the light gun-carriage was called, was used to a certain extent in South Africa. Dundonald was also in possession of a Secret Plan, the invention of his grandfather, Admiral Lord Dundonald, which could produce a great smoke screen concealing one's own troops from the enemy. He had promised that he would divulge the details of this plan only in a time of national emergency.

By one of those curious attempted evasions of responsibility that marked Buller's conduct throughout the campaign, he kept up a fiction that Clery commanded in Natal. The war correspondents were at first forbidden even to mention his presence at Frere, and all orders issued were sent out in Clery's name, although it was accepted by everybody that Buller was in command of operations. How was he to get across the Tugela? He had, for serious military purposes, no maps of the area. There was a military map of Northern Natal, done hurriedly in 1896 by Colonel Grant (who was now shut up in Ladysmith), but Grant had not gone south of Ladysmith because, as he said, his map seemed at the time to meet the necessities of the case. A defence of Natal, it is again evident, was never contemplated – it was to be simply a jumping-off point for British invasion. The only other maps available were one on the scale of 5 miles to the inch, compiled by an Inspector of Schools, an Intelligence Department map which had been discarded because all the contours were wrong, and Jeppe's map, which had been compiled from farm surveys and contained no military detail. It had the farm names and, Grant said with candour, 'if you told a man to go to a farm he could go somewhere within a square mile of where you wanted him to go'. There were also a few reconnaissance sketch maps, done by officers who had gone out before the war began, and these were of some limited usefulness. Buller had, however, no maps on which he could rely for details of the windings of the Tugela. It might be thought that he would send scouts or spies to discover the exact position of the Boer forces, or put out strong patrols to test their strength. Nothing of the sort was done. Such reconnaissances as were made were tentative, and revealed nothing more than Buller had already discovered with the aid of his telescope. The limit of Buller's guile was to send a message to White that he would send by searchlight false information in clear, as well as genuine news which would be heliographed in cypher. It is not likely that the Boers were deceived by this. They made frequent interceptions of the searchlight messages in clear to send ribald or insulting replies.

Buller made up his mind about the nature and position of the attack, then, without much help from maps or reconnaissance, and with the minimum of consultation. It is remarkable that his assessment was so nearly accurate. 'He possessed a wonderful memory, especially for the geographical features of country,' Dundonald said. 'I have heard him quietly correct some statement that some one had made about names or distance, or features of country, and he was always right.' Looking through his telescope Buller saw in front of him an open stretch of veldt, which offered little or no cover. On the British or southern side of the Tugela was Colenso itself, a collection of half-ruined tin houses, with a railway station and goods shed. On the other side, immediately opposite Colenso, was Fort Wylie, which was presumably occupied by the Boers, although Dundonald's reconnaissances had drawn no fire from them. The river ran directly eastwards for a little way from Colenso village, and then turned right away to the north. On the western side he could see that it moved for some miles in a series of bends, but it was not easy to discern the nature of these bends exactly without the aid of a map. On the Boer side of the river the nature of the ground was very different. It was broken up into a series of low ridges, afterwards called the Colenso kopjes, the first and most prominent of which was Fort Wylie, which showed itself above a reddish foothill. Behind the ridges were steep hills, which stretched almost in a semi-circle, and ran down in tiers to the river. Were trenches cut in those hills, were thousands, or merely dozens of Boers sheltering among the kopjes? There is a limit to what can be seen through a telescope, and Buller did not know. But he could see enough to be sure that the northern side of the river was excellent for defence, the southern side bad for attack. It would be necessary, therefore, to make a flank march, and he learned from a local farmer that if the Tugela was crossed a few miles above Colenso to the west, the country there was more open, and suitable for attack. He told Lansdowne that Colenso was too strong to be taken by a frontal attack, and outlined his plan. He would leave part of his force in position in front of the village, and with the remainder carry out one of those famous night marches, force the passage of the river at Potgieter's Drift, several miles to the west, and then advance on Ladysmith by the Acton Homes–Ladysmith Road. The plan carried the risk that Buller would be cut off from his line of communications perhaps for a week, but on 11 December, he was not prepared to consider this a serious deterrent. He gave orders for an advance by way of Springfield to Potgieter's Drift.

During the next forty-eight hours he received news of two defeats. In northern Cape Colony, near Stormberg, General Gatacre attempted a night march as prelude to a surprise dawn attack on the Boers. His guides lost their way, his force became hopelessly lost, and ran by accident into a Boer picket. A Boer commando arrived, attracted by the firing, and the British retreated in disorder, suffering ninety casualties. Not until Gatacre had returned to the starting point of his march at Molteno did he and his regimental officers notice that over 600 men, more than a third of the total number with which he set out, had been left behind. These men, who had not fired a shot in the 'battle', were taken prisoner.

After Stormberg, Magersfontein, Lord Methuen, with an army of 13,000 men, planned a night attack – yet another night attack – on the Boer lines, which had been carefully reconnoitred in advance. He announced his intentions with an intense artillery bombardment which he believed had destroyed the Boer defence works and demoralized their commandos. But the Boer lines were far in front of the position at which Methuen had placed them. A network of narrow trenches had been dug in the open and Methuen's bombardment, which caused only three casualties, was advance warning of an attack. The Highland Brigade, which had been chosen to lead the attack, was slaughtered and its leader, the famous 'Andy' Wauchope, killed. The battle that followed went on for most of the day and ended when the Highlanders, who had been exposed for many hours to a fire which they were unable to return successfully, ignored their officers' orders and retreated across the plain. Methuen lost nearly a thousand men killed and wounded, by far the greater part of them Highlanders of the Seaforth and Black Watch regiments. The Boer losses were not many more than two hundred. After the battle Methuen retired to the Modder River. There was obviously no question of an immediate relief of Kimberley.

These losses must be considered in relation to the total strength of the British armies. At Magersfontein Methuen had lost more than 7 per cent of his army, and nearly 20 per cent of Gatacre's troops had surrendered. But more shocking than the losses, to opinion at home, was the idea that British troops could surrender, and surrender to an amateur enemy, to farmers in ridiculous frock coats. 'We are not interested in the possibilities of defeat,' Queen Victoria told her visitors. 'They do not exist.' But this was a splendid denial of the facts. The Queen at Windsor, Chamberlain at Highgate, Milner at Cape Town, were all whistling to keep up their spirits. Wolseley suggested at once that Methuen and Gatacre should in future be used on lines of communication only, and that pending the arrival of a new commander Buller could 'send any good man you like to command the troops on the line of advance by which Gatacre is operating'.

On Buller himself these two defeats, coming in quick succession, had a temporarily stunning effect. He reported the Stormberg incident to Lansdowne with the comment that he did not think it would seriously compromise the position in the Cape, but after Methuen's failure he decided that he must not risk the abandonment of his own line of communications. He had expected Methuen to be successful, and had thought that the Boers would be disheartened, but 'the reverse unfortunately has occurred, and I (think) it too great a risk to make a flank march of 45 miles with an enormous wagon train across the front of a successful and active enemy'. He was therefore 'advancing to attack and try to force the direct road', and he went on to say, 'I fully expect to be successful, but probably at heavy cost'. Wolseley and Lansdowne must have been surprised to receive this telegram, for this was precisely the position that Buller had described on the previous day as one so strongly fortified that attack upon it must be extremely costly.

Joubert had been thrown from his horse by the explosion of a shell at the end of November, and had become seriously ill from shock. He had been sent to Pretoria for treatment, and in his absence the command of the force opposing Buller had been given to Louis Botha, one of those natural military commanders often thrown up by a citizen's army. Botha had been no more than a farmer, a member of the Volksraad who held the vague disciplinary powers of a Field Cornet over one single commando, when the war began. He had fought in the early Natal battles, and had been responsible for the fact that the defeat at Nicholson's Nek was so complete. If the Boers are to be believed Botha had no more than 6,000 troops, to face more than three times that number, but he had entrenched them in positions of very great strength during the days in which Buller had been slowly assembling his army at Frere. Trenches had been cut in the kopjes, and they had been cut also through much of the rest of the position, so that the Boers everywhere would have the greatest possible protection and the British would be continuously exposed.

There was one weakness even in this position. On the Boer left, and on the southern or British side of the river, rose a hill called Hlangwane. Possession of this hill by the British would enable them to cross the river with considerable protection and then roll up the whole of the Boer left flank, yet any Boer force on Hlangwane would have to be left to look after itself. The Boer burghers realized the dangers of the position so well that at first they positively refused to stay on Hlangwane. In the end eight hundred men, some of them volunteers, were persuaded to reoccupy the hill. They did so early on the morning of 15 December, an hour or two before the battle of Colenso began.

It was on the evening of 12 December, that Buller called his senior officers together and told them that the plans had been changed, and that he now proposed to make a direct frontal attack. Opinions about the feasibility of this attack, expressed after the event, varied. Ian Hamilton, who saw the position some months afterwards, wrote to Spenser Wilkinson: 'I only wish you could see the place. I trust I am right in saying that there are but a few subalterns in the British Army who would not recognize that an attack on Buller's lines must fail.' Roberts, looking at it years later, said that the attack was 'sheer murder'. On the other hand Lyttelton thought that 'either operation (the flank march or the direct attack) was feasible, provided it was carried out in the proper way, Colenso probably the easier'. Lyttelton said afterwards that Colenso had been one of the most unfortunate battles in which a British army had ever been engaged, that there had been 'no proper reconnoitring of the ground, no certain information as to any ford by which to cross the river, no proper artillery preparation, no satisfactory targets for the artillery, no realization of the importance of Hlangwane'. These things were said after the event, but at the time no criticism was voiced. Was Buller prepared to attack today the position that he had said yesterday was impregnable? Very well, then Buller must have his reasons. The campaign in Natal could never have taken the course it did, but for Buller's complete domination over his subordinate commanders. He had brought with him from the years at the War Office the habit of command, and at this stage it would have been as little possible for the divisional Generals to question his decisions as for a Catholic to doubt the Pope. As á Court says: 'Buller was a *grand seigneur*, blindly trusted by all until his limitations were revealed. He was an impressive, dominating and striking figure, and the curious mixture of obstinacy and vacillation which lay deep down in his nature was concealed from all but a very few by his firm, impassive and commanding exterior.'

He had ordered a direct frontal attack. His orders were now to be carried out.

Chapter Six *Colenso*

(i) *The Battle Begins*

The orders signed by Clery, but issued by Buller, at ten o'clock on the night of 14 December, provided for three separate points of attack. In the centre, facing Colenso itself, Hildyard's brigade was to cross the river by the iron bridge, and 'gain possession of the kopjes' on the other side of it. On the left Hart's brigade was to cross the river by a bridle drift just above the junction of the Tugela and the Doornkop Spruit, and then move along the northern bank towards the kopjes, attacking the Boer flank. On the right Dundonald, with most of the cavalry and one battery, was to 'take up a position' on Hlangwane, and from there enfilade the kopjes on the other side. Lyttelton's and Barton's brigades were to remain in reserve, ready to reinforce any weak point. There was to be artillery support for the attack in the centre from two batteries and six naval guns, separate artillery support for Hart, and general support from the 4.7 and 12 pounder naval guns which were placed midway between Hildyard and Hart. Buller himself would be near these guns. The preponderant weight of the attack was the centre and left. The attack on the right was a lighter weight affair altogether.

The plan was one which, as Amery says, could hardly have been justified 'against any enemy, at any period since the introduction of the rifle'. For once there were to be no night movements, so that the troops would have to get down to the river in the light of morning across absolutely open ground. While they were forcing the passage of the Tugela they would be exposed to Boer rifle fire, and when they were across they would be unfavourably placed to force the Boer positions. It is likely that Buller was so much misled by his almost complete ignorance of the Boer positions that he thought they were present only in small numbers, but of course the ignorance itself is inexcusable. Was he overwhelmed by the responsibility of his position, as Amery suggests, or was he simply deceived by the Boers' lack of response to the heavy shelling of the naval guns? Nobody will ever know. Botha himself guessed exactly the points at which Buller would attack, although it is not clear whether this should be interpreted as an inspired guess, or whether he had prior knowledge of the British dispositions through spies. He said afterwards that he did not make a single change in the Boer positions during the day. He had intended to let a considerable part of Buller's army cross the Tugela in the belief that no significant force was opposed to them, and then to blow up the Colenso Bridge, which had been mined. He would thus cut off the force on his own side of the bridge, which would be destroyed or forced to surrender. From this disaster, as will be seen, Buller was saved by the error of his artillery commander.

The morning of 15 December was very calm, clear, hot and windless. Between 4 and 4.30, before dawn, the British columns began to move across the plain. An hour later the naval guns began to shell Fort Wylie. The Boers made no reply, but the battle had begun.

(ii) *The Misfortunes of Hart*

It has already been remarked that among the Generals who commanded at Colenso the one whose ideas were most clearly a relic of the days of the Great German Sausage was Major-General Hart. He was not merely a believer in volley firing, but he liked to see an advance conducted in well-massed columns, with none of this new-fangled nonsense about open order. He gave instructions that the men of his Irish Brigade were to be kept well in hand – that is, they were to advance in mass formation. They might cheer in the event of a charge, but must not make a wild rush.

Breakfast was eaten at 3, but before then tents had been struck and packed. The men carried, according to the general instructions, only haversacks, water bottles, rifles, and 150 rounds of ammunition. They fell in at 3.30, and Hart spent the half hour that remained before they moved in drilling them. They marched off in perfect drill formation with the leading battalion, the Dublin Fusiliers, deployed in fours, and the men who followed them in massed columns. Hart rode in front, like some knight going to the Crusades, with his staff and a Kaffir guide. He received several warnings from the artillery batteries on his left that the Boers were present in force on the other side of the river, but preferred to trust the evidence of his own ears, which told him that the advance was going on unhindered. The Colonel in command of the Dublin Fusiliers tried to open out their ranks, but Hart promptly countermanded the order. At 5.20 they heard the first gunfire of the day, from the 4.7 Naval guns beside which Buller had made his headquarters. There was no reply to it. The naval guns continued to fire at rifle pits and trenches. No Boers could be seen.

The track along which they were advancing led directly to a bridle drift across the river, but the Kaffir guide now led them to the right, away from this drift towards another which might be crossed by ferry boat but hardly by swimming. Whether the Kaffir was in Boer pay, or whether he was genuinely under the impression that the British wanted to cross by this other drift is not known, but the effect of his guidance was to lead Hart's men into a big loop of the river which went deep into the Boer position, and was exposed to crossfire from three sides. No sooner had they moved into this loop than the firing began, first from the Boer guns and then, much more effectively, from their rifles. The guide disappeared and Hart, knowing nothing of the position in detail, ordered his men further into the loop.

There ensued complete confusion. The Dublin Fusiliers opened out their ranks willy nilly, but no sooner had they done so than they were joined by men of the Connaught Rangers, the Inniskilling Fusiliers and the Border Regiment. The men pushed towards the river, but there was practically no cover, nobody knew where the drift was, nobody understood what was happening, least of all Hart.

Faithful to his principle of massing men together, he ordered more and more reinforcements into the loop, leaving it to them to find their way across the river. The Boers were invisible, but they were obviously not far away if one crossed the river. Groups of men, determined to reach them, jumped up, dashed forwards a few yards, and lay down again. Other groups moved along the river bank, trying without success to find the drift. Others still assembled in a hollow, and waited for orders, which would tell them the direction of advance. But such orders were not likely to come from Hart, who simply brought up more and more men. No order from the higher ranks ever reached the firing line, nor did Hart ever send any order to the artillery batteries on his left, which had been detailed to support him. One group of the Dublins made a determined attempt to cross the river. A little bugler named Dunn, who had been ordered to the rear but had gone on with his company, sounded the advance. A number of men fixed bayonets and rushed down to the water. But the river here was ten feet deep and running swiftly. Several of the men were drowned, and a good many more were swept into mid-stream and shot by the Boers. No more than a handful reached the northern bank and there, finding themselves unsupported and still exposed to Boer fire, they turned to the water again and straggled back.

It was plain to Buller by this time that he was dealing with a considerable body of Boers. Watching from his vantage point beside the naval guns, he saw clearly the trap into which Hart had placed his men. He sent a messenger to order retirement, and then went down to the salient and confirmed the order in person. Afterwards he rode on to Lyttelton, who was acting as reserve for Hart's brigade. 'Hart has got into a devil of a mess down there,' he said. 'Get him out of it as best you can.' At this point, however, there was nothing that Lyttelton could do except cover Hart's retreat.

The attack, if one can call it by that name, had been in progress for less than an hour, but the confusion was so great that a retreat was more easily ordered than carried out. An officer of the Connaught Rangers volunteered to take Hart's written order for retirement to the front line, but when he had reached what was in fact the centre of the line he turned to his left, and many of the men did not receive the order. The retreat took place piecemeal, the first groups retiring at about 10 o'clock in the morning, some others staying in their positions until the afternoon, when they realized that their left flank was uncovered, and that a general retreat must be in progress. A few of them were taken prisoner. Hart's failure to understand the situation is shown by his optimistic remark to Lyttelton at about midday that all of his men had got back.

So ended this stupefyingly incompetent attempt to cross the river on the British left. In the hour or more that the Brigade had tried to cross the river they had suffered more than 500 casualties, the Dublin Fusiliers losing most men. Lyttelton said afterwards that he never saw a Boer all day, and the number who were killed by Hart's brave Irishmen could be counted on the fingers of two hands.

(iii) *In the Centre: Long and the Guns*

In 1887 the *Letters on Artillery* of the Prussian military theorist Prince Kraft von Hohenlohe-Ingelfingen were published in England. In these letters the Prince pointed out the comparative failure of the Prussian artillery in the war against Austro-Hungary, when it was kept in the rear, and the success of the artillery against the French in 1870, when it was pushed well forward. The conclusion he drew was that it was often advisable to take forward the artillery actually in advance of the infantry, so that accurate artillery fire at short range could pave the way for an infantry attack. Colonel Long was a firm adherent to this theory, which he put more simply by saying that 'The only way to smash those beggars is to rush in at 'em', and a victim of his own optimistic misinterpretation of it, for he extended the theory almost to the point at which artillery fire appeared of such supreme importance that it would play the major role in the destruction of an enemy, with the infantry conducting mopping-up operations afterwards. At Omdurman his impetuosity had been noticed by Kitchener. At Colenso it had fatal results.

Long had been told that he should move forward under cover of Barton's brigade, to a point from which he could prepare the crossing for Hildyard. The point itself was not indicated, and the phrase 'prepare the crossing' had an ambiguity about it, which may have encouraged Long to put his theories into practice. After the preliminary bombardment he left Barton, and the horses pulling his batteries trotted forward, with Long and his officers riding abreast of them. They must have looked a splendid sight as they moved over the plain towards Colenso. A splendid sight, and an astonishing one too, they must have seemed to the Boers, who can hardly have believed their eyes as they saw the batteries trotting towards them totally unsupported – for it was barely 6 o'clock in the morning, Hildyard's men were still a long way back, and Barton, having sent several messages to Long asking him to wait for his escort, halted and left the artillery to its own devices. The Boers had been told to hold their fire until they received a signal, and not a shot was fired as Long rode on and on, stimulated in his desire to get into battle by the sound of gunfire to his left, where Hart's men were advancing. Long had intended, as he said afterwards, to come into action at a medium range, that is about 2,000 to 2,500 yards, but 'the light was deceptive, and I got a bit closer'. Just how close he got is not certain. Long said that he unlimbered his field guns 1,000 yards from the river, but other observers thought that it was nearer 500 yards. The Boers obeyed strictly their orders not to shoot or to show themselves. Long's scouts, riding ahead, had almost reached the river bank without seeing any sign of the enemy, and no doubt Long thought that the long range artillery attack on Fort Wylie which had preceded his advance had driven them away. He was soon undeceived. No sooner had he given the order to commence action than the signal shot was fired at Botha's order.

'In spite of the sudden and rather unexpected fire that was opened, the field batteries came up perfectly steady, and were brought into action in an excellent line,' Long said. They were drawn up in the open as level as though they were on a parade ground. The six naval 12-pounder guns that accompanied Long came up more slowly, because they were drawn by oxen, and took up a position slightly to the left of his battery, and in his rear. Most of the native drivers of these gun teams bolted, but Lieutenant Ogilvy, who commanded them, was able to take up a reasonably protected position, although he could not move his ammunition wagons, which were jammed in a drift and under heavy rifle and shell fire. But Long's two batteries of field guns presented a perfect target to the Boer riflemen and, when they got the range, to their gunners. There was no infantry support within a mile of the batteries. They lay helpless, except so far as they could help themselves, upon the African plain. Within a few minutes two of the officers had been killed and four others wounded, and a little later Long himself was severely wounded by shrapnel. He was carried back to a little donga behind the guns, but refused attention until his men had been seen to. 'My brave gunners,' he muttered again and again, 'My brave gunners'. The gunners indeed showed exceptional courage. They kept up an energetic fire upon Fort Wylie, and succeeded in considerably reducing the rifle fire directed at them. Several requests for more men were sent to Ogilvy, and he sent men to replace the wounded, who were wounded in their turn. After an hour, however, Long's batteries had used up all their ammunition, and Long sent his staff officer to Buller to tell him the situation. The gunners, carrying their wounded, retired to the shelter of a large donga. The guns were – as Long hoped, only temporarily – silent.

Among the mistakes committed by Buller on this day the failure to give the guns any support during this vital hour is among the least excusable. He said himself that Long's batteries were firing so rapidly that he was convinced they were too close to the Boers, that he sent an officer to find out if they were suffering under fire, and that the officer returned and said that the batteries were all right. Long seems never to have seen any such officer. Probably the truth is that Buller was concerned at this time with extricating Hart's Brigade from its trap, and that he paid little attention to Long and the guns. Not until they ceased firing, and he learned the situation from Long's staff officer did he make any move to support them. It was now just after 7 o'clock in the morning, and the only part of the British force that had come into action was Hart's Brigade. If the purpose of an attack is to bring pressure on several points simultaneously, this attack of Buller's had failed from the start.

He had already seen Lyttelton, and given instructions for Hart's withdrawal. Now he galloped to the rear to see Hildyard, and to tell him that the guns had got into trouble. If Buller was culpable, Hildyard and Barton among his subordinates were hardly less so. It is true that Barton was told to remain in reserve, to support either Hildyard or Dundonald, but Hildyard had explicit instructions telling him to move out at 4 o'clock and attack the iron bridge crossing the river, and it is not easy to understand why at 7 o'clock his attack had not begun. Buller said gloomily to Hildyard that he thought it would be impossible to attack at all that day, and added that he was going to try to extricate the guns. He told Hildyard to advance two battalions to the left of them, where they could provide covering fire, but on no account to involve himself seriously. Then he rode down with Clery and some staff officers to a donga some 800 yards behind the guns. This was an intrepid move, for the horsemen were only partly covered by Hildyard's advancing infantry, and they attracted a good deal of Boer shell-fire.

The advance of Hildyard's battalions was carried out with the skill so noticeably lacking in Hart's attack. The men of the Queen's and Devon Regiments advanced in a widely extended line. They crossed the railway, passed by the deserted guns, and actually moved in front of them to occupy the ruined houses and sheds of Colenso. They were in the village, and a few men got on to the road bridge, but they were not across the river. Although they were well under cover in the village, and able to counter Boer rifle fire, they were not able to advance further without artillery support. This further artillery support, however, Buller had no intention of giving. He wanted nothing now except to withdraw and get this unhappy battle over. He countermanded an order for more ammunition to go up to Long's guns and told one of his ADCs, Captain Schofield, to try to get the guns away. Schofield called for volunteers.

(iv) *On the Right: Dundonald and Hlangwane*

Dundonald had been convinced from the first of the importance of Hlangwane. He had carried out reconnaissance in the early days of December in company with an Engineers' officer who had prepared a map, which showed the importance of the hill. Dundonald took the map, together with a report, to Buller who, he said, 'pretended to be very annoyed that I had taken this officer out with me'. Although Buller had paid little attention to the map, and designed the move on Hlangwane chiefly as a device to occupy the Boer left, Dundonald decided to try to capture the hill.

He had a force of about 1,000 men, and the battery assigned to him, and with this he devised a partial enveloping attack. It was the only move carried out during the battle in which a British commander used the whole force at his disposal. He placed his battery on a low gravelly hill south of Hlangwane, from which it was within range both of the hill and of the kopjes north of the Colenso Bridge, and made a simultaneous attack upon the south and south eastern sides of the hill. Hlangwane, however, was more strongly held than either Buller or Dundonald had expected, and the Boers threatened to outflank the attack on the south-eastern side. He went off to see Barton, whose 6th Brigade had been told to support him, and asked for a battalion which would go round Hlangwane on the Tugela side and threaten to cut off any Boer retreat. But Barton had now received orders not to commit his brigade, and he refused to support Dundonald with so much as a company. By doing so he would certainly have exceeded the exact limit of his orders, but he might have forced the evacuation of Hlangwane by the Boers. As it was Dundonald, well established on the slopes of the hill, but lacking men to force home his attack, could do no more than hang on.

(v) *The Abandonment of the Guns*

The position at 9 o'clock in the morning was that Hart's attack had been given up, and that the Irish Brigade were preparing confusedly to retreat. Hildyard's demonstration in the centre had been successful in occupying Colenso village, but he could get no further. Dundonald's move on the right, which was full of promise, had been held up by Barton's refusal of co-operation. The army had been checked, but not defeated. Nothing was lost. It would have been easy for Buller to have protected the two silent batteries by gunfire and to have switched the focal point of his attack to Hlangwane, or to have turned Hildyard's demonstration into a real attack. As the historians of the German General Staff were to say later, it was not the Army, which had been defeated, but its commander. Buller, munching sandwiches, stood in the donga under heavy shell-fire. He paid no attention to this shell-fire, even when his staff surgeon was killed beside him, and did not reveal until the end of the day that he had himself been struck and badly bruised by a spent fragment of shell. We have no record from any witness close to him of anything he said, but there seems no doubt that behind the impassive exterior his mind was in turmoil. Certainly his dominant thought was to break off the action. Before he could do this, the tradition of the Army demanded that he must get away the guns. The task was perilous, for it involved crossing some four hundred yards of open ground, limbering up the guns and bringing them back, under fire the whole time. Nevertheless, when Captain Schofield called for volunteers, two limber teams and two officers came forward immediately. One of the officers was Captain Congreve of the Rifle Brigade. The other was Clery's ADC, Roberts' son, the Honourable Fred Roberts.

Only a couple of months earlier Roberts had written to Wolseley, saying that he hoped his son might get to the Staff College, and had been warmly answered. 'If your son was not to have a nomination for the SC who should have one? Besides, he has a very good reputation of his own as a soldier.' But the young man was eager to go to South Africa, and went out there. He wanted to join Dundonald's Mounted Brigade, but Dundonald's request for him was refused, because Fred Roberts was an only son, and mounted men were so constantly in action. It was thought safer for him to be ADC to Clery. Now, with the others, he galloped across the veldt towards the guns, laughing and waving his stick with a circular motion, like a jockey encouraging his horse. Lieutenant Salt, of the Royal Welch Fusiliers, who died four months later of enteric fever, described the rescue attempt in a letter home:

> I was on a rise of a hill to their right, and could see every inch of the ground from start to finish. One could see the bullets striking all round them, and it seemed a marvel that they were not hit. When they were about halfway across, one team came to grief and had to lie where they were under a hot fire. Another was struck, and became a struggling mass before they reached the guns. Three got to the guns, hooked on their teams,

and started to gallop back. A shell, as far as I could see, struck one of the guns, and turned it right over, but the other two got safely back. It was an awful sight, but fearfully exciting.

Roberts was one of those hit. He fell from his horse, struck by three bullets. As they reached the guns Congreve also was badly wounded by a bullet which killed his horse. Schofield and the others succeeded in limbering up two guns and riding back with them. Congreve crawled back across the ground towards Roberts, and a medical officer crawled out from the donga. Together, they succeeded in bringing him back. A little later Captain Reed, of the 7th Battery, which was supporting Dundonald, made another attempt to rescue the guns, riding across the plain towards them with three wagon teams. He turned back without reaching the guns after he had himself been wounded in the leg, and had lost 7 men out of 13, and 13 horses out of 22.

Now Buller seems to have been struck by panic and remorse. He was a tender-hearted man, and he had been visibly shocked earlier when Lyttelton told him that the losses of Hart's Brigade probably amounted to four of five hundred. Now the sight of men killed uselessly under his eyes, combined with the pain of his injury and the stress of the burning sun, was too much for him. (It must have added to his distress to have known that one of the wounded men was young Roberts, whom he had tried to keep out of harm's way.) He sent word to Hildyard to withdraw his men from Colenso, rode across to Ogilvy and told him also to withdraw, and then rode to Dundonald and told him to disengage all his men from Hlangwane. His incessant personal activity on this day was partly a reflection of his failure to make proper use of his staff, but it surely sprang also from a desperate frustration that could find relief only in action.

The disengagement took a period of several hours. Dundonald's brigade took nearly three hours to get away from Hlangwane, even though they were covered by the 7th Battery and supported at last by Barton. The difficulty of communicating the retirement order to all of Hart's men has already been mentioned. And although the retirement in the centre was orderly and skilful, the order to retire did not reach Colonel Bullock, the commander of the Devons, who was in a small donga in front of the silent guns. At 2.30 in the afternoon the battle was over, but Bullock and his men remained on the field. About two hours later the Boers, crossing the river by the road bridge with wagon teams to take the guns away, were met by a hot fire from this sole remaining British group in action. The Boers halted and their commander, Botha's brother-in-law, Field-Cornet Emmett, went up with a British ambulance orderly and asked Bullock to surrender. He refused, but in the meantime the Boers, who were no great respecters of the Red Cross, had surrounded the donga. When Bullock drew his revolver one of them clubbed him with a rifle. The rest of the soldiers surrendered and as the sun set the Boers, unmolested, took the ten guns, with the same number of ammunition wagons, back across the river.

Up to the time that the guns were abandoned, Colenso might have been regarded as no more than an unsuccessful reconnaissance in force. The loss of the guns converted a repulse into a defeat. It was not merely that the loss of almost two whole batteries was a blow to prestige. There was the further, very practical point that these batteries were almost half the field artillery that Buller had with his army, and that they were more than all the field artillery with Botha's force. Would it not have been possible at least, it was asked afterwards, to send men out to dismantle the breech blocks, so that the guns would have been temporarily useless? Buller's lame explanation was that if he had tried to send men by night to dismantle the guns they would have met the Boers crossing to capture them, and 'we should have had a rough and tumble on the banks of the Tugela, in which I fully believe we should have been worsted'. Perhaps: but at the possible cost of a hundred or two hundred men the attempt should have been made, and Buller as well as his Generals must have known it. Yet none of them dared to say so as, morose and savage, he rode off the field. His nerve had failed utterly; he saw no hope of victory in the battle; and, taking Hildyard's and Barton's Brigades with Dundonald's men back to Chieveley, and Lyttelton's and Hart's men further back still to Frere, he asked for an armistice to collect the dead and wounded, which Botha granted. The British casualties numbered just over 1,100, and almost half of them had been sustained by Hart's Irish Brigade.

Many of these casualties were not seriously wounded. The Boer losses were negligible, perhaps a dozen men killed and twice that number wounded. Very few of the British saw a Boer during the day. They did not appear until sunset, when they came over the bridge to take guns, and sometimes valuables, off the dead. Buller's losses, it will be seen, were actually less than those incurred by the capture of the Nicholson's Nek column. It was the abandonment of the guns that made Colenso so resounding a defeat.

The four little field hospitals, each capable of taking about a hundred patients, had been pitched close to Buller's original vantage point near the naval guns. Each hospital had a central marquee, which served as an operating and dressing station, with a number of bell tents around it for the wounded. To these tents the hospital wagons came, jolting their patients across the uneven ground, each wagon driven by a Kaffir and drawn by ten mules. The wounded came to the tents silent, listless, their faces covered with dust and sweat, their bodies blistered by heat, their blue army shirts stiff with blood. Round the operation marquee men sat or lay on the ground, waiting for their turn at the surgeon's hands. Boxes, panniers, canteen tins and cooking pots lay around, with heaps of dusty rifles. The shirt-sleeved surgeons operated speedily, wearing riding breeches, and helmets to protect them from the tremendous heat. Some orderlies heated soup over camp fires, others went round to the wounded with water and bread. There was plenty of morphia and plenty of chloroform, to drug the men before the surgeons operated. The wounded were meant to be brought in and taken out of the marquees one by one, but occasionally a man was left in by mistake. On one occasion a leg was being amputated at a table beneath which lay a man who had been shot in the face and was apparently dead. His head was enveloped in bandages, his big moustache clotted with blood, his eyes closed. When the leg was dropped upon his body, the apparently inanimate man raised his head and opened his eyes.

Sir Frederick Treves, after working all the afternoon in the field hospitals, went back to Chieveley, where he hoped to get something to eat. He had been there only a short time when an orderly arrived to tell him that Lieutenant Roberts had been brought in wounded, and asking him to return at once. He went down by rail, travelling in the engine. He examined Roberts carefully, and came to the conclusion that 'from a surgical point of view the case was hopeless, and had been hopeless from the first'. Nothing could be done, except to keep him comfortable. On the following day he was removed to Chieveley on the hospital train, and he died there that night. He was awarded the Victoria Cross, as were five others who had taken part in the rescue attempts.

By 5 o'clock on the afternoon of the battle Buller was back at Chieveley. An hour later he sent a telegram to Lansdowne reporting his 'serious reverse'. Later that evening, without consulting his Generals, he sent Lansdowne another telegram, which began: 'A serious question is raised by my failure today; I do not now consider that I am strong enough to relieve Ladysmith.' He spoke of the lack of water, the exhaustion of his men, and of the 20,000 men who, as he thought, had opposed him. 'I consider I ought to let Ladysmith go and to occupy good position for the defence of south Natal and so let time help us. But I feel I ought to consult you on such a step.' The best thing, he said, was to fall on the defensive and 'fight it out in a country better suited to our tactics'.

Just what he meant by letting Ladysmith go was made clear in the telegram he sent on the following morning to White. He could get over the river at Colenso, he said, only by what he called siege operations which would take 'one full month to prepare'. He went on to ask how many days White could hold out, and continued:

After which I suggest your firing away as much ammunition as you can, and making best terms you can. I can remain here if you have alternative suggestion, but unaided I cannot break in.

He added at the end of the message a reminder to 'burn your cipher, decipher and code books, and all deciphered messages'.

Later on, Buller was to deny that he had ever suggested to White that he should surrender. He had merely meant, he said, to stir up this slothful General to some kind of action. White had, he said afterwards,

A better force theoretically, a more experienced force, and a larger available force to help himself than I had to help him. The onus of his relief was thrust upon me, and practically he had got into Ladysmith and was directing me, as he did then and afterwards, to bring the whole forces of the Empire to get him out. I am satisfied in my own mind that if I had been in Ladysmith with that force I could have come out any morning or evening that I wished to from Wagon Hill and along the line of the watershed.

Perhaps Buller was right about White's supineness. Perhaps it would have been possible to co-ordinate a movement to get out of Ladysmith, but the suggestion of surrender caused by his own failure of nerve is clear enough and can never be evaded. To White, safely ensconced in Ladysmith, and troubled more by dysentery than by the Boers, the suggestion seemed so incredible that at first he thought the Boers must have penetrated their cipher and sent the message. When he understood that Buller was serious, he replied with vigour:

I can make food last for much longer than a month, and will not think of making terms unless I am forced to... The loss of 12,000 men here would be a heavy blow to England. We must not yet think of it.

White was much opposed to Buller's retirement, because he thought that it would precipitate a violent attack upon him. Buller replied, less angrily than plaintively, to the rebuke he had received. He could not take Colenso, he said, and could not stay in force near there because water was lacking, but he would do his best to help. 'Can you suggest anything for me to do?' he asked. White said reasonably enough that it was difficult for him to make suggestions beyond 'getting every available reinforcement in men and guns and attacking again in full force as early as possible'. He repeated that 'abandonment of this garrison seems to me the most disastrous alternative on public grounds'.

These words of White's confirmed the sharp reply Buller had received from Lansdowne to his first despairing suggestion of 'letting Ladysmith go':

The abandonment of White's force and its consequent surrender is regarded by the Government as a national disaster of the greatest magnitude. We would urge you to devise another attempt to carry out its relief not necessarily via Colenso, making use of the additional men arriving if you think fit.

This telegram was sent on 16 December. Before Buller had answered it, he received another:

The prosecution of the campaign in Natal is being carried on under quite unexpected difficulties, and in the opinion of Her Majesty's Government it will require your presence and whole attention.

It has been decided by Her Majesty's Government under these circumstances to appoint Field-Marshal Lord Roberts as Commander-in-Chief, South Africa, his Chief of Staff being Lord Kitchener.

Chapter Seven *The Appointment of Roberts*

The idea that Roberts was the proper commander for any expeditionary force sent out to South Africa had been advanced by his friends ever since his appointment to the Irish Command. And not only by his friends. Roberts himself had persistently suggested since early in 1896 that he might lead an expedition either in the Sudan or in South Africa. Soon after the Jameson Raid he wrote to Lansdowne that if the troubles should prove more serious than was anticipated, he hoped that he would not 'be considered too senior, or too old, to be employed'. He added that if necessary he would be prepared to serve in the field as a General instead of as a Field-Marshal. Lansdowne politely brushed aside the suggestion, saying that the idea of sending a British force to the Sudan was not contemplated, and that there would not be room for a Field-Marshal in South Africa. This refusal was not taken as final by Roberts or his friends. Lansdowne's regard for the Indian Army officers, and his personal liking for Roberts, were foundations on which something surely could be built. Articles and suggestions were pushed through Spenser Wilkinson. On one occasion Roberts asked Wilkinson to write a letter to Lansdowne for him, saying 'I think it should go direct from you', and at another time, when putting forward his ideas about the north-west Frontier, he said that this was all strictly private and confidential and that he felt sure 'you will not make any allusion to me in any articles you may write on the subject'. From India, Nicholson kept up a barrage of suggestions and, nearer home, Rawlinson in 1897 stressed the importance of approaching

Lansdowne directly, and put forward some of the almost wholly fictitious theories of war at the War Office which encouraged the Indian Army officers to endure neglect:

> I understand...that Wolseley himself would like to take command, but that the state of his health coupled with his position as C in C render this impossible. As far as the WO are concerned, therefore, it rests between Buller and Wood, for as may be imagined your name has not been considered by them.

Buller, he went on to say, was likely to resign if Wood were appointed, and Wood had threatened to do the same if Buller were sent. When knaves fell out in this way, must there not be an opportunity for honest men – provided they had the help of Lansdowne and Chamberlain? Roberts wrote to Chamberlain, who told him that such arrangements would of course be in the hands of the Secretary of State for War. He approached Lansdowne again, to be told that the Secretary of State did not think an expedition to the Transvaal was at all likely. 'Should I be wrong I will bear your name in mind. I expect there will be competition.' The response could hardly have been less encouraging: evidently there was no intention of employing him. During the following two and a half years, however, Roberts kept up a correspondence with Lansdowne on the possibilities of detailed changes in the Army, advocating his favourite three year service scheme for a selected number of men, stressing the defects of the linked battalion system, and casting general doubt upon War Office administration. When war came, he wrote to Lansdowne on 8 December (that is, at the time when Buller was actually massing his force at Frere) a letter for 'your eye alone', although he added that Lansdowne was welcome to show it to the Prime Minister, or to Chamberlain. He pointed out that 'not a single commander in South Africa has ever had an independent command in the field', and acutely suggested that Buller was weighed down by the responsibility placed upon him. The tone of Buller's telegrams, he said, caused him considerable alarm, and – stressing that he was prompted by the gravity of the situation and his own strong sense of duty – he said that he thought he should himself be placed in supreme command. He added:

> I would ask you to do me the favour not to let anyone besides those I have named read this letter, and not to mention its contents to any of the authorities at the War Office; for, impossible as it may seem, I am sorry to say I cannot help feeling they would prefer running very great risks rather than see me in command of a British army in the field.

Lansdowne replied that Buller had so far made no mistake, and that it would hardly be possible to supersede him merely because he sent gloomy telegrams. Perhaps he would achieve a brilliant success on the Tugela within the next two or three days? He would show the letter only to Salisbury, and the proposal would be 'constantly in my thoughts'. This letter was written on Sunday 10 December. On the following Friday he received in the evening Buller's telegram describing the defeat at Colenso.

When Lansdowne received this telegram he asked Balfour, then first Lord of the Treasury, to come to see him at Lansdowne House. Balfour occupied an important position, as one of the 'moderates' in the Cabinet, and his assent to a change in the command was almost essential. Lansdowne told Balfour that he thought Buller should be superseded by Roberts, and that Roberts had already ascertained that Kitchener would be prepared to serve under him as Chief of Staff. (It had been suggested that Kitchener should occupy this post under Buller, but in the end he had not been appointed because it was thought that the two might not work easily together.) Lansdowne's view was strongly reinforced, and Balfour's feelings must have been affected, by Buller's second telegram in which he suggested the abandonment of Ladysmith. On Saturday a meeting of the Defence Committee was held in Salisbury's room at the Foreign Office. Chamberlain was away in Ireland, receiving the honorary degree of LLD at Trinity College, Dublin, but he wholeheartedly approved of what was done. Lansdowne submitted the draft of a telegram, which pointed out that the surrender of Ladysmith would be a national disaster. This telegram was amended, and sent after the meeting. The proposal that Roberts and Kitchener should go out was also put to the meeting. It received further backing from soundings taken by Balfour at the Intelligence Branch before the meeting on Saturday. Balfour had hoped to see Ardagh, who was ill in bed. In Ardagh's absence he talked to Robertson, who expressed the opinion that Buller should either hand over his Natal command and resume central direction of the war, or a new Commander-in-Chief should be appointed. Final approval of the appointments was postponed, pending word from Kitchener. On Sunday morning Roberts, who had come over from Ireland at Lansdowne's request, formally accepted the command, saying that he believed he would be able to stand the physical strain of the campaign, and Kitchener accepted the position of Chief of Staff. Roberts had already heard from Buller that his son was wounded, and had been recommended for the VC. In the evening the news of the boy's death arrived, and Lansdowne had to break it to him. 'For a moment I thought he would break down, but he pulled himself together,' Lansdowne wrote afterwards. 'I shall never forget the courage he showed, or the way in which he refused to let this disaster turn him aside from his duty.'

The problem of consulting Wolseley about Buller's replacement as Commander-in-Chief must have been present in the minds of all the members of the Cabinet, and foremost in the thoughts of Lansdowne. It was farcical that a Cabinet Minister should ask the opinion of Robertson, a mere Staff Captain, and ignore that of the Commander-in-Chief. It seems, indeed, unthinkable that a new supreme commander for South Africa should have been appointed without prior consultation with Wolseley. Nothing shows the Government's distrust of the War Office and their fear of Wolseley better than the fact that they not only thought of the unthinkable but actually did it, feeling no doubt that if they consulted Wolseley and then rejected his advice, they would be flying too obviously in the face of accepted military authority. The prospect of consulting Wolseley must, in any case, have caused Lansdowne some apprehension, for the Commander-in-Chief was inclined to blame the Colenso defeat on the division of authority within the War Office. On Sunday morning he had had a great row with

Lansdowne, 'and, my temper being up, thumped the table and told him he had started a system at the War Office that was impossible for war, and must break down'. Wolseley thought that his outburst had had some effect. He did not guess that Lansdowne's meekness concealed his knowledge of the decisions reached behind the Commander-in-Chief's back. Nor did he suspect what had happened even when Bigge came to him from the Queen, who disapproved of Roberts' appointment, and asked if he had been present at the Defence Committee meeting on Saturday. Wolseley said that he had not been asked to attend, and Bigge told him nothing of what had happened. The news, when it came from Lansdowne on Sunday afternoon, was a complete surprise:

He sent for me to say that the Cabinet *yesterday* decided to send out Lord Roberts as C in C to South Africa, with Kitchener as his Chief of Staff. He had previously given me no inkling of this, although I had seen him yesterday after the Cabinet, and this morning... I was nearly struck dumb and said I thought it was a very unwise decision and that in my mind and according to my opinion Buller was much the abler soldier of the two, and that of course he would resign. I said: 'Were I in his place, I should resign at once, and I think you will have his resignation back as the answer to your telegram'. Of course they expect this, and have I presume discounted it. What a set of people to serve. In the meantime news just in to say that young Roberts has died of his wound. I feel for Roberts and his vulgar wife from my heart.

Buller did not resign, but replied that he agreed with the reasons guiding the Government's action. Lansdowne, however, typically anxious to ameliorate the effect of what he had thought it proper to do, had sent a personal telegram (for good measure, he sent a letter in much the same terms to Evelyn Wood) saying he feared the decision would be distasteful, but that it seemed inevitable. 'I have seen Lord Roberts, and I am quite sure you need have no misgivings as to your relations with him,' he said. Buller made no personal reply to this at the time, although he said caustically that the message read like one to a girl who was being put in charge of a strict governess, but four months later he wrote to Lansdowne:

> I received two telegrams on the 18 December 1899, one from the Government I thought brusque, the other from the Secretary of State for War I thought brutal. I confess I deeply resented the cruel and, as I thought, quite uncalled-for sneer contained in the latter.

The events of 'Black Week', as it was called, and the appointment of Roberts and Kitchener, were the signals for a great spontaneous effort on the part of the nation, spontaneous in the sense that it received acquiescence rather than encouragement from the Government. The inception of the Imperial Yeomanry as a force to fight in South Africa, the raising of volunteer battalions, and the decision to use the Militia, all came in Black Week. The first Militia battalions to leave England since the Crimean War sailed on 4 January, the various Yeomanry depots were crowded with men eager to fight, and the City Imperial Volunteers were only the first and most famous of many Volunteer groups that went out to South Africa. Their stories do not come within the scope of this book, but it is important to understand the upsurge of anger and enthusiasm with which the announcement of the defeats was met. After them the war was a national one, no longer something simply in the province of the War Office.

In this blaze of enthusiasm Roberts made his preparations for departure. Kitchener was to be in effect his second-in-command although it was impossible to give him a local rank senior to the other Generals, as he wished. Roberts had decided, as he told Butler, that 'to carry out the original plan of campaign and advance through the Orange Free State in force appears to me the best way of co-operating with you when I arrive in South Africa'. With his accession Wolseley's reign was over, and the Roberts Ring came at last into its own. Roberts asked particularly for Nicholson, and he was brought straight over from India, to be first of all Roberts' Military Secretary, and then his Director of Transport. G F Henderson, professor of strategy and tactics at the Staff College, and a warm friend of Roberts, joined the Headquarters Staff as Director of Intelligence. A host of smaller fry went out with him, or were asked for by the new Commander-in-Chief.

He went to Windsor to kiss the Queen's hand, and when she spoke of his son, said: 'I cannot speak of *that*, but I can of anything else.' It was necessary also for him to pay a call on Wolseley at the War Office, and this went off as well as could be expected. Wolseley wrote to his wife:

> I was as 'gushing' as possible to him, so much so that he told Lansdowne afterwards I had been most cordial. He said 'the one unpleasant thought he had in going was that it must naturally have been a great disappointment to me as his senior not to have been sent.' My ready answer was, 'I never expected to be asked', which was quite true. But added I, the man I was sorry for was Butler. However, we parted the best of friends, and I said everything that was nice to him both officially, and on account of his sad loss in our last battle.

On 23 December, a raw and cheerless morning, Roberts left London. The scene was strikingly different from that which had marked the departure of Butler, although the enthusiasm was no less. Almost all of those present wore black, as a mark of sympathy for Roberts in his loss. Many of the officers who went with him were old friends from the Indian Army. At Southampton 'the little, vigorous, resolute, sorrowful man in deep mourning', as *The Times* called him, went on board the *Dunottar Castle*.

Chapter Eight *The Coming of Warren*

There was a time after Colenso when the armour-plated complacency that covered Butler's self-distrust cracked, and he realized fully that he was not mentally fitted to devise the strategy of an army. It is this mood which is shown in the messages to the War Office, the surrender telegram to White, and the desperate question: 'Can you suggest anything for me to do?' But the crack quickly healed. His Generals did not question his strategy, nor did his men lose faith in their commander. They were infuriated rather than distressed by the facetious Boer signals which said, 'How is Mr Buller today', and 'What has Mr Buller done that Roberts is coming out?' There were those, it is true, like the grey-haired Sergeant captured by the Boers at Colenso who, when asked what he thought of the attack, replied: 'Brute force and bloody ignorance, and we poor soldiers have to do the brute force part,' but for every man who thought in this way there were twenty others who worshipped Buller, like the private in the Devon Regiment who said: 'When there is any fighting on, General Buller does not stay far in the rear. He is always in the front, where the shot and shell are thickest.' In an era when personal courage was regarded as the highest qualification of a good soldier, Buller's courage was exceptional. He rode about the battlefields of the war as serenely as though he were on his Devonshire estates, and combined with this disregard for his own safety a care for the welfare of his men greater, probably, than has ever been shown by any other British General. A civilian engineer sent out to South Africa records a fragment of dialogue with a soldier, which is typical of the ranks' feeling for Buller:

'You don't know the fighting line. Some Generals don't know it.'

'Then who the dickens does know it?'

'Buller knows it. He sends boxes of biscuits along the fighting line. Buller knows it. And them Generals that don't know the fighting line, we don't fight for them, we don't.'

The return to Chieveley and Frere, although it depressed many of the junior officers, was cheerfully accepted by the men. It was very hot and intensely dusty, with a wind that blew down the improvised shelters made as protection from the dust. There were scorpions, tarantulas, millions of flies. The men slept seventeen to a tent, compared with the officers' three. Yet it was the officers who felt humiliated and disillusioned. The men retained faith in what they called their Fighting Buller.

The Fighting Buller had also recovered faith in himself. When he was told that he might use the additional men now arriving, and that Field Artillery to replace the lost guns would also be sent, he cheered up. He ordered the 5th Division, which had recently arrived, to Natal, passed on to Lansdowne a message from White that he should be able to hold out for another six weeks, and said that when his reinforcements arrived he would try to relieve Ladysmith by short stages. 'There is only one stretch for 10 miles without water, and rain perhaps may fall then,' he said. 'Today the heat is terrifying.'

Sir Charles Warren, who had come out in command of the 5th Division, was one of the most eccentric and colourful figures in the British Army. This son of an Indian Army officer who became a General and was much decorated for his services in the Crimean War, had chosen the Army as a career as a matter of course. At Sandhurst and at Woolwich he showed an unusual aptitude for science and mathematics, and passed out so high up on the list that his choice of the Royal Engineers in preference to the Royal Artillery was automatically granted. He was sent out to Gibraltar, and there almost his first activity was to make a vast trigonometrical survey of the Rock, on the scale of 50 feet to an inch, and two great models of Gibraltar, each of them over 30 feet in length. He had been sent out to South Africa in 1876 to survey the borders between the Orange Free State and Griqualand West, which at some points included territory rich in diamonds. There he had become involved in the now-forgotten Transkei War and distinguished himself in this struggle against the Kaffirs and in the subsequent military occupation of South Bechuanaland sufficiently to receive the Brevet of Lieutenant-Colonel. He later led a military expedition, which did not have to undertake any actual fighting, to reimpose British rule in the territory, where a Boer-provoked rebellion had taken place. When he returned from Bechuanaland he accepted an invitation from the Liberals to stand in the newly formed Hallam Division of Sheffield. He refused to accept party funds to pay his expenses, and insisted on standing as an Independent Liberal, but this did not save him from coming into conflict with the War Office. Wolseley, who was then Adjutant-General, pointed out that an officer on half-pay, as Warren was, could not undertake any other employment without special permission from Staff Headquarters. Wolseley urged Warren to withdraw, but he refused, saying that he was already pledged to the electors. Wolseley told him that he could never expect another appointment in the Army.

The principal points in Warren's election address were advocacy of free elementary education for all, together with more physical training in State schools, the granting of 'the fullest possible measure of local self-government' to Ireland, the abolition of primogeniture, entail and life pensions, the drastic reform of the House of Lords, and the enaction of legislation 'for the repression of criminal vices that involve the suffering and ruin of the weak and helpless'. It is surprising that he was defeated by only 609 votes. Thinking that his military career was at an end, he turned after the election to the formation of a Lodge of Masonic Research, which dealt with archaeology. He had already played some part in the discovery of the Moabite Stone, a Semitic lapidary record supplementary to the narrative in the second Book of Kings. From his position as first Master of the Lodge he was removed suddenly by an appointment to serve on the Staff of the Army in Egypt, and to command the troops at Suakim. His surprise at the appointment was increased when he learned that the recommendation for it had come from Wolseley. At Suakim he found that the official servants and batmen were all convicts. He appointed a convicted prisoner to make the coffee, and made sure that he drank the first cup of each brew.

After a month at Suakim he was offered, and accepted, the post of Chief Commissioner of the Metropolitan Police. He succeeded Sir Edmund Henderson, whose seventeen years' reign had been marked by scandals about illegal arrests, corruption, and inefficiency – in 1886 a body of police called out to check a riot had marched to the Mall instead of Pall Mall, with ludicrous consequences. During his three years as Chief Commissioner, Warren provoked as much controversy as his predecessor had engendered in seventeen. To check an outbreak of rabies he insisted that the Muzzling Order of December 1885 should be strictly enforced, and that all dogs on the streets should be not only muzzled but led. All unmuzzled dogs found in the streets were taken to a Dogs' Home and destroyed. At times it is difficult to regard Warren's activities as anything but comic. No other Commissioner of Police, surely, has issued orders in rhyming prose. ('The Commissioner has observed there are signs of wear on the Landseer lions in Trafalgar Square. Unauthorized persons are not to climb on the Landseer lions at any time.') He caused unfriendly laughter by appearing at a Socialist and unemployed demonstration in Trafalgar Square wearing, not only the eyeglass which he invariably used to assist his short sight, but an old-fashioned chimney pot hat with his Commissioner's uniform. Late in 1887 his attempt to suppress Socialist meetings by forbidding the approach to the Square by any 'organized procession' led directly to 'Bloody Sunday', when a huge crowd led by Annie Besant, Eleanor Aveling, William Morris, John Burns and R B Cunninghame-Graham, clashed violently with the 4,000 constables, 300 Grenadiers and 300 Life Guards called out by Warren to deal in a military fashion with the marchers. More than 150 people were taken to hospital, and when the Grenadiers brought their bayonets to the charge a blood bath was averted only by the officers and sergeants rushing in front of their men and ordering them to put up their arms. The Home Secretary, Henry Matthews, disapproved of Warren's militance, and relations between the two men, deeply frayed by various petty incidents relating to police expenditure and the fact that the CID was independent of the Chief Commissioner, snapped altogether when at the time of the Jack the Ripper murders Warren wrote a magazine article complaining about the independence of the CID and defending his Trafalgar Square action. 'The strategy was admired not only by the experts at the Clubs, but by the social democrats themselves; and there is a most interesting letter on the subject by Mr Morris in one of the democratic newspapers,' he wrote. The writing of such an article was in absolute defiance of regulations, and when Matthews reproved him in public, Warren resigned. Within a few weeks he was appointed as the first GOC at Singapore. He was still only a Colonel on the Staff, but he had the temporary rank of Major-General.

The position at Singapore was a delicate one. The troops there had been under the Hong Kong command, but Warren was sent out as an independent commander charged with constructing fortifications, building up the garrison, and settling an argument between the civil and military authorities about the exact proportions of the bill for the work payable by each, since the Colony was supposed to pay only for what was needed to provide local defence. Warren plunged into this problem with his accustomed vigour. Within weeks he had infuriated the inhabitants and upset the Governor by apportioning for local defence 27 per cent of the Colony's total treasury revenue. Both Warren and the Governor wrote angry letters home. During his leaves Warren made extensive tours all over India, and in Ceylon, Siam, Java, Japan and China. In his five years at Singapore he played a part in founding the Straits Philosophical Society, and was responsible in his capacity of District Grand Master of the Eastern Archipelago for founding several Masonic Lodges. During this period also he was promoted to the rank of Major-General.

When he returned to England he spent a year without employment and then was given the command, suitable to a man on the verge of retirement, of the troops in the Thames District. He took his responsibilities with his usual seriousness and when appointed to the command of a division on manoeuvres borrowed the kit of a private soldier and marched in it for several miles to test the strain of carrying the weight. After this command also came to an end, he settled down in a house at Ramsgate. He was fifty-eight years old, and it must have been in hope rather than in expectation that, a fortnight after the outbreak of war, he wrote to Wolseley asking if there was any service on which he could be employed. He received a reply asking if he were in every way strong enough for work, and said that he could do a hard day's work in the saddle, walk 35 miles a day against the best, and play golf all day, cycling to and from the course, without feeling the least fatigue. He went up to London and had an encouraging interview with Wolseley, but he must have been surprised as well as pleased to learn on 7 November that he had been appointed to command the 5th Division.

It is easier to understand than to excuse the appointment. Warren had had experience of South Africa (that fatal recommendation) in the Transkei War and the Bechuanaland campaigns. He was a man of strong and independent opinions, a characteristic which Wolseley respected, and even his enemies acknowledged that he had original ideas. And he was a man Wolseley knew, one of his own generation. It was one of Wolseley's most unfortunate weaknesses in old age that he could never wholeheartedly accept the worth of the younger Generals like Kitchener, but clung to those who had made their reputations in his own shadow. There were many things against Warren, apart from his age. His experience of active warfare was practically confined to encounters with native tribes, and he had not fought in any kind of war for nearly fifteen years. During this period he had, unlike Buller, been a long way from the seats of power, with little chance to see or experiment with new arms or methods of warfare.

His worth as a commander was, thus, largely unproved, and his ideas were likely to be out of date. Most important of all, perhaps, was his well-known irascibility, tactlessness, and dislike of criticism. Nobody but Wolseley, who was always sympathetic to the tactless and the rebellious, had for years succeeded in working with Warren as a superior, and he was generally disliked by the officers who had to work for him. Roberts went so far as to say that his disagreeable temper unfitted him for holding any important position in the field. Warren and Buller had known each other since the days of the

Transkei War, and although Warren dismissed their frequent differences of opinion as 'arguments and chaff', relations between them were not good. During Warren's long battles with the Governor of Singapore Buller wrote to him, much more in exasperation than in sympathy, from the War Office:

> We are inundated with long correspondence regarding squabbles between you and your Governor.
>
> In each case I have done my level best to support you as far as possible, and I quite see that you have not a very comfortable berth; but I am bound to say that you seem to make a good many of the pricks for yourself, – that though is perhaps not my matter, – all I want to say is, for heaven's sake leave us alone, do not write and send everything here. If you have to fight the Governor, fight him, though I pray you fight as little as possible, surely the sun is hot enough in Singapore, but if you do fight him, trust us, let him send home what he likes. You may be assured you will have your say in due time.

Buller's distrust and dislike of Warren was increased when he learned that he had been given the Dormant Commission. When Buller went to Natal it became obviously necessary to appoint somebody who should take command if he were killed or badly wounded. This appointment was called the Dormant Commission, and Warren was favoured for it by Wolseley and by Lansdowne, both on the ground of seniority and because of his forceful personality. This appointment was decided after Warren had sailed, and when he arrived at Cape Town, a couple of days before Colenso, he found the news waiting for him. A letter from Wolseley said: 'I look to Sir Redvers Buller and you to put an end to this folly. Our men and Regimental Officers have done splendidly. Our Generals so far have been our weak point.'

Warren left Ramsgate on 24 November among scenes of great enthusiasm, and at Broadstairs, Margate and Westgate crowds gathered to cheer him. Most of his staff sailed with him, and as soon as they had got their sea legs, Warren indulged one of his particular preoccupations by engaging with them in a daily war game. They played on maps, and Warren acted as umpire. One of his officers commanded the Boer Army and the other the British, and plans were made for flank marches, countering Boer mobility, using guns in bush country, and forcing the passage of the Modder (Warren expected to be sent up in support of Methuen, and therefore did not play the war game on the Natal front). He had had to abandon another pet project, that of making 'skiographs', or X-rays, of the soldiers' feet so that they might be given boots which improved their marching ability. It is likely, however, that he impressed upon his staff the importance of mnemonics, in which he had a faith hardly justified by his own experience. When he wished to remember the name of Butcher's Island he had created in his mind a picture of a butcher's shop, with legs and shoulders of mutton hanging up – but then when writing to a friend who lived there he had addressed his letter not to Butcher's, but to Leg of Mutton Island. The difficulty, as he said, was this: 'A word is turned into a picture, and the picture after many months is turned into a word, but what certainty is there that it is the same word?'

The struggle for power between the civilian and military sides of the War Office, and the division of responsibility between London and South Africa was the cause of considerable confusion when Warren arrived at Cape Town. A telegram from the War Office told him that he was to supersede Methuen in command at the Modder, but Buller took the strongest exception to this, and to Wolseley's suggestion that Methuen and Gatacre should be employed upon lines of communication. On the day after Colenso he had telegraphed countermanding the supersession of Methuen, and had justified himself in a cable to London:

> I cannot agree with the Commander-in-Chief and allow Methuen, who has done very well, to be superseded by Warren. Commander-in-Chief, comfortable at home, has no idea of the difficulties here. It would, I think, be a fatal policy to supersede every General who failed to succeed in every fight, but I may say that, as I myself have since failed, I offer no objection in my own case, if thought desirable.

An objection so forcibly stated was bound to carry weight. Buller was told that Methuen might stay in command of his Division.

Warren went up by railway to join him, with his staff and some of his troops. But this raised a point of protocol. Warren was senior to Methuen and held (although nobody knew it but the War Office and Buller) the Dormant Commission: therefore Methuen must be subordinate to him. This delicate problem was solved by Buller's decision that the 5th Division should come to Natal. Warren, when he had travelled 500 miles in the direction of Methuen and the Modder, was met at De Aar junction by a young Major who produced a telegram from Forestier-Walker at the Cape saying simply: 'You will instruct General Warren to return at once.' It is not surprising that Warren was annoyed by this impersonal order, and complained that he was regarded as a shuttlecock to be ranged about up and down the line. During the twenty-four hours he spent in Cape Town on his return he had a long conversation with Milner, and resisted the High Commissioner's attempt to induce him to give up the 5th Division, and organize the defence of the East District of Cape Colony.

On 21 December, Warren and his staff embarked on board the *Mohawk* for Durban. Maps of the Natal district had been bought in Cape Town, and much time was spent on the four-day voyage in playing war games. 'There was a general conclusion that the route by Hlangwane was the most passable, but it was not taken in the exercises because General Buller had given it up, and it was therefore assumed that there must be some unknown difficulty that way,' Warren wrote in his diary. At Maritzburg he was astonished by the atmosphere of gloom and indecision, which seemed to affect everybody from Hely-Hutchinson downwards. The important thing, Warren knew, was constant contact with the Boer, and he said this when he met Buller at Frere. Warren found Buller 'rather reserved', a condition which in later years he attributed to shell shock. The reserve, or shell shock, did not stop him from showing irritation at Warren's suggestions about a possible advance by Hlangwane. 'What do you know about it?' he asked.

Warren felt his reply to be a little weak. 'General knowledge, and war games.'

Chapter Nine *Plans for the Second Attempt*

Roberts was anxious that Buller should turn the Boer position on the Tugela and relieve Ladysmith as soon as possible. He envisaged his own sweep up into the Orange Free State as the move that would bring victory in the campaign, and thought that once Buller had relieved Ladysmith it would be a good idea for him to evacuate the town and hold the line of the Tugela until a general advance was made in which he would take part. What troops would Buller be able to spare, he asked, after Ladysmith was relieved? But the idea of sparing any troops was far from Buller's mind, for the problems ahead loomed larger and larger as the days passed. He made a calculation by which he reckoned that the Boers had 145,000 men in the field, 85,000 of them from the Transvaal, and that about 46,000 of these were in Natal or on its borders. So far from releasing men, it was clear to him that the force he had was hardly sufficient to cope with this invisible, multifold army. In fact, the total Boer force in Natal did not exceed 20,000 men, half of whom sat round Ladysmith while the other half opposed Buller. An acidulous note from Lansdowne to the effect that the total population of both sexes in the Transvaal before the war was only 90,000 did nothing to improve Buller's temper. In the week that succeeded Colenso he did nothing, but brooded on what might be done. The Boers were equally inactive. They did not attempt to take Ladysmith, or to attack the British positions at Chieveley and Frere. Many men in the commandos, bored by inaction, drifted away and went home.

During this time of inaction the British soldiers remained cheerful. Their food was excellent, one pound of fresh meat and a quarter pound of bacon each a day, with bread, cheese, potatoes and either tea or coffee, with an occasional issue of lime juice. On Christmas Day and Boxing Day there were sports both at Chieveley and at Frere. The programme included cutting the lemon, tent pegging and tug-of-war, as well as horse, mule and donkey races. The men threw stones for prizes at bottles hung in rows, ran races in their stockinged feet, and wrestled on horseback stripped to the waist. The atmosphere was that of a fair, rather than of an army at war a few miles from the enemy. In frizzling heat a band of sailors made the rounds, led by one on horseback carrying the Union Jack who was followed by two seated on a gun-carriage, representing John Bull and Kruger. The soldiers were issued with a quart of beer a man, and had bacon, fresh bread and farm milk, with 'fine cuts of good Natal oxen'. What Buller ate is not known, but it may be taken for granted that he drank champagne. The menu of the Irish Fusiliers' Officers' mess, at which the officers of the Naval Brigade were guests, began with Soup Colenso, continued with Salmon Tugela, and included among the drinks Champagne HMS Forte, Port Terrible, Whisky Powerful and Maritz Beer de Plucky Natal. Prince Christian Victor ran Hildyard's mess, where the officers ate sucking pig and two turkeys, which had been fattened on Quaker oats. On Boxing Day a furious dust storm interrupted the festivities. 'We are suffocated and can only fill our lungs with air by breathing through a handkerchief while struggling with the ropes and inflated tent,' wrote Dickson, the picture-taker with the biograph. The dust storm was succeeded by heavy rain, which flooded many of the men out of their tents. Scorpions and tarantulas came out in hundreds. This was the usual weather, searing heat by day and then often a storm, which could be seen coming in the form of a high, forbidding wall of darkness. The effect of the storms was miraculous. They washed away the dry khaki-coloured face of the country, replacing it by a world of sparkling and tender colours backed by the grey-blue bloom of the distant mountains.

After three weeks of inaction, however, both officers and men were becoming perplexed. The war correspondents were annoyed because Buller made it as awkward as possible for them to send dispatches. The Boers sent over signals from across the river: 'How's Mr Buller? When is he coming for his next hiding?' The British signallers replied in kind, but still the signals did not cure their frustration. With the arrival of Warren's Division Buller had under his command some 30,000 men. What was he waiting for? Perhaps he did not know himself, perhaps he would have remained inactive for weeks but for the fact that on 6 January the Boers made their first, and only, determined attack on Ladysmith.

The spirits of those inside Ladysmith were a good deal lower at Christmas time than were those in the force that was doing so little to relieve them. Hunger had been added to boredom and enteric fever as dangers to be faced as the siege wore on, with Buller's coming continually rumoured. When news of his impending attack on Colenso was known, it had an immediate cheering effect. 'Only two days more, we thought, or perhaps we could just stick it out for another week,' wrote H W Nevinson. Then the correspondents were summoned to the intelligence office and there Altham told them that the attack had failed, and that Ladysmith would not be relieved as soon as expected. The correspondents – there were almost a dozen of them – balloted for turns to send a short heliogram. Then they left the Intelligence Office, having been warned that it was their duty to keep the town cheerful.

This was more easily said than done. Everybody was sick of the siege: the inhabitants in their caves and dumps, the soldiers who had little to do and suffered increasingly from enteric and dysentery, the officers who were disturbed and depressed by inaction. Relations between the inhabitants and the soldiers were not always good. A deputation, headed by the Mayor, asked that the bathing parties of soldiers on Sundays should be stopped, because they shocked the feelings of the women left in the town. The petition was indignantly denied, but it did nothing to improve tempers on either side. Yet a tremendous effort, characteristic of the period and of the people, was made to celebrate Christmas. A Christmas food market was arranged, in a nook between the main street and a side alley, where fifty people might gather together without attracting notice from the gunners on Bulwana. There was enough food to fill only one long table, and it was auctioned, for the most part to mess-presidents of regiments. Prices were high. A pair of ducks or fowls fetched a guinea, eggs were a shilling each, tinned butter was sold for eight and sixpence a pound. Twenty-eight new potatoes fetched thirty shillings. Two privates of the Gordons listened to the bidding, and then one said to the other: 'Come awa mon! We dinna want nae sour grapes.' But still, the men ate roast beef and plum pudding for their dinner in the sweltering heat of midday, and some plum puddings were even provided by the Boers, who sent over shells marked 'With the Compliments of the Season', which contained puddings partly cooked by the heat of explosion in gun barrels. There were sports, less elaborate than those of the relieving army, but still lasting from 10 o'clock in the morning until near sunset. The morning train to the Intombi Spruit hospital, which was outside the British lines, was laden with fruit, and such flowers as could be obtained. There were now 900 cases of enteric in the hospital, and the position was worsening every day. There were few doctors and nurses, perhaps one to fifty patients, the food was unsuitable and inadequate, and there were frequent complaints that supplies were stolen in the course of distribution. Steevens, the gifted correspondent of the *Daily Mail*, died of enteric early in the New Year.

Perhaps the most remarkable aspect of the Christmas celebrations was the children's party, organized by Cecil Rhodes' brother, Colonel Rhodes, and Major Karri Davis of the Imperial Light Horse. The auction rooms were decorated, and contained four Christmas trees, labelled Great Britain, South Africa, Australia and Canada. A big trooper of the Light Horse wandered about dressed as Santa Claus, his swansdown costume shedding flakes wherever he walked. The two hundred and fifty children left in Ladysmith emerged from their burrows starched and radiant. Each child had a ticket, and each ticket earned a present. White came out of the house in which he spent most of his time and watched the scene, with Hunter and many of the staff officers. Yet Christmas comes but once a year, and when it was over the besieged were unhappily aware that their resources were steadily lessening and that there was no prospect of relief. 'The oxen are skeletons of hunger, the few cows hardly give a pint of milk apiece, the horses are failing,' Nevinson wrote. 'Nothing is more pitiful than to feel a willing horse like mine try to gallop as he used, and have to give it up simply for lack of food.' He wondered whether they would have to feed the cows and starve the horses, or kill the thinnest horses and stew them into broth for the others. The idea that they might themselves have to eat the horses had not occurred to him.

A poet writing in the *Ladysmith Bombshell* expressed the general feeling of disillusionment:

> The New Year comes, so let us fill
> The flaming bowl with right good will
> Though Buller's at Colenso still,
>   Marking time...
> We dreamed of battles fought and won,
> We dreamed our scattered foes would run
> Before us – but we haven't done
>   Marking time.
> Our lingering faith is growing small.
> 'Where's Buller?' is the weary call,
> 'Where's French, where's Clery?' They are all
>   Marking time.

If the Ladysmith garrison were miserable, the Boers were far from happy. Buller might say that 46,000 of them stood between him and Ladysmith, White might fear getting to grips with them, but they knew very well that the combined British forces were much superior in numbers to their own. The stream of burghers who gave themselves leave and went home was swelling. Joubert's policy of masterly inactivity was producing no results. It was positively necessary to do something, and a Krygsraad decided, against Joubert's wishes and advice, on an attack aimed at capturing Wagon Hill and Caesar's Camp, on the southern side of the Ladysmith perimeter, while a holding attack was launched at the opposite side, on Observation Hill, and general demonstrations were made elsewhere. Caesar's Camp was the highest point overlooking Ladysmith, and possession of it would have given the Boers a large measure of command over the town. The garrison had discounted the likelihood of such an attack by this time, and the Boers who engaged in it carried it through with a skill and tenacity from which both Buller and White could have learned lessons. There were lessons for the Boers also, however. The Generals in command made no attempt to involve themselves personally in the attack (as Buller and his Generals were involved at Colenso), nor, having made their plan, did they take steps to see that it was carried out. Those burghers who flinched from the assault remained unpunished for hanging back.

Ian Hamilton, who was in charge of this section of the defences, had constructed several forts, with underground magazines and telephone connection with headquarters in Ladysmith, on Caesar's Camp. On the adjoining Wagon Hill a single fort had been placed with some other, lighter shelters. It was on the lightly defended Wagon Hill that the Boers made their first attack, just before three o'clock in the morning. They crept up the steep slopes of the hill, surprised and shot a sentry, and reached the summit. They did not, however, achieve anything important through their surprise, nor did they capture any vital position. Among a good deal of confusion, with the Boers and the Imperial Light Horse firing at each other sometimes at almost point blank range, the attack was repulsed. The Boers remained on the hill in a position from which it was very hard to dislodge them, although it was almost as difficult for them to attack the British defenders. This attack was accompanied, a little late, by a attempt to storm Caesar's Camp. One Boer party of about fifty men actually got on to the top of the hill, overcoming one of Hamilton's pickets, but they could get no further. The attack on Observation Hill, which was meant to stop the British from sending reinforcements to the southern end of the perimeter, was also a failure, some half of the men refusing to take part in it. The rest were never able to disturb the Devons in the fort and trenches on Observation Hill, although a small party made a determined effort to get into the trenches.

A rifle and artillery duel continued all day, terminating in a tremendous thunderstorm. Under a sky completely black, broken only by long trickling streams of lightning, with hailstones falling as big as shillings, the mounted infantry of the Manchester Regiment combined with the Gordons and the Rifle Brigade to drive the Boers off the crest of Caesar's Camp and away from the hill. Shortly afterwards three companies of the Devons, specially ordered up by Hamilton, charged the Boer positions on Wagon Hill. They were subjected to concentrated fire as they ran, with drawn bayonets, across the open ground which separated the positions, but as they approached the Boers turned and ran. They then retreated in good order, stopping to fire again as they went down the hill. The battle, which had lasted all day, ended with the British positions untouched, although, largely because of the Devons' charge on Wagon Hill, their casualties were heavier than those of the Boers. They might claim to have won a victory but nothing had been gained. As Colonel Rhodes put it, 'We are a victorious army surrounded by an inferior enemy'.

Chapter Ten *Spion Kop*

(i) *The Centipede Crawls*

When the struggle for Caesar's Camp and Wagon Hill was at its height, White had sent a heliograph to Buller asking him to make a diversionary attack. Buller's only response had been a demonstration against Colenso handled by Clery, a demonstration which was quite obviously nothing more than that, because the Tugela was in flood and could not be crossed at Colenso. When the fighting was over both the Queen and Buller sent congratulatory telegrams. White acknowledged them, and told Buller that his men were much played out, and that a large proportion of the officers were killed, wounded or sick. He added: 'I would rather not call upon them to move out from Ladysmith to co-operate with you; but I am confident the enemy have been very severely hit.' Later he told Buller that his sick list amounted to 2,000. Obviously an attempt must be made to relieve White without further delay, and Buller decided to disregard the telegrams he had received from Roberts diplomatically suggesting caution. 'Although I should be delighted to hear of your joining hands with White, still the status quo until the 6th Division has landed does not appear to be altogether undesirable,' the new Commander-in-Chief said. Personal motives, as well as the desire to relieve White, moved Buller to action. He had accepted Roberts' appointment without complaint, but he would have been inhumanly modest if he had not hoped for a decisive victory which would silence his detractors.

The question of where the attack should be made was, this time, the subject of discussion. There was a school of thought which wished to advance by Hlangwane, and another that urged the quick seizure of Potgieter's Drift, so that a force might be established firmly on the northern side of the Tugela. Buller, however, had made up his mind to a course that did not involve anything so adventurous as the sudden capture of the Drift. What he proposed was to march there with his whole army and supplies. This march would take four days to cover sixteen miles, and on the fifth day he would be ready to attack. There was to be no attack elsewhere, and this crossing of Potgieter's was not at all the same as the earlier flank attack, which he had abandoned in favour of the move at Colenso. That would have been a flank march. What he proposed to do now was to shift his whole centre of operations from Colenso to Springfield, and then make another frontal attack. The basic reason for this extremely cumbrous move, which would be made in full view of the Boers and absolutely excluded any possibility of speed or surprise, was Buller's faith in the railway. The vital importance of the railway system had been firmly impressed upon all of those 'modern' Generals who had learned their paper lessons from the Franco-Prussian War. Without a railway system you could not bring up supplies, nor could you advance troops quickly. The railway marked for you always a logical line of advance. Buller's first suggestion to Roberts, when he was asked for advice before the Commander-in-Chief embarked, was the construction of a railway line which would enclose a quadrilateral area roughly 100 miles square, which could be 'subjugated completely' and would provide a base from which mobile columns would operate. But such a plan was clearly not practicable in Northern Natal. Where were the engineers? And how would one get the railway across the Tugela? The other way of achieving mobility would have been by the liberal use of cavalry, but Buller had largely deprived himself of mounted troops. There was therefore, as he saw it, no alternative to the centipede crawl of an army encumbered by the whole of its supply column. The idea that a striking force might range fifty miles away from its supplies without the benefit of a railway line was one that he was not prepared to contemplate. Those who came out to Natal after Colenso, like á Court, with the optimistic idea that they might be able to persuade Buller to adopt a different course from the one on which he had decided, were soon undeceived. á Court, who favoured an advance by Weenen, very much further on the British right, told his ideas to Colonel (later Major-General) Wynne, who was acting as Chief of the Staff. But Buller had little contact with his staff and Wynne simply told á Court that it was useless to object. á Court then went to Lyttelton and asked him to try to get the plan changed, but Lyttelton also was unwilling to argue with Buller. He went to see Warren who, no doubt mindful of the scornful rebuke he had already received, said that he knew too little to express any opinion about the situation. Bolder than the others, however, he went to see Buller, but without success. Buller refused to listen to him, and on 10 January the centipede began its crawl. Barton's brigade was left behind at Chieveley as a containing force, with roughly a quarter of the mounted troops, but the army that was moving to Springfield was one of some 23,000 men, to which were opposed certainly not more, and very likely a good deal less, than 15,000 Boers. The command of the Field Force had been reorganized with the coming of Warren. Clery was in command of Hildyard's and Hart's Brigades, and of Dundonald's mounted troops. Warren commanded the remainder of the army.

In one of his letters to Roberts, Buller had said that their water difficulties had been great, but that the rainy season should make things much easier. The rain certainly provided water, but it also churned up the route between Chieveley and Frere and Springfield into a sea of mud. In this mud the guns sank axle deep and the wagon train – mile after mile of it – floundered. One of the war correspondents described it:

> The rain came through the still air in a steady, teeming, straight downpour that threshed in one's ears. I wore an oilskin coat, but it was useless; the rain found assailable chinks or else beat its way through. The hills seemed to melt down like tallow under heat; the rain beat the earth into liquid, and the thick, earthy liquid ran down in terraced cascades. From Estcourt to Frere the division waded, sliding, sucking, pumping, gurgling

through the mud; the horses floundered or tobogganed with all four feet together; the wagons lurched axle-deep into heavy sloughs and had to be dragged out with trebled teams of oxen.

A few steam traction engines had been brought from England, and these did good service with Warren's column, pulling an ox-wagon out of the mud when a span of eighty oxen had failed to move it. Warren was in his element. He acted as a leading hand or ganger with the teams pulling the wagons out of the mud. After a day or two he was recognized (all ranks in the 5th Division were dressed alike, by Warren's order), and the men were delighted to see him working with them.

At last the march through the mud was completed, but then there were the gathering of provisions, the filling up of supply depots and the medical arrangements to be settled. The whole infinitely laborious operation took a week. In the meantime the question arose of whether, after all, it was possible to cross successfully at Potgieter's. There was the little ferry, with its boat, which was brought over to the southern bank by some troopers of the South African Light Horse. But as Winston Churchill, who had escaped from Pretoria and returned to the Field Force, saw it, the position was a very difficult one. He looked at it from the heights on the southern side:

The ground fell almost sheer six hundred feet to the flat bottom of the valley. Beneath, the Tugela curled along like a brown and very sinuous serpent. Never have I seen such violent twists and bends in a river. At times the waters seemed to loop back on themselves. One great loop bent towards me and at the arch of this the little ferry of Potgieter's floated, moored to ropes which looked through the field glasses like a spider's web.

To cross the river here would be easy enough, but what then? On the other side was a smooth grassy slope, which was enclosed by the river on three sides. It was completely exposed to enemy fire from a large horseshoe of hills in which the Boers could be seen busily entrenching. While Churchill was brooding on the difficulties of the

215

position Buller himself rode up with his staff, lay down, and peered through a telescope for the best part of an hour before going off to breakfast. To what purpose? Churchill did not know, but like so many others he had complete faith in General Buller.

The extreme deliberation of the British movements gave the Boers the chance to construct excellent defences. Buller looked at them through his telescope, and let them dig. He censured General Talbot Coke, a brigade commander who had set his men to work making defensive schanzes in front of Springfield Bridge. He told Coke that the work was folly, although it may be thought that anything that made the soldiers better able to defend themselves was useful. At this time, if Buller had not been so much concerned about getting up a fortnight's supplies, he could have crossed the river, at Potgieter's or elsewhere, without great loss. As the days passed Botha sent reinforcements, yet this was by no means so favourable a position for the Boers as Colenso, unless Buller crossed at Potgieter's Drift and nowhere else. They were strongly concentrated opposite Potgieter's, but both left and right wings – especially the right – were much weaker.

Buller now abandoned the idea of making his main attack at Potgieter's. In company with Captain Hubert Gough of the 16th Lancers he reconnoitred a position some miles further up the river. They decided that a crossing here, and the subsequent turning of the Boer right flank, were perfectly feasible, and on 13 January, he sent a telegram to Lansdowne from Spearman's Camp, where he had established his headquarters. He said: 'I propose that Warren – taking 36 guns, Field Artillery; 3 brigades and 1,500 mounted men – shall cross 5 miles to the west at Trichard's Drift; the mountain which forms right flank of enemy defence will be turned by his advance, while we do the best we can here with 1 brigade and 3 battalions, howitzer battery and Naval guns. He agrees to this...'

'He agrees to this': but Warren had done nothing of the kind, and at this time had not even seen the Drift. He reconnoitred it two days later at Buller's request, and reported that he thought a crossing could be made there, but that if it was made the hill of Spion Kop should be taken at once, because according to the Intelligence Report there were two Boer long range guns on the Kop. Warren thought that he should have long range guns of his own to oppose them. Buller brushed aside this suggestion. He said that he did not believe that there were Boer long range guns on the mountain, that if the guns existed the British guns would be able to deal with them from a distance and need not be attached to Warren, and that in any case his plan did not involve capturing Spion Kop, but moving round it until he gained the open plain beyond. Once in the plain Warren would command the rear of the Boer positions. Warren was the only one of his Generals who ventured positively to contradict Buller, and relations between the two men were very strained. Perhaps Buller did not clearly explain his ideas; certainly it does not seem that Warren ever properly understood them. Denied the long range guns to which he attached so much importance, he signified his awareness of his own difficulties by setting thirty of his officers the problem of crossing a river commanded at long range by enemy artillery.

The plan proposed by Buller could hardly fail to succeed – when was it difficult for a General with so great an advantage in numbers to devise a successful plan? – but it did demand reasonable speed in execution for the certainty of success. Unfortunately, Warren was even more convinced than Buller of the need for troops to be accompanied by their supplies. Tents and camping equipment were left behind, but even so the column of wagons and guns for Warren's force was fifteen miles long, and it was calculated that on a level road this procession would take thirteen hours to pass any point. The wagons carried ammunition, ambulance equipment, and the three and a half days' food supply which it was thought necessary that the men should take. The idea that the crawl of this monstrous centipede precluded surprise did not occur to either General, and instructions against talking, smoking and showing lights at the beginning of the march were issued just as though this were to be a dash across half a mile of ground.

The most extraordinary thing about Buller's orders was the system of command they envisaged. He was the Commander-in-Chief of the Natal Field Force, but he did not propose to command it during this operation. He was to stay at Spearman's Camp, on the south side of the river almost opposite Potgieter's Drift, with his

217

entire staff. Some eight miles away Warren, with the staff only of an infantry division, was to direct and conduct the fighting. In front of Buller, Lyttelton was to demonstrate before Potgieter's, and to attempt a crossing at Skiet's Drift, four miles to the east of it. Buller was thus rather in the position of a critical commentator, or umpire at manoeuvres, and he actually claimed later that he was not in command, nor even present, during the battle. The reason for these remarkable orders can be looked for only in terms of Buller's personality. The self-distrust behind his façade of utter assurance made him wish always to place responsibility upon others, and to this self-distrust there was joined personal dislike of Warren, and annoyance at the way in which this 'strong man' had been thrust upon him. He had been sent out as Second-in-command, given the Dormant Commission, ordered to supersede Methuen. Very well, then: let the people at home see what Warren could do. A blend of vacillation, dislike of Warren, and indignation at his own replacement as Commander-in-Chief led Buller to place Warren, who had never so much as seen 15,000 British soldiers together at one time, let alone command them, in charge of the offensive that was to relieve Ladysmith.

(ii) Warren Checks Dundonald

Early on Wednesday 17 January, Buller and his staff, perched on the heights of Spearman's, saw a narrow strip of black stretched across the river five miles to the west. Seen through the telescope this strip of black became a pontoon bridge with men, horses, guns, wagons, moving steadily across it. On the other side of the bridge the infantry filed up into masses of khaki, then went forward in open lines. Warren was crossing the Tugela, and doing so with little opposition. Below again, but nearer, part of Lyttelton's Brigade had crossed at Potgieter's, and could be seen on the other side. They were not advancing, but skirmishing among the kopjes, creating a 'demonstration' which did not deceive the Boers.

Seen from nearer at hand, as it was by Winston Churchill, the main characteristic of Warren's operation was its amazing deliberation. When, on the evening of the 16th, Warren's force assembled opposite Trichard's, everybody made sure that pontoon bridges would be built during the night, so that the infantry might cross at dawn. But this was not Warren's way. Pontoons were launched in the morning, and the West Yorkshires were ferried across. The pontoon bridge grew by span after span, and was finished by 11 o'clock in the morning. The Engineers made a second bridge over the river and across this the artillery, the ammunition columns and the rest of the wheeled transport moved. The whole day was occupied with the crossing, with which the Boers interfered very little. No doubt, then, the attack would begin on the following morning? Not at all. Warren was heard to say that his artillery had not yet finished crossing, and that in any case there was no hurry. On the 18th the wagons continued crossing. No fighting took place. The Boers, who were now in no doubt at all where the weight of the attack was coming, spent the time in strengthening their defences.

Surely, the soldiers and civilian onlookers thought, an attack must be launched on the 19th? It seems hardly possible that Warren should have contemplated another day of preparation. Yet in fact the 19th January was occupied in moving the wagons to Venter's Spruit, three miles to the west of Trichard's Drift, and no attempt was made to engage the Boers with the mass of British infantry. This delay was in accordance with a curious theory of Warren's that before a battle it was vital to have a dress rehearsal. One had practice and rehearsals, as he said afterwards, for cricket, football, golf and theatricals. Why not for war? All that the soldiers needed to fight the Boers successfully, he thought, was a three days' acquaintance with them, and he must have considered it fortunate that the Boers were considerate enough to give them these three days. What acquaintance the soldiers could get with the Boers during a period in which they did not see them, but were subjected to more or less distant rifle fire, is not apparent.

One part of Warren's force had gained acquaintance with the enemy more closely. Dundonald and the cavalry had not crossed at Trichard's Drift, but about half a mile lower down, at a deep and dangerous ford called Wagon Drift. There were a good many duckings during this crossing, and one man of the 13th Hussars was swept away and drowned. Dundonald's own horse slipped into a hole and blundered, so that he was thoroughly soaked. His instructions were to protect Warren's force from flank attack and (a true Bullerian phrase) 'act according to circumstances'. He did not realize that Warren intended to spend three days in dress rehearsals, and conceived that he should move westward across the Boer position, probing at it and trying to find a way through. (It must be remembered that Warren had no accurate maps to guide him, so that the way round Spion Kop which Buller blithely assumed to exist had to be discovered.) On the 18th, when Warren was getting the last of his artillery across the river, Dundonald set off with his 1,500 men towards the road that was known to run from the Orange Free State through Acton Homes to Ladysmith. If the British could command this road they would force the Boers out of their positions in a matter of hours. Dundonald reached Venter's Spruit, where he left 300 men of Thorneycroft's Mounted Infantry, and arranged that sketches should be made of the Tabanyama Hills as they appeared from this point. Very soon afterwards he received a message from Warren, telling him to send back 500 mounted men at once to guard the oxen in the camp. Warren explained afterwards that he had thousands of oxen, which must have their grazing, and he needed quite 500 men to act as cattle guards. The idea that the cavalry might be better employed than in acting as cattle guards does not seem to have occurred to him. The infuriated Dundonald was compelled to send back the Royal Dragoons, so that, with the men he had left to guard the Venter's Spruit position, he was now reduced to 700 men. With these he pushed on towards Acton Homes.

He now had with him two squadrons of the 13th Hussars, 300 of the South African Light Horse, and almost as many of the 'Composite Regiment'. In the afternoon the commanding officer of the Composite Regiment saw some 300 Boers coming down the Acton Homes road from Tabanyama. He lay in wait for them, and engaged them. The South African Light Horse supported him, and the Boers were surrounded. Winston Churchill, who took part in this engagement, described their surprise. 'The Carabiniers and the Imperial Light Horse held their fire until the scouts walked into their midst, and then let drive at the main body, 300 yards range, mounted men, smooth open grass plain. There was a sudden furious, snapping fusillade. The Boer column stopped paralysed; then they broke and rushed for cover.' They left behind them nearly twenty dead and wounded, and twenty-four prisoners. The British losses were a mere half dozen. Dundonald now found himself in an extremely strong position in some kopjes on the Acton Homes–Ladysmith road. He occupied them, making the natural but unfortunately quite mistaken assumption that the infantry would be following his line of advance. One of his officers told him that the Boers had a gun on the upper part of the road, and Dundonald sent back word to Warren asking for artillery support to knock out the Boer gun, and asking also for the return of the Royals.

A combination of dashing skill and good fortune, very much resembling one of Buller's own exploits twenty years earlier, had placed Dundonald in a place of vital importance. By giving him artillery support at once, and following this up with the infantry, Warren would have achieved the immediate objective of turning the Boer flank, and the road which led direct to Ladysmith would have been open to him. This, however, was not at all the light in which he saw the situation. His view was that an army could not move without its supplies, and that its progress must therefore be that of its slowest ox wagon. Besides, although Dundonald's men had taken some Boer prisoners, they had not the necessary practice and rehearsals before doing so. He acknowledged that they had done splendidly, but they were mere novices in mountain warfare, and an advance of this sort really could not be allowed to continue. He sent back one and a half squadrons of the Royals, but ignored the request for artillery, and did his best to check his impetuous subordinate by stopping his supplies. 'Whose wagons are those?' he asked the Transport Officer of the Mounted Brigade.

'Mounted Brigade, sir.'

'Can't pass,' said Warren. 'If I let them go, Lord Dundonald will try and go on to Ladysmith.'

The Transport Officer managed to get the supplies forward when Warren was out of sight, and Dundonald remained at Acton Homes until he received an order to return for an interview which he felt he could not ignore. On the morning of the 19th he rode back to

Venter's Spruit. He found Warren seated on the bank at the ford, 'taking an active part with his voice in urging drivers to do their best'. There followed a sharp altercation. Warren said that he must have the cavalry close to him. Dundonald insisted that he was trying to carry out Buller's orders.

'I want you close to me,' Warren said again, and shouted at the wagon drivers.

Dundonald repeated his arguments in favour of pushing forward by way of Acton Homes. He asked for all the mounted men possible, and some guns. Warren made no immediate reply, but went on staring at the Drift and shouting to the drivers. At last, ignoring Dundonald's arguments, Warren ordered him to return Thorneycroft's Mounted Infantry. Dundonald, with his much-weakened force and without any artillery, went back to Acton Homes.

It was plain, however, even to Warren, that he must make some sort of decision about an advance. On the evening of the 19th he assembled his principal officers and their staffs (with the exception of Dundonald) and told them his views. There were two possible ways of advance, he said, one by way of Acton Homes and the other by Fair View and Rosalie. The first he rejected as being too long and his officers, who knew nothing in detail of Dundonald's moves, agreed with him. He reported to Buller: 'The second (Fair View) is a very difficult road for a large number of wagons, unless the enemy is thoroughly cleared out. I am, therefore, going to make some special arrangements, which will involve my staying at Venter's Laager for two or three days. I will send in for further supplies and report progress.' The Fair View and Rosalie road led directly between the mountainous plateau known as Tabanyama and Spion Kop, and what Warren seems to have meant by 'special arrange-ments' is the capture of Tabanyama. Having clung to his wagons up to this point he now proposed, after the capture of Tabanyama, to send them all back over the Tugela and then, giving his men three or four days' food to carry in their haversacks, to fight his way across the plain behind Spion Kop. There was obviously no point in Dundonald's continued presence at Acton Homes if no attack was to be made along that road, and on the 20th Warren sent a message in triplicate directing his return. Having got the mounted force back into the fold, Warren as nearly as possible ignored them thereafter.

Lyttelton had continued his demonstrations in front of Potgieter's, and a mountain battery had been got across the river. But Lyttelton, like Warren, was operating almost independently and he began to communicate with Warren direct in an attempt to find out what was happening. There was a total absence of any central direction from Buller, and it is difficult to see what he and his staff were doing on these days. On the 17th he was with Warren at Trichard's Drift, watching the crossing. On the 18th and 19th he seems to have done nothing at all. He kept in touch with Warren and Lyttelton, but gave them no instructions and offered no suggestions about their course of action. He afterwards wrote that he saw on the 19th that things were not going well.

> I ought to have assumed command myself... I blame myself now for not having done so. I did not, because I thought that if I did I should discredit General Warren in the estimation of his troops; and that if I were shot, and he had to withdraw across the Tugela, and they had lost confidence in him, the consequences might be very serious.

All this hypothesizing took place after the event. At the time Buller approved the plan for capturing Tabanyama, totally opposed though it was to his original conception of Warren throwing his left forward and refusing his right – which was, of course, exactly what would have happened if the attack had been made by way of Acton Homes.

(iii) *The Attack on Tabanyama, 20–23 January*

> South African hills are like the sea: at a distance they seem smooth, but look close into them and you will find unsuspected valleys and crests. Nothing on the face of South African nature is what it seems. You see the British trenches up there, seeming to lie immediately under the Boer trenches, but if you go up you will find that they are on different hills, and a deep valley

223

lies between. You see troops march out on to a sheer plain; and when they have disappeared suddenly in their march you learn for the first time that the plain is no plain but is full of dips and rises, dongas and unremarked kopjes.

This was written by J B Atkins of the *Manchester Guardian*, with Tabanyama and Spion Kop particularly in mind. Warren's simple plan ignored such subtleties. He held the lower slopes of Tabanyama leading up to Three Tree Hill. He proposed first to capture the hill by artillery fire supported by an infantry advance, then to move on and gradually push his way to the plateau of Tabanyama, getting eventually round to the back of Spion Kop. Lacking any proper maps of either hill he relied for guidance on a Colonial Scout named Schwikkard, who knew the country well. He made no attempt to reconnoitre the ground before attacking, and it would be a mistake to think that he was greatly worried by the fact that he knew the configurations of Tabanyama no more precisely than Atkins or the other newspaper correspondents. Both Buller and Warren seem to have felt that, while maps were important for marking the general physical features of a country and estimating distances, they could really be dispensed with when one was engaged in close-range fighting.

Lieutenant Charlton, a young officer attached to the Lancashire Fusiliers, wrote years later, in the third person, of the emotion of moving off early in the morning to take the position on Three Tree Hill:

He was nudged into wakefulness by his colour-sergeant, who whispered that the men were falling in. In less than a minute he had joined his company and was listening to the captain's orders. The instructions were simple in the extreme. All they had to do was to extend in an interval of five paces between each man, lie down, and await the word to advance. It was then a question merely of pressing forward, keeping the line intact and firing occasional volleys at the crest of the hill ahead. If any one were wounded it was strictly forbidden to stop and render assistance. The stretcher-bearer contingent would see to all that.

By 6 o'clock in the morning Three Tree Hill and part of the plateau to the east of it had been occupied, and the men were told to entrench. Here arose a difficulty that had occurred before, but now was seen for the first time in its full gravity. The soldiers had had little practice in making trenches, and that little had been done in such places as the Dover Downs, where the ground was comparatively soft. Such easy digging was no preparation at all for making trenches in the rock hard ground of the South African kopjes. The men carried as standard equipment the Wallace spade, which proved so utterly useless for the job of entrenching in South Africa that many of them threw it away. The Wallace spade, Hildyard said afterwards, was a poor weak thing, more like a toy than anything else, and there was an overwhelming consensus of opinion that this spade, which had been in use for fifteen years, was nothing more than an encumbrance. The Boers, by contrast, chose the placings for their trenches very deliberately in advance and dug them with effective spades, or erected thick stone walls which provided good shelter.

Warren had entrusted the command of operations to that master of minor tactics, Clery, but now, as the two Generals rode up to Three Tree Hill, they saw what advance scouting might have told them, that the hill so easily taken had given them no advantage. The Boer defences on Tabanyama extended in a great semi-circle in front of them. Botha had been given ample time to make preparations, and his defences against a frontal attack were very strong indeed. It was such an attack, however, that Clery chose to make without hesitation, not across a river this time, but over the varied slopes of a hill which he did not know. The prospect did not deter him. He brought up his field artillery to Three Tree Hill and battered away at the Boer positions. After four hours of artillery bombardment he judged that the time for attack had come, and sent Hart, in command of four and a half mixed battalions of Lancashire Fusiliers, Dublin Fusiliers, Inniskilling Fusiliers, Border Regiment and York and Lancasters, forward to reach and take the Boers positions. There was a good deal of cover but the advance was difficult, as the Lancashire Fusiliers, who were leading it on the right, soon found. Charlton wrote:

Before long, owing to the roughness of the surface, to fatigue and faint heart, the line became disordered, and an uncontrollable tendency asserted itself to collect in pockets of the ground for shelter, for breathing space, and for the summoning of resolution for further advance. On the first few occasions the halt was momentary, but the impulse to linger ever grew until finally, as the sense of physical danger overpowered the mental resolve, and as the hills loomed more threateningly ahead, the laggard progress stopped for good and all, and the tired and dispirited attackers longed only for dark.

It was Charlton's first day in battle, and perhaps he was inclined to exaggerate the fatigue and faint-heartedness of those around him. To others it seemed that the infantry advanced with great heart, dropping behind shelter when it was available, and watching their chances to come forward with caution. From Three Tree Hill, Warren and Clery watched their progress, a progress which, mapless and in the most literal sense of the word clueless, they were unable to guide intelligently. At a quarter past one a Boer pom-pom and two other guns suddenly opened fire on Three Tree Hill, scattering the two Generals and the group of staff officers and newspaper correspondents who were watching the battle. By 3 o'clock Hart's men, with some 300 casualties, had reached a point about 600 yards from the Boer lines. Across this considerable distance there was no cover whatever. Hart, among whose defects lack of courage was not numbered, was prepared to lead his men in a suicidal dash for the Boer trenches. 'There is nothing apologetic about General Hart,' as one eyewitness wrote, 'gallant fiery Irishman, too hot with the *ignis sacer* of fighting to see anything ridiculous in a sword angrily brandished at an enemy a thousand yards away.' But now Clery intervened. Whether he was disturbed by the fact that the Boer rifle fire had not in any way decreased as a result of the artillery bombardment (which, like so much artillery fire in this war, was extremely ineffective), or whether he flinched from the slaughter ahead, he stopped the advance. Warren agreed with this course of action, saying that a flank attack would be 'more suitable', and that they would continue the advance tomorrow, if they could not do so that night. But nothing further was done, and a party of the Lancashire Fusiliers who had got close to the Boer position were ordered back to rejoin the rest of their regiment. Charlton was one among several small groups feeling their way back under cover of darkness. He wrote:

> When they arrived at the bivouac, they threw themselves down where they stood and slept. He found he had lain down near the Colonel, who was also in a state of wakefulness. They exchanged a few remarks in tired and subdued voices. The colonel said that about two hundred good fellows had been killed and wounded, and that they were to try again next day.

For Warren there was always another day.

A chance of making the flank attack was opened to Warren by the initiative of Dundonald, who took advantage of the fact that no specific orders had been given him. Seeing opposite to him a great hill, which took its name from its bastion-like shape, the cavalry leader decided to reconnoitre it. He sent the South African Light Horse galloping over the open ground to the foot of the hill. There they dismounted, fanned out, and began to climb. One of them, Corporal Tobin, went up hand over hand, ascending the slope as though it were a bell tent. He reached the top, and waved his helmet on his rifle. The few Boers on Bastion Hill had retired. It was thus captured without loss, although the Boer fire from the ridges beyond killed a very few men, including Major Childe of the South African Light Horse. It was Childe's first day in action, and on the previous night he had not only prophesied his own death, but had suggested his epitaph, a sad, neat Victorian pun, which was cut on a cross at the bottom of the hill: 'Is it well with the child? It is well.' The capture of this height was important because it commanded the position, so that Dundonald was able to signal back useful information to Hart on the adjoining Sugar Loaf Hill and to Warren on Three Tree Hill. The hill faced directly the Boer extreme right, so that an advance from it offered a real opportunity of turning the Boer flank.

Buller had stayed during the day at Spearman's Camp on Mount Alice, from the heights of which the troops were plainly visible, as though they were tiny figures being moved about on a map. Mount Alice was, as one of the correspondents said, a hill fit for Xerxes to watch from. Buller watched, made critical remarks to his idle staff (idle because he gave them nothing to do), and before breakfast on the 21st rode over to Warren. Acting, as Amery puts it, in his capacity as impartial umpire, he criticized Clery's dispositions freely. Why were his batteries all crowded on the inner flank? Why was no attempt made to turn the Boer right? Now, it had been plain to Warren on the previous day that Clery's varicose veins made him comparatively inactive. He had therefore given Hildyard command of the left of the position, and had relegated Clery to control only of the extreme left flank. This was exactly the point at which Buller wished to attack, but Warren pointed out triumphantly that it was Clery himself who had halted the attack on the previous day. Perhaps, he suggested, Clery should be placed on the sick list until his leg got better? Buller, perhaps interpreting this as an attempt by Warren to obtain greater power for himself, refused to listen to the suggestion, and went to talk to Clery. He later said that he found that Warren had 'divided his fighting line into three independent commands' (Clery, Hildyard, and General Woodgate on the right), 'independent of each other, and apparently independent of him, as he told me he could not move any batteries without General Clery's consent'. It might be added that Warren was similarly 'independent' of Buller, and that this independence was really a means of evading final responsibility.

As a result of Buller's criticism the 19th and 28th batteries were brought round to the left of Hildyard's position, and the infantry, who had relieved Dundonald's men on Bastion Hill at dawn, carried out an attack on Sugar Loaf Hill. They were under the command of Kitchener's brother, Colonel Kitchener. The plan was that four companies of the East Surrey Regiment should work their way round the western slope of the hill, while a direct attack across the plateau was made by men of the Queen's and West Yorkshire Regiments. Nobody except Buller, however, was very keen about this attack. Clery disapproved of it, and Warren had no faith in it at all. He saw an action going on for which he had no orders and assumed, as he says, that 'General Buller was trying his hand at a little warfare on his own account'. Buller, having made his criticisms, had in the meantime recrossed the Tugela and gone back to watch, not quite like Xerxes, from his headquarters at Spearman's. The attack, which began at about 11 o'clock on the morning of the 21st after some hours of heavy firing, was never pushed very hard. It met with strong resistance from the Boers, but some ground had been made, and Kitchener was confident of success, when he received an order from Clery that the attack was to be stopped at once. So ended this gesture, for it was hardly more, towards turning the Boer right.

It is difficult to know what Warren really wanted to do at this time, and perhaps he hardly knew himself. He had always favoured pushing straight through from Three Tree Hill, and now he seems to have returned to this idea, with the proviso that any attack should be preceded by three or four days of intense artillery fire. He asked Buller for the 10th Brigade, commanded by Major-General Talbot Coke, and requested also that he should have some howitzer and long-range guns. (He still had in mind those two long range guns of the Boers.) Buller sent the 10th Brigade and four howitzers, but ignored the request for long-range guns. He also retained on his own side of the river the balloon, which might have been immensely useful to Warren, and certainly performed no important function at all on the wrong side of the Tugela.

So passed Sunday the 21st, a day on which nothing had been achieved. The British forces remained exactly where they had been, Lyttelton demonstrating on the north side of Potgieter's, Woodgate and Hart making no progress, Kitchener encamped on Bastion Hill. Warren, however, had not expected to make progress, and he was surprised and hurt when Buller, paying his early morning visit on Monday, expressed utter dissatisfaction with the course of the attack, which was now in its sixth day. Warren pleaded for a couple of days' further artillery preparation, but Buller absolutely refused to consider this, nor would he accept Warren's suggestion that after the hills were taken (but when would that be?) they should send back the supply wagons and advance with three or four days' provisions in haversacks. Bluntly he put before Warren three possibilities: a wholehearted attack on the Boer right which, as he said, was in the air; the retirement of Warren's whole force across the Tugela; or an assault on Spion Kop. The idea of taking Spion Kop was now mentioned for the first time, and it entered the discussion only because of Warren's insistence that they must advance by the Fair View road. They could not go that way, he said, without taking Spion Kop first, and to this Buller irritably replied: 'Of course you must take Spion Kop.' So the capture of this hill, which had never even been considered, was now taken for granted. Warren said he would lead the attack himself, but Buller immediately forbade this, saying that Warren went too much in advance, and that he ought to remain in one place and get reports from his Generals. Warren later observed this suggestion quite literally, with unhappy results.

Buller now went off to look again at Bastion Hill, rather in the spirit of a schoolboy contemplating forbidden fruit, leaving Warren indignant at the way in which his attack was being hurried. In the afternoon he received a plan from Buller, suggesting that a night attack should be made from Bastion Hill on the Boer right. Disturbed, he called Clery, Hildyard, and the newly arrived Talbot Coke, who was still lame from the effect of a recently broken leg, into conference, and asked their advice. Clery was emphatic against Buller's suggestion, saying that if it succeeded it would commit them to taking the whole line of the Boer position (which one might have thought the purpose of the operation), and that they might not be able to hold the position after they took it. Warren agreed. He explained afterwards that he 'concurred in ruling against the enterprise so long as it was in General Clery's hands', and the idea of taking it out of Clery's hands does not seem to have occurred to him. Hildyard agreed with Clery, and Talbot Coke seems to have expressed no particular opinion. Dundonald was not consulted. Nobody wanted to retire; Warren and Clery were against the attack on the Boer right; and so, by a process of elimination, it was settled that an assault should be made on Spion Kop. Few military decisions can have been arrived at more haphazardly. Nobody wanted it, nobody really believed in it. For Warren it was no more than an adjunct of the main design printed ineradicably on his mind, of pushing through by the Fair View road to Rosalie. For Buller it was an excuse to stir Warren into action of some sort. The result of the decision so lightly taken was to be one of the most ludicrous episodes in the history of British arms.

The decision had been taken, but nothing was immediately done about it. The artillery and the howitzers were busy. The Boers replied with their Maxim, Vickers and long-range guns. The soldiers hung on to their positions, hot and unhappy, wondering what had happened to the attack. Warren was busy rearranging his command yet again. It was divided now into halves. Clery was placed in command of all troops west of Three Tree Hill, and Talbot Coke was appointed to the command of the Fifth Division, and entrusted with the task of taking Spion Kop, Colonel Hill replacing him in command of the 10th Brigade. Coke, however, pointed out that the battalions chosen for the assault, the Middlesex and Dorsets, and Thorneycroft's Mounted Infantry, were still at Venter's Spruit. The hill had not been reconnoitred – something that Warren, in his anxiety to circumvent Buller's threat of withdrawal, seems to have thought supererogatory. Coke suggested that it would be useful to have a guide up the hill, and when he was told that there was nobody who knew the way, he asked that the attack should be delayed for a day. It was so dark that he lost the way back to his own bivouac, and had to sleep out.

At 4 o'clock on the following morning, the 23rd, he and Warren rode out to make a reconnaissance, and decided a line of attack. They examined Spion Kop, a hill, which could not quite be called a mountain, from a valley joining it to Tabanyama, and from a hill on the right of their position, and as a result of these examinations they decided on a line of advance. But of course they could not go up the hill or look at it in any detail, and Spion Kop resembled all the other South African positions in this area, in being utterly deceptive to the eye. In default of an expedition made by experienced scouts, any examination was very much a matter of guesswork.

A little later on in the morning Warren was visited by the wrath of Buller. The Commander-in-Chief, furious that nothing had been done during the past twenty-four hours, and perhaps suspecting that Warren's agreement to the attack was a cover for the continuation of his own plan of incessant bombardment, was peremptory. He told Warren that he could either attack that night or retire over the Tugela. Warren said that he would prefer to attack and showed Buller the orders he had drafted. But Buller was now not in a mood to agree to anything. He criticized the appointment of Coke to lead the attack and suggested that Woodgate who had, as he put it, two sound legs, was better adapted for mountain climbing. The word 'suggested' is used, but Buller's suggestions were in effect orders. He delegated á Court, from his staff, to accompany Woodgate. Having fulfilled what seems to have been a psychological necessity for him at this time by interfering with Warren's arrangements without taking any responsibility for them, he drew á Court aside and told him that he was to accompany the assault column. The staff officer naturally asked what the column should do when it had taken the hill. Buller thought for a moment and then said, 'It has got to stay there'. When the staff officer said that they would want guns, the mountain battery at Frere was ordered up. 'The only other request that I made to Sir Redvers was to point out to me on the ground the exact point which he wished us to take, as the maps were so bad that we scarcely ever referred to them,' á Court says. Commenting ironically on the project afterwards, he remarked: 'There was no plan except that we were to take the hill and stay there. Some 1,700 men were to assault a hill 1,740 feet high in the centre of the Boer position, and the rest of Buller's 20,000 men were to look on and do nothing.' There was no attempt at co-ordination, no arrangement made for a supporting attack by Clery or by Lyttelton which might have drawn off the Boer from Spion Kop. Buller's attitude was not that they must so co-ordinate their movements as to make the night attack succeed, but rather that if it succeeded then it might be supported. The whole scheme exemplified both the incaution and the timidity of the British command. This was realized by á Court and some others, but nothing was said of it at the time.

Warren and Coke passed the rest of the day in making preparations for the night attack. Woodgate, who was now in direct command of it, selected from his own 11th Brigade the Lancashire Fusiliers, six companies of the Royal Lancasters, and two companies of South Lancashires. To these were added half a company of engineers, and two hundred of Thorneycroft's men, who were to proceed dismounted. The mountain battery, which Warren had for some reason supposed to be at Potgieter's, had not arrived, but Warren and Coke selected various points on which the artillery at Three Tree Hill was to fire to check a possible counter-attack, and an artillery officer was chosen to accompany the force to report on the effect of this fire. Arrangements were made for a dressing station on the top of Spion Kop and a hospital at the bottom of it, for a water supply, and for the assaulting column to be supported if necessary. Buller had promised to send native water carriers, but these did not arrive, and one of Warren's staff improvised an arrangement by which twenty-five pack mules were to accompany the assault force, each carrying two biscuit tins containing nearly twenty gallons of water. The men took 150 rounds of ammunition apiece, and a full day's rations.

These arrangements, considered in themselves, were adequate enough, but the all-important question of the assault itself was left comparatively vague. There was a long, strongly-marked spur running down Spion Kop to the south and south-west, and when this spur was reached it would serve as a guide on the way up. But neither Warren nor the leaders of the assault force nor anybody on the British side had any real idea of the configuration of Spion Kop, except that there was a plateau on the top of it. Lyttelton, who had more than once asked Warren how he might help, was told nothing of the intended attack, and Barton, who commanded a force left behind at Chieveley, was similarly kept in ignorance. Nor did the attack have any real purpose. Warren seems to have conceived of it as a defensive move, and to have thought that once the troops were on top of Spion Kop they could entrench, and so facilitate his plan of forcing a way through by bombardment. Buller's conclusion, as we have seen, was that 'They have got to stay there', and his thoughts seem to have gone no further than that. At 8.30 on the evening of the 23rd the 1,700 victims of their Generals' inefficiency and incapacity to plan assembled at the starting point, a gully south of Three Tree Hill.

(iv) *The Assault on Spion Kop, 23–24 January*

It was 11 o'clock when the assault force started the march up the hill. There was no guide who knew the way up, but Woodgate and á Court agreed that Thorneycroft should lead the way, as he had some knowledge of the ground. The Colonel, who had raised his regiment of mounted irregulars very early in the war, was a man six feet two inches tall, and of great bulk. When asked how much he weighed he said, 'With my wire-cutters and map and pencil, not an ounce under twenty stone'. Now, in a darkness so intense that it was impossible to see a hand in front of the face, he set off, followed first by his own men and then by the Lancashire contingents. They marched first of all in fours, and then in single file. Progress was extremely slow and many of the men, who had been for a week under arms, took the chance to sleep at every halt, so that á Court and the regimental officers had to round them up continually. At one point a large white dog, a regimental pet, suddenly appeared at the head of the column and had to be sent back in charge of a bugler. The spur was found successfully, and they moved up it. Woodgate, who, although he had two sound legs, was fifty-five years old and far from well, had to be helped up the rockier parts of the slope.

They had been climbing up under the crest of the ridge, but now they came to a point where the track broadened out. The men in front deployed and lay down, and slowly the Lancashire troops came up and joined them. They had been on Spion Kop now for more than four hours, and dawn was breaking, but with the dawn came a thick white mist, which confined visibility to no more than a few yards. Cautiously they moved forward and suddenly a Boer voice shouted: 'Wer da?' This was answered, possibly by an attempt to reply in the same language, possibly by the countersign, 'Waterloo'. The Boers fired, but Thorneycroft's men were lying down, and nobody was hit. Then Thorneycroft sprang to his feet and gave the order to charge. His men, and some of the Lancashire Fusiliers, charged, and the Boers ran. One of them was bayoneted, the others disappeared into the mist. They were on the central plateau at the top, they had captured Spion Kop. They gave three cheers, a signal prearranged with Warren to let him know that they were on the plateau, and set about entrenching themselves. There was a brief investigation of the position, which was in any case hampered by the mist, and then Major Murray of the Royal Engineers taped out positions for the trenches, and the men began to dig. Again the Wallace spade proved its total ineffectiveness. After eighteen inches of earth the men came to an almost solid bed of rock. The engineers had brought up some 200 picks and shovels, and these made an impression on the rock. Sangars were hurriedly built of stones, with loopholes for firing. Sandbags would have been invaluable, and a supply of them had been ready at the meeting place below, but by one of those pieces of utterly incompetent staff work that marked the Natal campaign, Woodgate's men had not drawn them.

Now the mist lifted a little, and it could be seen that the placing of the trenches was far from ideal. Murray and his men had gone round the edge of the plateau and made sure that the ground sloped away from the entrenchments, so that they would command the widest possible range of fire. Now, however, they saw that although the ground certainly sloped away for something less than 200 yards from their main northward-facing trench, it shelved so steeply afterwards that the Boers would be able to climb the hill and remain under the ridge in perfect safety. A hurried attempt was made to entrench on what was now seen to be the true edge of the hill, but the sappers who went to do the work found the ground almost impermeable, and in face of some scattered firing by Boers who had crawled up the slopes they retired. The regiments were left to make their own arrangements for holding the crest line, and if they could push forward little groups towards the edge under cover of rocks they did so. The resultant confusion is excellently conveyed by Charlton, who had come up with the Lancashire Fusiliers, and had fallen asleep on top of the hill:

> When he opened his eyes it was to find that the light had come bringing with it a dense white cloud that enveloped the mountain-top and blotted out vision beyond a distance of fifty yards at most. There did not seem anything for him to do, so he continued to lie on in drowsiness... There was a certain commotion in the vicinity. The colonel's distinctive tone could

235

be heard speaking in a peremptory manner, and the company next door was moving forward at a run.

He knew that it would be the turn of his own company soon but was determined not to bestir himself until the last moment. His captain's name was called, and Charlton watched him scurrying to receive his orders. It seemed that affairs were taking a serious turn. In the darkness and confusion an hour or two ago the position which had been chosen from the point of view of defence had turned out to be faulty. The enemy was already attacking under cover of the mist and would gain a sure foothold unless new dispositions were taken immediately. The order was for them to leave their present cover and occupy the forward edge of the plateau, trusting purely to luck for natural shelter from the stream of bullets which went sleeting by.

If ever he felt like a faint-heart it was then, but fortunately for his self-respect he found that, with the eyes of his men on him, it required less moral courage to smother his hesitation and spring up and on than to falter and hang back.

Holding themselves in a crouched position and mindless of the weight of their equipment they plunged forward, and as they did so the air around seethed with the hiss and crack of rifles fired at short range. Looking neither to the right nor left, nor backwards, he held straight on and at last flung himself down behind a heaven-sent boulder in a fringe of such, already in the occupation of others of the column, mixed and jumbled.

In this spot for hours on end he was pinned by a fierce, short-range fire which plastered his shelter and held him for a long time motionless.

The Boers had reacted quickly to the capture of Spion Kop. The report of their picket spread considerable alarm in the laagers, and a number of the burghers favoured immediate flight. Some of the commanders believed, wrongly but not at all unreasonably, that the capture of the hill was the prelude to a major offensive designed to split their force in two. Volunteers to recapture the hill were asked for, and small parties from several commandos started up the slopes. On the Boer right Louis Botha hurriedly collected men at the north-western spur of the hill and sent them forward, while he arranged to bring round from Acton Homes the two long-range guns that had caused such alarm to Warren, and to place them in a position at the rear of Tabanyama from which they could enfilade the top of Spion Kop. It was these burghers, no more than a few hundred in all, who, having reached the edge of the plateau, were firing on the British. Their activities, troublesome though they were to Charlton and his comrades, did not present any serious threat to Woodgate, and the commander, although no doubt regretting the mistake about the placing of his main trench, was on the whole very satisfied with his position. He sent down most of his engineers to lay out a road for reinforcements, and to make slides for the guns which he hoped would be brought up to the plateau. At 7.15 in the morning he had a dish of tea with á Court, and then sent the staff officer down the hill to Warren with a letter (signal communication was impossible because of the mist). In this letter Woodgate said that they had captured the hill, and mentioned the mist.

> I pushed on a bit quicker than I perhaps should otherwise have done, lest it should lift before we got here. We have entrenched a position, and are, I hope, secure; but fog is too thick to see, so I retain Thorneycroft's men and Royal Engineers for a bit longer.
> Thorneycroft's men attacked in fine style.

Woodgate and á Court agreed that the staff officer should ask verbally for some 12 pounder naval guns, and for support from Lyttelton. On the way down á Court passed the headquarters of Coke, and also the piquets of the Connaught Rangers, who were entrenched to provide help in case of a reverse. At the bottom of the hill he met a man of the Royals, borrowed his horse, and reached Warren just before 9 o'clock in the morning. He presented the letter and told Warren about Lyttelton, the naval guns, the sandbags, and the water. A small spring had been discovered upon the plateau, and although it was muddy, á Court thought this should provide a water supply. The news was upon the whole pretty cheerful. Warren signalled to Coke to ask if Woodgate needed any support, and was told by Coke that he had been trying for an hour to open signal communications with the summit, but had been unsuccessful because of the mist. Warren told Coke to send up a battalion in support, and Coke sent up first the Imperial Light Infantry and then the Middlesex Regiment, telling the first of these units to work their way along the south-eastern kopjes, instead of taking the route of the previous night. á Court stayed with him while these instructions were given and was about to leave when, at 9.50, the first signal from the summit came in. It was from the commander of the Lancashire Fusiliers, Colonel Crofton, and it read:

Colonel Crofton to GOC Force. Reinforce at once or all lost. General dead.

(v) *The Tragi-Comedy of Command*

It was some half-hour after á Court had left the summit, between 8 and 8.30 in the morning, that the mist completely cleared, and revealed to Woodgate that, far from being safely entrenched on the summit in a commanding position, his men were in a death trap. Through haste, carelessness, and ignorance the engineers had completely failed to notice the existence of a hill called Aloe Knoll to the east of the British position. This hill dominated the main British trenches, which were facing north, and on the eastern side the only protection was a few roughly made curved sangars. The Boers had climbed the hill not only upon the north and north-west sides, which faced the main British trenches, but also upon this eastern side. Now they poured in rifle fire upon the eastern side of the main trenches, and upon the advanced sections on the forward crest. No provision at all had been made by Woodgate or the sappers for an attack upon the eastern side, and the return fire which they could bring to bear was comparatively feeble. The British were at first so much exposed to attack from this side that, according to Botha, seventy of the men afterwards found dead in the trenches were shot through the right side of the head. To rifle fire there was soon added the menace of the Boer artillery. Botha had sent a heliograph and signallers up to the Aloe Knoll and they were immensely helpful in signalling the British positions, but in any case the Boer guns were brilliantly placed. There were very few of them – the two guns and a pom-pom brought up from Acton Homes to the northern slopes of Tabanyama, a gun that faced the main British trench, a gun from the east firing at about 2,000 yards, and a pom-pom which was firing also from this direction but was much nearer – yet they were far more damaging than the British guns which greatly outnumbered them. It had been arranged that the batteries on Three Tree Hill should shell the north-western side of Spion Kop and so they did, but this had practically no effect on the Boers who were clambering up on the northern side. The artillery signallers on the summit tried to send messages to direct the fire from Three Tree Hill, but so furious a fire was directed upon them that they gave up this attempt, and the batteries on Three Tree Hill had to trust to luck rather than to judgment in their attempts to put the Boer guns out of action. They shelled points where they imagined the guns might be, but did no damage.

Woodgate, who was conspicuous equally for his gallantry and his military ineptness, had little idea of exactly what was happening. He walked along the trenches with his staff encouraging the men and ordering them forward. He also told the signallers to ask for reinforcements, although in truth his urgent and vital need was not for men but for guns. The signallers moved from their exposed position round to the south-eastern side of the spur, and transmitted a message to the signal station by Buller's headquarters on Spearman's. It said: 'Am exposed to terrible cross-fire, especially near first dressing station. Can barely hold our own. Water badly needed. Help us. Woodgate.' Probably the wording of this message was not Woodgate's, but only a signaller's version of his general instruction. In fact there was not at this time a shortage of water. Very soon after the message had been sent Woodgate was shot in the head. He was not killed, but was fatally wounded. He was carried to the dressing station, which had been established behind some rocks on the south-eastern side – a point which had been thought to be completely protected, but was found to be under fire from Aloe Knoll. It was thought that Woodgate was dead and his brigade-major, Captain Vertue, went across to tell the senior Colonel,

Crofton. He told Crofton, and was killed himself immediately afterwards. Crofton then sent down the message which Warren received in á Court's presence, a message which again was changed by the signaller from the original. The original message said: 'General Woodgate dead. Reinforcements urgently required.' With Woodgate believed dead, á Court gone, and Vertue also dead, there was nobody on the summit who had much knowledge of the situation.

When Warren received the message he consulted á Court who was inclined, not exactly to pooh-pooh it, but to suggest that Crofton had lost his head. His own view, based on what he had seen before leaving the summit, was that the position could be held till Doomsday, and he suggested that a sharp message should be sent back to this excitable Colonel. Warren accordingly signalled that help was on the way up, and added: 'You must hold on to the last. No surrender.' He had the news relayed to Buller, and sent a message to Lyttelton asking for assistance. All this was done within a few minutes of receiving the message from Crofton. á Court then rode off to cross the Tugela and rejoin Buller, eight miles away on Spearman's, and Warren bent his mind to the problem of replacing Woodgate by another commander. He had originally wanted Coke to lead the assault, and now he rode over to the place where Coke was stationed, at the foot of the hill, and told him to take command on the peak towards which two of his battalions were already moving. Just after 11 o'clock in the morning Coke, bad leg and all, set out to climb the hill with men of the Dorset Regiment, who had been given sandbags to carry up with them. 'Mind, no surrender,' Warren said to him, and Coke assured him that Spion Kop would be held. Warren did not tell Buller that he had put Coke in command on Spion Kop. Perhaps he felt that it was none of Buller's business, and that he should be able to make his own appointments. Perhaps he simply forgot. It was to prove an important omission.

The incident shows clearly the abilities and the limitations of Warren. On the immediate issue involved in the telegram he moved quickly and efficiently, but in relation to any of the wider problems involved in the battle he had no ideas at all. Only a small part of his force was engaged in the action on Spion Kop and the most obvious way of helping them was to order an attack elsewhere. Now and throughout the day, however, he rejected the idea that Clery and Hildyard, his left and centre, should push forward to relieve pressure on Spion Kop. In view of the Boers' paucity of guns such an attack could hardly have failed to succeed, but Warren was haunted, even more than Buller, by the idea that many thousands of Boers were lurking on his left, waiting only for a rash move to mount an attack. He was determined not to give them the chance. Clery and Hildyard, not loth to be inactive, stayed where they were.

It took á Court something like an hour to cross the river and reach the umpire on Spearman's, a sufficient commentary on the absurdity of Buller's position. He was now receiving most of the signals from Spion Kop before Warren, and passing them on to him. Both Warren and Buller were influenced by á Court's conviction that the position on Spion Kop was a splendid one, and that Crofton must have lost his nerve. The staff officer was full of praise for Thorneycroft's energy and ability, and after talking to him Buller, unaware, of course, that Coke had already been appointed to the command, sent a heliograph to Warren:

> Unless you put some really good hard fighting man in command on the top you will lose the hill. I suggest Thorneycroft.

Warren's actions on receiving this message are inexplicable, and completely inexcusable. He might have questioned Buller's authority to 'suggest' such an appointment, might have said 'Thorneycroft is a junior officer, and I can't accept your suggestion', might have told Buller that he had already appointed Coke. He did none of these things. He sent a signal to Crofton that Thorneycroft was to be placed in command on the summit, with the local rank of Brigadier-General, but having done this he did not inform Coke, who was making his way up the hill. Both Coke and Thorneycroft, therefore, assumed that they were in command on Spion Kop. When Coke reached the plateau he sent back to Warren a message which showed that he believed himself in command. Warren did nothing to undeceive him.

Warren's next move was to squash the first effective artillery attack made on the Boer position. Early in the morning Lyttelton had been demonstrating against Brakfontein, but Buller, as insistent as Warren upon involving the smallest possible number of men, ordered him to withdraw. When he received Warren's appeal for help, however, Lyttelton began a very vigorous diversion. He sent a battalion of the Scottish Rifles, who were on the wrong side of the Tugela, to cross it by a Kaffir Drift, and go to the help of Spion Kop, and a battalion of the 60th Rifles to cross the drift and attack the hills called the Twin Peaks, well to the east of Aloe Knoll. At the same time Lyttelton's guns, eight naval 12 pounders and two how-itzers, opened fire on the eastern slopes of Spion Kop and upon Aloe Knoll. The two 4.7 inch guns on Mount Alice were also turned upon them. On the top of Mount Alice the air was bracing and the atmosphere extremely clear, so that very long distances could be seen. The naval gunners had an excellent view of the Boers on Aloe Knoll through their telescopes. They were a fine target, but the gunners had been firing for less than half an hour when Warren sent an urgent message to both Buller and Lyttelton:

We occupy the whole summit and I fear you are shelling us seriously. Cannot you turn your guns on the enemy's guns?

Warren had received no word from the summit, which gave him any reason to say this. His message proceeded from his fixed conviction that the assault force had occupied the whole of the summit, instead of the western half of it, and he never wavered from this mistaken view throughout the day. After receiving such a message Lyttelton felt bound to stop firing, and although artillery attacks were renewed from time to time during the day, each attack was checked by a complaint from Warren that the guns were firing on their own men. Lyttelton was not in a position to see the effect of his guns, but Buller on Spearman's had a perfect view, and could see that Warren's complaints were baseless. By the strained courtesy that governed this ridiculous situation, however, he did not use his superior knowledge to ignore Warren and continue firing, any more than Warren had thought of denying his 'suggestion' that

Thorneycroft should be placed in command on the summit. The only artillery attack that could have been seriously effective in helping the assault force was stopped by the General in command of it, with the connivance of his Commander-in-Chief.

These hours, during which Coke's men were slowly moving up the hill (those who had been told to go round the south-eastern side found the way too steep, and wasted an hour in moving circuitously back to the other route), and the Scottish Rifles were crossing the Tugela and coming over the kopjes, were a period of torment for the men on the summit.

(vi) *On the Summit*

I will describe the scene as I saw it from below. I shall always have it in my memory – that acre of massacre, that complete shambles, at the top of a rich green gully with cool granite walls (a way fit to lead to heaven) which reached up the western flank of the mountain. To me it seemed that our men were all in a small square patch; there were brown men and brown trenches, the whole like an over-ripe barley field... I saw three shells strike a certain trench within a minute. The trench was toothed against the sky like a saw – made, I supposed, of sharp rocks built into a rampart. Another shell struck it, and then – heavens! – the trench was men; the teeth against the sky were men. They ran forward bending their bodies into a curve, as men do when they run under a heavy fire; they looked like a cornfield with a heavy wind sweeping over it from behind...

The Boers had three guns playing like hoses on our men. It was a triangular fire. Our men on Spion Kop had no gun. When on earth would the artillery come?

Guns on the summit would have been invaluable to the British, but no urgent attempt was made to get them there. The mountain battery had not arrived, and a report had been made by the artillery officer on Spion Kop that the 15 pounder guns at Three Tree Hill were too heavy to be dragged up, although he thought that 12 pounder naval guns might be got up the hill. Buller was dilatory in sending these, and Warren did not press him.

The men on the summit were not aware of how urgently they needed guns. They knew only that they were exposed to intense and continuous fire, and their immediate reaction was concern for self-preservation. Very few of the men or the junior officers knew what was happening, or why. The confusion was increased by the fact that all badges of rank had been given up, so that the Boers should not concentrate their fire on officers, as they had done in the past. As Charlton found, it was difficult to know exactly what one was doing, and reactions were automatic rather than intelligent:

His own men seemed to have evaporated into space in some mysterious way. He had even parted company with his captain and found himself in the midst of strange men of other units, each one as concerned as he was to fit the kindly shelter, which Providence had supplied.

After an interval, not reckonable in time, he became more accustomed to the situation, and he began to use his rifle, urging his next-door neighbours to do the same. The enemy fire was slightly lulled. He peered round his cover. A few paces away he saw the crown of a slouch hat behind a large boulder, and as he gazed, transfixed, it rose slowly bringing into view a face which was all beard. So they were as close as this, were they, and that was why the fire had slackened. He fired point blank into the beard and instantly took cover again.

They were as close as this. During the hours up to midday the Boers crawled and shot their way on to the crest of the hill, and drove back the advanced British line. The pressure first became intolerable on the right of the line, where the rifle fire from Aloe Knoll was most deadly. At 11 o'clock Thorneycroft, who had not yet received the message appointing him to command, led some forty of his Mounted Infantry and Lancashire Fusiliers in a charge to clear the Boers off the crest. The Boer fire was too intense. The charge failed. Thorneycroft twisted his knee, but was otherwise unhurt. On the left Crofton found himself similarly unable to maintain an advanced line, and had to retreat to the main trench. It was just after the failure of the charge that Thorneycroft heard of his promotion. An orderly sent by Crofton (who may reasonably have felt aggrieved at being deprived of authority) was killed, but Thorneycroft's orderly officer, Lieutenant Rose, had seen the message. He crawled towards Thorneycroft and shouted: 'Sir Charles Warren has heliographed that you are to take command. You are a General.' Thorneycroft did not know much more of the overall situation than many of his soldiers and for the moment was quite unable to take any action in accordance with this surprising news. He was occupied simply with keeping off the Boers, and when he heard from Rose that reinforcements were coming up, he ordered them round to the right, where he was hardest pressed.

Now there occurred an incident, which shows the confusion of the battle. It was vaguely seen by Charlton: 'There was great commotion a hundred yards or so away on the right. Men were standing up and gesticulating. Surely those others with them could not be some of the enemy. The commotion died down, and firing went on as before.' What had happened was that some of the Lancashire Fusiliers on the right of the line had shown the white flag. Others had gone on firing. The Boers jumped over into their trench, and the firing stopped. Some of the men were under the impression that the Boers were surrendering, but others had raised the white flag because, wounded and thirsty, they had had enough of the battle. A sergeant of Thorneycroft's Mounted Infantry, coming on the scene and seeing what had happened, went to find his Colonel. Thorneycroft rushed up to the Boers and shouted, 'I'm commandant here. Take your men back to hell, sir. There's no surrender'. When he realized that some of the men would not go on fighting Thorneycroft, with those who wished to fight on, rushed back to shelter behind rocks, and reopened firing.

Within minutes of this surrender, which involved more than a hundred and fifty men, reinforcements arrived. These were the Middlesex Regiment, the second battalion sent up by Coke (the first, after their wanderings among the lower slopes, arrived soon afterwards). They now came into the line – although *line* is much too orderly a word to convey any impression of the confused situation on the plateau. The Middlesex averted a threat to the centre of the main trench, and the Boers were temporarily swept away from the crest, although they took most of their prisoners with them. The arrival of the Middlesex, and of the Imperial Light Infantry who followed them, halted the Boer attack but did nothing to improve the British situation permanently. There were too many men in the trenches, and there was little cover for them elsewhere on this part of the hill. There was not enough water, the distribution of it was bad, and there were not enough doctors to look after the wounded. Thorneycroft had been fighting the whole time in the front, where he had been a continuous inspiration to his men, but this very fact meant that he lacked any clear idea of what was happening elsewhere. In particular, he was unaware that the chief danger came from the east, and the Boers on Aloe Knoll. At 2.30 in the afternoon Thorneycroft sent along a note to Coke. He had no signalling apparatus, and he sent the note by a member of Buller's staff, Colonel Sandbach, who had been sent up to see what was happening. Thorneycroft told Coke that his force was not adequate to hold such a large perimeter, and that they were troubled by guns from the north-west and the east. He added that they were badly in need of water and that there were many killed and wounded, and ended:

> If you wish to really make a certainty of hill for night you must send more Infantry and attack enemy's guns.

Thorneycroft wrote as commander on the hill, but of course Coke did not know this and Colonel Sandbach, strangely, did not tell him. At 3 o'clock Coke sent the note down to Warren, endorsing it with the remark that he had sent up the Scottish Rifles and a company of the King's Royal Rifles to reinforce. He added, perhaps on the advice of Sandbach, 'We appear to be holding our own'. A little less than an hour later Coke dragged his bad leg actually on to the summit – it had taken him four and a half hours to get there. He did not go into the main trench firing line, but was told that the men were holding their own on that side, although they were exposed to shell-fire. He saw no reason to get into touch with Thorneycroft, whom he regarded only as (to use his own words) 'a junior brevet Lieutenant-Colonel in command of a small unit'. Coke knew that he was himself in supreme command on Spion Kop, for Warren had told him so, and he had no doubt that the actual fighting commander was Colonel Hill of the Middlesex Regiment, the officer who had been placed in command of Coke's own 10th Brigade when Coke was appointed to the 5th Division.

Hill had been occupied in resisting the most serious attack of the day, an attempt by the Boers to encircle the forward British troops by coming round their right. Rifle fire from Aloe Knoll and the main ridge made it impossible to move from the trench where Thorneycroft and Crofton were established towards the right, and the Boers attempted an attack here which, had it succeeded, would have cut off the original force completely. The Middlesex, the Imperial Light Infantry and the Scottish Rifles resisted them, making most gallant and costly charges across the plateau. After two hours' fighting they restored the position and a British attempt to outflank Aloe Knoll was now made, by moving along the southern crest of Spion Kop, but the Boers were fully aware of the vital importance of this position. The officer who led the attempt was severely wounded and his men suffered heavily. Some were left where they lay, and the rest crawled back to the main force – that is, to Hill's force. In effect, the British troops were now operating as two independent units, commanded by Thorneycroft and Hill. There was no contact between them, because the Boer rifle fire made it impossible.

It was to Hill, then, that Coke talked about the position, after he had had a general discussion with his staff officers about the situation in the main trench. Coke had been shaken by what he called himself the 'scene of considerable confusion' which he found on top of Spion Kop. Units were intermingled, officers were separated from their men, wounded were lying about everywhere, and men who had had enough of the fight were leaving the summit for less risky positions on the lower slopes. This confusion is nicely conveyed, again, in the recollections of Charlton, who was near to the main trench, and whose saga was at this time completed by an act of courage. Charlton saw to his surprise the adjutant of another

247

regiment walking towards him across the open space to the rear 'in apparent oblivion of the fact that to show a finger even in that inferno of bullets was to have it shot off'. The officer suddenly collapsed, and Charlton hastily looked the other way so that he should not be involved. A private in the adjutant's regiment, however, called his attention, saying, 'Sir, sir, our adjutant!'

This supplied the necessary spur to courage. One might act the coward to oneself... But one could not show hesitation or fear before the men, for to do so was to lose every sense of shame and be followed by whispers through life. So he intimated to the man that he would see to it and took several long breaths.

By dint of stooping and crawling he had almost reached his goal in safety when he felt his flesh just above the left knee to be as if threaded in lightning swiftness by a red-hot bodkin, and at the same time he was knocked over on to his side. So utterly novel, and outside all calculation, was this effect from an, apparently, impersonal cause, he was slow to realize that he had been wounded. It seemed incredible that he, whose star was lucky, should have been brought low by a chance shot. But was it a chance shot? Was he perchance the deliberate target of an enemy marksman? While these conjectures were passing through his mind and while he was still gathering his wits, a most remarkable thing happened. The wounded officer, whom he had set out to rescue and who until then had lain crumpled and motionless, suddenly started to his feet, clapped both hands to his face, and ran, as if the devil were after him, towards the rear and safety.

Charlton, regardless of his wound, did the same. He flung himself behind a rock, and discovered there the captain of his own regiment. 'The captain knew nothing either of what had become of the men. A fingertip had been touched by a bullet. His senior was in a rather shaken condition and most gloomy as to eventualities. He bound his wound, which was stiffening but by no means painful... They lay talking and the day wore on.'

At about 4 o'clock in the afternoon Winston Churchill rode up the hill with Captain Brooke of the 7th Hussars, to try to find out the exact situation. They passed through the ambulance station and, leaving their horses behind climbed the steep spur. What they saw shocked them:

> Streams of wounded met us and obstructed the path. Men were staggering along alone, or supported by comrades, or crawling on hands and knees, or carried on stretchers. Corpses lay here and there. Many of the wounds were of a horrible nature. The splinters and fragments of the shell had torn and mutilated in the most ghastly manner. I passed about two hundred while I was climbing up. There was, moreover, a small but steady leakage of unwounded men of all corps. Some of these cursed and swore. Others were utterly exhausted and fell on the hillside in stupor. Scores were sleeping heavily.

The two men went back to tell Warren what they had seen.

Imagine the enaction of a hundred scenes like this, and it is easy to see why Coke was disturbed. There was a great shortage of water, and it was proving extremely difficult to move and tend the wounded. Just before 6 o'clock Coke, after conferring with Hill, wrote a despatch to Warren which distinctly hinted that it would be advisable to retire. Unless the enemy's guns could be silenced, he said, 'Today's experience will be repeated, and the men will not stand another complete day's shelling'. He considered, and rejected, the desperate idea of charging forward from the main trench, which he had not seen, said that he had men in hand to cover a retirement, and asked for orders. Coke sent this message down by hand, returned to his signal station well below the summit, and repeated it by signals. He received no reply from Warren. Coke now stayed at the signal station, leaving the actual fighting command on the summit, together with the unenviable task of restoring order out of confusion, to Hill.

In the meantime Thorneycroft, without leaving the main trench, had been trying to discover the exact position about his command. He had talked to Colonel Cooke of the Scottish Rifles, and Cooke

249

had then seen and talked to Coke, who confirmed that the fighting command on the summit rested with Hill. Cooke suggested that Hill should come over to the main trench, but Hill said that he could not now spare time to come over, although he would do so in a few minutes. Cooke went back and told all this to Thorneycroft, but in the meantime Thorneycroft had seen Crofton in person, and had received confirmation of his appointment as Brigadier-General. He therefore had no doubt that he was in command, and accordingly sat down and wrote a despatch to Warren. It was to much the same effect as Coke's. The troops who had marched up last night were 'quite done up', they had no water, ammunition was running short, casualties were very heavy.

> The enemy are now (6.30 p.m.) firing heavily from both flanks (rifle, shell and Nordenfelt), while a heavy rifle-fire is being kept up on the front. It is all I can do to hold my own. If my casualties go on at the present rate I shall barely hold out the night.
>
> A large number of stretcher-bearers should be sent up, and also all the water possible.
>
> The situation is critical.

He sent this despatch by messenger to the signal station.

Half an hour later darkness fell. Just before the sun sank Charlton, whose leg was now very painful, went with his captain in search of their men. They found them, thirsty, exhausted by the heat, and dispirited. Here and there a man slipped away, but most of them stayed on. With darkness the firing died. Thorneycroft's men, hungry and thirsty, lay in their trench, and their commander waited for the promised visit from Hill, and for instructions from Warren. But Hill did not come. He heard nothing from Warren. Time went by.

(vii) *And Down Below*

The most obvious fact about the battle of Spion Kop is the total breakdown of British communications. They were hampered at first by the mist on the summit, and then by the firing that drove the signal station off the north-western side to a point on the south-west from which signals could be seen easily by Buller on Spearman's, but not by Warren, a most maladroit arrangement. At about 2 o'clock in the afternoon clouds obscured the sun and the heliograph could be used only intermittently, so that messages had to be signalled by hand. This method was not only slow, but for those on the summit also dangerous. Recourse was had to messengers, but those who tried to carry messages from the signal station to the fighting area did so at risk of their lives. Messengers going up and down the hill also took far longer than the seventy minutes, which Warren reckoned as a possible time under ideal conditions. There was no reason, as Amery says, why a telegraph line should not have been taken up Spion Kop by the engineers as soon as the assault force was established on top – except that nobody thought of it.

The result was that there was no regular communication between the officers on Spion Kop and Warren down below, and this unhappy situation was exacerbated by Buller's occasional messages to Warren – he no doubt thought it against protocol to send messages direct from Spearman's to Spion Kop. Between 1 o'clock and 2.30 Warren peppered the signal station with messages addressed to 'Officer Commanding Spion Kop'. The first reply he received was Thorneycroft's message sent in the afternoon, and endorsed by Coke. This reached Warren at about 4.30, and he regarded the news as good. There was a request in it for more infantry, but seven battalions were on or about the hill. The message asked that an attack should be made on the Boer guns. Warren's own batteries were still attacking, although quite ineffectively, the Krupp and the pom-pom on the north-west side, and he pinned his faith on their eventual success, and on the arrival of the mountain battery. This had reached Trichard's Drift by 2.30 but Buller, ever careful of his men's welfare, ordered that the men with it must have rest before going on. It was 7.30 at night before this battery reached the foot of Spion Kop. At about 8.30 the two 12 pounder naval guns sent round by Buller arrived. The combination of these reinforcements, Warren thought, should cover the request for guns. And then there were requests for water and food. Warren assured himself that boxes of meat and biscuits were being taken up by hand

and that the water supply, contained in those biscuits tins, was continuous. Colonel Morris, one of Coke's staff officers, said that in his opinion the men were not suffering very badly from want of water. Morris had been with Hill's men and not in the main trench, but Warren accepted his assurances. It did not seem to him that he could do anything more. He still did not think of asking Clery or Hildyard to act in support of the attack, he left Dundonald guarding the baggage at Venter's Spruit. While those on the hill waited for instructions from below, Warren waited for news from on high.

There was no word from above, but there was advice from the side. At about 4 o'clock Warren received a long message from Buller. It told him that the mountain battery was on the way, and said that they must have a rest before going up, it expressed in an impartial manner the view that there were too many men on the hill, it suggested that two battalions should be entrenched strongly and the other two supporting battalions brought down, and it made completely clear Buller's ignorance of what Warren had done in connection with his 'suggestion' about Thorneycroft:

> I think it is want of head in the CO rather than want of strength which makes the difficulty. They tell me that Colonel Crofton is not much good. I have telegraphed to you to put Thorneycroft in command... Pray tell C of S if I can help you and how, but above all put a good fighting man in command at the top.

Buller, however, had spent most of the afternoon in signifying his disapproval of, and finally stopping, the very telling diversion begun by Lyttelton in attacking the Twin Peaks. The battalion of the 60th King's Royal Rifles who undertook it split into two as they approached the Twin Peaks and climbed the precipitous hillsides, under fire from the Boers but much assisted by the fire of the naval guns from Lyttelton's position and from Spearman's. At 5 o'clock in the afternoon the eastern peak was captured by a bayonet charge which was supported by the naval guns and by rifle fire from the half-battalion on the left, and a few minutes later the western peak was captured also. The effect of the capture of these hills was to force the Boers to take away the Krupp gun and the pom-pom which had so well supported the Boer rifle fire on Aloe Knoll. But the attack might have had much more far-reaching consequences if it had been supported by the advance of Lyttelton's other troops from their position on the Maconochie Kopjes against the Boer left. Botha was hard pressed for men, and a threat to another section of the line might have led to a break through, or prompted a Boer retreat. This gesture of Lyttelton's, made with a single battalion, showed at once how vulnerable were the Boers to pressure exerted simultaneously in two or more places.

This was not at all the interpretation placed in it by Buller. When Lyttelton reported what he had done, Buller was furious. The Scottish Rifles and Bethune's Mounted Infantry, it will be remembered, had gone to reinforce Spion Kop. Buller demanded to know why Lyttelton had separated his battalions so widely, and in effect rebuked Lyttelton by asking for copies of the orders issued during the afternoon. He said further that the battalions attacking the Twin Peaks were unsupported, and, casting aside his role of impartial adviser, ordered that they should be brought back at once. Buller's peremptoriness bred doubts in Lyttelton, who had devised the manoeuvre. Perhaps the 60th Rifles were bearing too far to the right, away from Spion Kop? As he said frankly years afterwards:

It was not till later that I realized how very important this diversion really was... There is little doubt that it was this pressure which relieved that on Thorneycroft.

Even if he had not felt such doubts he would have found it impossible to ignore the increasingly angry orders for the return of the 60th Rifles sent to him by Buller through staff officers. Throughout the afternoon, from 3 o'clock onwards, Lyttelton on his part sent messages to Colonel Buchanan-Riddell and Major Berwicke-Copley, commanding the two half-battalions, telling them to retire. These messages were ignored and it was not until 6 o'clock, when Buchanan-Riddell had been killed, that Berwicke-Copley, who had already brought up ammunition and water mules and entrenching tools to his position on the Twin Peaks, accepted the

253

inevitable. Lyttelton had told him that they could not be supported. They would have to retire. At 8 o'clock they did so, in good order and unhampered by the Boers. A bonfire showed them the position of the pontoon bridge across the Tugela, and by midnight they had recrossed the river. It was a poor reward for their skill and courage to leave the Peaks they had captured, and their thoughts must have been bitter.

As darkness fell Buller, down below, was reasonably content. He had checked that dangerous move of Lyttelton's, and he assumed that the men on top of Spion Kop were safely entrenched. Tomorrow the mountain battery and the two naval guns would be on top of the hill, and he had given very particular instructions – or offered particular suggestions – that epaulements eight feet thick must be made for the naval guns, so that they would be adequately protected. Warren too was busy in his way. He had discussed with Colonel Sim of the Royal Engineers arrangements for making the epaulements, had sent over to Spearman's for another company of Engineers and for the balloon – the usefulness of which had belatedly occurred to him – and had made provisioning arrangements for the following day. He had heard nothing from the summit since 4 o'clock, but this does not seem to have worried him. It was with a shock that he read, at about 7.30 in the evening, the message that Coke had written almost two hours earlier. It came by the hand of Colonel Morris – the signalled message sent by Coke had not been received – and Morris confirmed that the situation was critical. Thorneycroft's later message, which said the same thing in more urgent language, did not reach Warren until early the following morning.

Warren might have been disposed to doubt Morris's estimate of the situation, as earlier he had doubted Crofton's, but at this time Winston Churchill returned to camp, rushed up to one of Warren's staff officers, Captain Levita, and appealed to him not to let Spion Kop be a second Majuba. Levita said that he was busy and suggested, perhaps ironically, that if Churchill had any ideas he could pass them on to Warren, who was pacing up and down nearby. Churchill immediately began to harangue Warren, who listened, glared, and said to Levita:

'Who is this man? Take him away. Put him under arrest.'

'This is Mr Winston Churchill, sir, Member of Parliament and newspaper correspondent,' Levita replied.

Warren was not inclined to listen to Churchill, and Levita, perhaps to get the correspondent out of the way as much as for any other reason, called him over and said that a message must be got through to Thorneycroft, confirming that he was in command, telling him that guns were coming up, and asking for information. Churchill said that he was quite ready to go and find Thorneycroft. Levita wrote the message, and Churchill went off to play his part in the end of the drama.

In the meantime Warren, although it was not in his nature to accept advice readily, had been disturbed by Coke's message. He sent a signal by oil light asking Coke to come and see him and then, at 9 o'clock at night, in total darkness, ordered Sim to begin to make the epaulements which had been only a matter for discussion in the daylight hours. He also gave Sim a letter for Thorneycroft, urging him to hold the hill and to carry on. Sim organized a tool-carrying party and this party began to climb the hill.

Coke, at his point below the upper slopes, received the message asking him to return, the first message he had received that day from Warren. He was feeling much more cheerful than when he had been on the plateau at the top. There were, after all, plenty of fresh troops, and no doubt the guns would come up tomorrow. He was deeply irritated by the thought of stumbling down the hill in darkness, hampered by his bad leg. He composed a message in reply:

Night so dark and country so rough that the whole night would be taken up in journey. Is it not possible to give orders without my presence?

This message, however, could not be sent because the oil in the signaller's lamp had given out, and after waiting half an hour, Coke felt that there was nothing for it but to obey Warren's order. He began the journey down the hill.

But Warren's late preparations to construct epaulements, Churchill's journey up the hill and Coke's down it, had all by now become irrelevant. At 8.15 in the evening Thorneycroft had begun to evacuate Spion Kop.

(viii) *The Abandonment of Spion Kop*

The difficulties of Thorneycroft's position must be understood. He had received verbal messages that he was in command, he had then been told that this was not the case and that Hill was in command, he had expected a visit from Hill but had never seen him, he had not seen Coke, he had heard nothing from Warren. He knew nothing of the capture of the Twin Peaks, which had eased his own position. He and many of his men had been under shell and rifle fire for nearly twenty-four hours, and the men were too exhausted to entrench further in the darkness. There was no water or food, there was no sign of the mountain guns. He had sent off the message asking for instructions at 6.30, but after sending it he seems to have had a revulsion of feeling against staying on the hill another night and offering his men up for more useless slaughter in the morning. He had a conference with Crofton and Cooke, and they agreed with him in thinking that the Boer artillery, which apparently could not be silenced, was too much for them. 'They were both of opinion that the hill was untenable. I entirely agreed with their view.' Thorneycroft had no basis for making such a decision. He did not know the number or position of the other troops on Spion Kop, he had made no attempt to find out from Coke what reinforcements and supplies were on the way. In fact there were sandbags and there was water three hundred yards behind him, but the failure of communications was so complete that nobody had given news of these supplies to any of the three Colonels in the main trench. Thorneycroft knew only that his men were thirsty, hungry – the bully beef sent up was in six pound tins, and much of it never reached the summit – and that Warren, Coke and Hill had all failed to get into touch with him. Perhaps Coke and Hill were dead, or mortally wounded like Woodgate. In any case he was in charge, and the decision rested with him. 'Better six battalions safely off the hill than a mop-up in the morning,' he said to Cooke and Crofton, and they agreed.

Thorneycroft's action has been called inexcusable, but in retrospect it is difficult to condemn wholly a man who, having fought with such conspicuous courage, now showed the readiness to assume responsibility from which Buller, Warren and Coke had all in their different ways flinched. He lacked the qualities required in an overall commander as distinct from a fighting man, and what he did proved to be disastrously wrong. Yet although Warren, in an article written afterwards, quoted Wolseley's dictum that 'an officer in command who abandons the defence of a post, as long as one-third of his garrison remains effective, ought to be shot', the final blame must rest much less with Thorneycroft than with his superiors.

An effort was made to line up the men in some sort of order in the darkness, with the reinforcements from the Middlesex Regiment in the van and those from the Scottish Rifles forming the rearguard. In some parts of the line, however, the shouted order was for each man to make his way independently off the hill. Some of the wounded had to be left, but as many as possible were taken, among them Charlton. His story may stand for those of many who were not too seriously hurt:

He started off with others, supported by a man on either side, but progress in this fashion was so slow that the bottom would never be reached. They came to a dressing-station deserted by all except one orderly, who was on the point of leaving and had only remained in order to destroy the last of the supplies rather than that they should fall to the enemy. Many dead were lying about and these he regarded with a curious fascination. A stretcher was found and on this he was put. His two supporters enlisted two others, and by these four stalwarts he was borne through the night and finally deposited at a clearing-station for wounded which had been hastily improvised at the foot of the hill.

Long before Charlton reached the foot of the hill there had occurred the climactic comic point of the battle, the meeting of the two 'commanders' left on Spion Kop. Colonel Hill, who had for so many hours been too busy to go to see what was happening in the main trench, now belatedly decided to go over in the darkness – not indeed to see Thorneycroft, whom he regarded as a comparatively junior officer, but to consult with Cooke. He had hardly started when, to his astonishment, he met a company of his own Middlesex Regiment marching off the plateau. He halted them, found Thorneycroft, and discovered that he claimed to be in command. There was an altercation between the two, but Thorneycroft responded to Hill's protests with such vigour and authority that the senior Colonel was overborne, and agreed to the retreat.

In the meantime Churchill had been toiling again up the stony and uneven track. He found all the battalions hopelessly intermingled. Little parties of companies and half-companies had been collected by officers, and although there was no demoralization there was also no order. Some of the men knew nothing about the retreat, and were making arrangements to hold the position. At the top of the hill, coming on to the plateau, he met Thorneycroft:

> Everyone seemed to know, even in the confusion, where he was. He was sitting on the ground surrounded by the remnants of the regiment he had raised, who had fought for him like lions and followed him like dogs.

Churchill passed on his message from Levita, and said that naval guns were on the way up the hill. Thousands of sandbags, he said with some exaggeration, were also on the way. But Thorneycroft was adamant. He said he had received no word from Warren, and 'having heard nothing and expecting no guns, he had decided to retire'. He handed Churchill a written note to this effect, to be given to Warren, and the descent continued. At midnight Colonel Sim, working his way up the hill with the tool-carrying party, and by then about a quarter of the way up the slope, met Thorneycroft and gave him Warren's letter urging him to hold on. Thorneycroft said that it was too late and that the men, unsupported by guns, could not stay.

One more attempt was made to check the retreat. Coke had left one of his staff officers, Captain Phillips, in charge at the signal station. Phillips had fallen asleep, but at 11.30 was wakened by the sound of men moving past him down the hill. He found out what was happening, and tried to stop it. Thorneycroft had already passed him, but Phillips had an argument with Cooke. Phillips said that the retirement had no authority whatever. Cooke replied that Thorneycroft had authorized it, and that he would return to the summit only on a positive order from Coke. He was prepared to wait while Phillips signalled to Warren, but there was still no oil, so that signalling was impossible. There seems to have been no attempt to obtain oil since the time, two and a half hours earlier, when Coke had obeyed Warren's order and gone down the hill. Phillips, in his way as vigorous and determined as Thorneycroft, issued a written protest to all the commanding officers he could find:

The withdrawal is absolutely without the authority of Major-General Coke or Sir Charles Warren... Some one, without authority, has given orders to withdraw, and has incurred a grave responsibility. Were the General here, he would order an instant reoccupation of the heights.

Most of the men had now gone down, but this powerfully-worded protest had the effect of checking the descent of the Scottish Rifles, the Dorset Regiment, and Bethune's Mounted Infantry, who remained on the slopes above the signal station, ready to reoccupy the summit. Three hours later, at 2.30 in the morning, Phillips managed to get some oil, and sent a signal to Warren by his lamp.

Summit of Spion Kop evacuated by our troops, which still hold lower slopes. An unauthorized retirement took place. Naval guns cannot reach summit before daylight, would be exposed to fire if attempted to do so by day.

About half an hour before this, at 2 o'clock, Coke had at last arrived at the wagon which served as Warren's headquarters. This wagon had been shelled during the previous afternoon, and so Warren had ordered that it should be moved a short distance. The unfortunate Coke had been unable to find it. He had arrived at

259

Three Tree Hill shortly after midnight, and had been stumbling about in the darkness for nearly two hours. In all, he took nearly four and a half hours to reach Warren. The meeting between the two men cannot have been very warm, for Coke resented having been called away from the hill, and Warren really had little to ask him. Almost at the same time there arrived the message sent by Thorneycroft at 6.30, which had somehow taken almost eight hours to get down the hill. And within a few minutes Warren's cup of trouble was brim-full as Thorneycroft arrived, before the message he had sent through Churchill, and told the two Generals in person what he had done. The scene of this triple confrontation in Warren's wagon, by the flickering light of the oil lamps, must have been a dramatic one.

What was Warren to do? It has been said that there were still 1,600 troops on the slopes of Spion Kop, and that Warren might immediately have issued an order that set them climbing up again to the summit. To suggest this, however, is to attribute to him far greater vision, mental agility, and indeed knowledge, than he possessed. It seemed to him that there was no reversing what had been done, or at least that he could not reverse it. Now, in time of trouble, he made the characteristic gesture of British Generals in the Natal campaign, that of trying to shift responsibility on to somebody else. He tried to telegraph Buller, but was unable to get through to the telegraph clerk. He sent a mounted orderly with the message that Thorneycroft had abandoned Spion Kop on his own authority, and that the hill was being evacuated. 'Can you come at once and decide what to do?' he forlornly asked. It was the first request he had made for Buller's presence since he had been given his command.

The rich, ripe absurdity of the British evacuation of Spion Kop was not known until later. This was the fact that the Boers also had abandoned the hill. The capture of the Twin Peaks by Lyttelton's men seemed to Schalk Burger, in command of the Boer commandos on the left, to be decisive. It has been said already that the Boers thought it no shame to retreat, and now Burger's men melted away, acting as individuals, but with their panic spreading from individuals to groups. Deneys Reitz has told of the certainty among the Boers that 'the morning would see them (the British) streaming through the breach to the relief of Ladysmith, and the rolling up of all our Tugela line'. From this belief there was practically only one dissentient, Louis Botha. He was confident that the British had been severely mauled, and that they would abandon their positions during the night. Botha rode about among the wagons, from commando to commando, alternately exhorting and threatening the men. Some of them gathered round him, or stayed at the foot of Spion Kop, but those who remained were only a small fraction of the total force. If Thorneycroft or Hill had remained on the summit and sent out scouts they would have discovered the Boer positions unoccupied, there for the taking. At about 2 o'clock in the morning there was nobody at all on the summit of Spion Kop, except the dead and the wounded. At half past three a few burghers who had climbed the hill to search for the body of a comrade found no life, no movement, on the British side. Reitz, at the foot of the hill, has told how the Boers learned the news:

> We woke with the falling of the dew and, as the sky lightened, gazed eagerly at the dim outline of the hill above, but could make out no sign of life.
>
> Gradually the dawn came and still there was no movement. Then to our utter surprise we saw two men on the top triumphantly waving their hats and holding their rifles aloft. They were Boers, and their presence there was proof that, almost unbelievably, defeat had turned into victory – the English were gone and the hill was still ours.

The orderly sent by Warren to Buller added one final touch to the tale of bungling by losing his way. He did not arrive at Buller's headquarters until 5 o'clock in the morning. An hour later Buller was with Warren. His feelings must have been mixed. Regret at the failure of the attack was, of course, one thread in them, and there may have been present in his mind the thought that he might himself have done something more, but it does seem that his dominant emotion was one of satisfaction. He had given Warren his chance and Warren had failed, as he had expected. Perhaps now all those armchair critics at home would think again before they criticized Buller. Some such thoughts as these certainly moved in his mind. Amery says that he could scarcely conceal his satisfaction at the turn of events, and on arrival at Warren's headquarters he briskly dismissed any suggestion that the action might be resumed. Warren said that they could reoccupy Spion Kop, Levita told him that the Boers had gone – although this was no longer true, for they had returned, not in large numbers. Buller would have none of it. He had thought of another approach to Ladysmith and now, resuming direct command of the whole army and relegating Warren again to the command of the 5th Division, he ordered a general retreat. Churchill has left a memorable picture of this retreat. They awoke on the morning of the 25th, he says, with the most gloomy forebodings:

> The army was irritated by the feeling that it had made sacrifices for nothing. It was puzzled and disappointed by failure, which it did not admit nor understand. The enemy were flushed with success. The opposing lines in many places were scarcely a thousand yards apart. As the infantry retired the enemy would have commanding ground from which to assail them at every point. Behind flowed the Tugela, a deep, rapid, only occasionally fordable river, eighty-five yards broad, with precipitous banks. We all prepared ourselves for a bloody and even disastrous rearguard action. But now, when things had come to this pass, Buller took personal command. He arrived on the field calm, cheerful, inscrutable as ever, rode hither and thither with a weary staff and a huge notebook, gripped the whole business in his strong hands, and so shook it into shape that we crossed the river in safety, comfort, and good order, with most remarkable mechanical precision, and without the loss of a single man or a pound of stores.

The 'amazing ease' with which Churchill said that the operation was conducted was largely due to the fact that the Boers had not fully recovered from their panic on the night of the 24th, and were happy to see the British retreat. But for Churchill and for some of the other correspondents, Buller got the credit. 'Buller himself – not Buller by proxy or Buller at the end of a heliograph – Buller himself managed it... We believe that Buller gauged the capacity of one subordinate at Colenso, of another at Spion Kop, and that now he will do things himself, as he was meant to do,' Churchill wrote. In truth, it was Warren and his staff who were chiefly responsible for managing the retreat, which was conducted for the most part in a steady downpour of rain. It was about 4 a.m. when the last battalion tramped over the worn-out chesses of the pontoon, which swayed beneath their weight, and as they did so a single shell sang in the air and fell with a splash into the muddy water. When it was all over, Buller moved Warren's division almost to Springfield, and Clery's out of range of the Boer guns. Lyttelton remained where he was, on the right side of the Tugela as it might be called, on Maconochie Kopjes. The battle for Spion Kop was over. The cost to the British had been very heavy in relation to the size of the force engaged. Nearly 900 officers and men had been killed or wounded, and some 300 had been made prisoner by the Boers, including the wounded who had had to be left on the field. The losses fell most heavily on the units involved in the original attack, Thorneycroft's Mounted Infantry, the Lancashire Fusiliers and the Royal Lancasters. The Boer losses were no more than a quarter of the British. During the 25th, British stretcher parties and doctors moved about the hill, collecting those wounded men who had not been taken prisoner, and taking them down the hill.

It was over, and nothing had been gained. The confidence of Buller's senior officers in their Commander-in-Chief had been much shaken. Lyttelton said in a letter home: 'I have lost all confidence in Buller as a General and am sure he has himself.' But the men had not lost confidence. After the withdrawal had been accomplished, and extra rations had been issued, Buller made a vague but inspiring speech to them, in which he represented the attack on Spion Kop not as an outstanding success perhaps, but as a vital move which had given him, he said, the key to Ladysmith. 'Lavater would have been puzzled by that square impassive face,' said one who listened to him. 'Never a soul of the thousands there, nor, it appears, of the millions at home, understood his abrupt, cryptic sayings; but they, nevertheless, lifted a weight from hearts unconsciously heavy.' The men were greatly cheered, and Churchill reflected: 'Everyone has been well fed, reinforced and inspirited, and all are prepared for a supreme effort in which we shall either reach Ladysmith or be flung back truly beaten with a loss of six or seven thousand men.'

Chapter Eleven *The Inquest*

Warren regarded himself as being on friendly terms with Buller. 'He used often to come over to lunch with me, or I lunched with him, and on these occasions, both to myself and also to my Staff, from the character of our conversation he appeared to be most friendly towards me,' he says, adding that officers outside his own Division would ask him to bring matters to Buller's notice 'on the assumption that I was the only officer in the force he would allow to speak out to him'. He had no idea of the deep-seated dislike and distrust of him that appears in Buller's dispatches.

From the first Buller looked for a scapegoat in relation to the Spion Kop action. He first of all considered Coke as a candidate, telling Warren that he heard Coke had been asleep during the action. He said nothing at all by way of criticism to Coke personally, although they saw each other daily, but put down severe censures in his dispatches. His most savage criticism, however, fell upon Warren. In three separate dispatches written on 30 January, none of which was seen by Warren at the time, Buller blamed himself (if one can call such a comment self-blame) because he had not assumed direct command on the 19th. He must leave it to higher authority, he said handsomely, to decide whether or not he had acted rightly. But of one thing he was sure:

> We had really lost our chance by Sir C Warren's slowness. He seems to me a man who can do well what he can do himself, but who cannot command, as he can use neither his Staff nor

subordinates. I can never employ him again on an independent command.

As for Thorneycroft, Buller thought that in view of the 'want of organization and system' Thorneycroft had exercised a wise discretion in ordering a retirement. His own responsibility, he thought, had ended with his failure to relieve Warren of command on the 19th. So far as Spion Kop was concerned, he maintained that he had really not been there at all, and in writing to Roberts he said that the dispatches he enclosed from Warren, Coke and others were 'original documents written by Commanders of troops in three independent operations at which I was not present'. Roberts sharply replied that he could not accept this argument for a moment. 'Though portions of the force were engaged in different localities under subordinate commanders, you were present during the operations and in Chief command.' Since that was so, Roberts told Lansdowne, the principal blame must be Buller's. He stigmatized Thorneycroft's assumption of authority for retirement as 'wholly inexcusable', although he added praise of his gallantry, and of the troops' behaviour. He ended by castigating Buller:

> Whatever faults Sir Charles Warren may have committed, the failure must also be ascribed to the disinclination of the officer in supreme command to assert his authority and see that what he thought best was done.

It had been hoped by some optimists among the Boers, who still thought in terms of Majuba, that the British would make peace after Spion Kop. They were undeceived by the reaction in Britain. There was a great deal of press agitation about the mistakes of the War Office, the anti-war Radicals and Liberals increased their propaganda, and during the course of a six-day debate in the House of Commons Lloyd George made a savage attack on Chamberlain, whom he accused of starting the war on behalf of the Johannesburg mine owners. But when the thunder of Lloyd George and the more measured censure of Sir William Harcourt, who led the attack for the Liberals, had died away, the Government majority was 352 to

139, and Chamberlain had triumphed not so much by any feat of oratory as by his apparent persuasiveness and sweet reasonableness. After the debate it was apparent that the war would be fought with larger forces and firmer determination.

A reflection of this was the large increase in men and artillery given to Wolseley. Before Spion Kop the Commander-in-Chief, who had now lost all but the framework of power, had been threatening to resign on the ground that the increases Lansdowne thought he could induce the Cabinet to accept were inadequate. Lansdowne and the Government would have been happy to see the back of him, but his resignation at this time would have been extremely damaging, and this Wolseley understood. 'I am so sick of my position here that I positively *long* to resign,' he wrote to his wife, 'but my resignation must have good grounds and those grounds must be of such a nature as will be accepted by Englishmen as sufficient and commend themselves to all the educated classes.' He arranged one of his code systems with her. If he resigned he would say, 'Joseph has given warning'. He would convey the news from Buller by saying that Joseph's character was very good, good, indifferent or bad. He cherished the hope that the news would be good. As early as 12 January, he was hoping that Buller would 'shake hands with that ass White tomorrow', but a few days later he was more doubtful. 'I don't like the undertaking as far as I understand Buller's plan.' On the 19th he wrote to his wife that he had just left 'that horrid War Office':

I have had a good tumbler of milk and am somewhat revived in strength by it, though not brightened in spirit by a long sitting on the Defence Committee. 'Go, my son', says the great Swedish Minister, 'and see by what fools the world is governed.' Well, I always come away from these meetings of Ministers in saddened frame of mind when I have listened for some time to the military folly talked by most of those who comprise that Committee. Hicks Beach talks the greatest nonsense, but my little French Jew, Lansdowne, runs him close. I have made up my mind that he is the greatest obstruction to any effective precautions being taken against invasion.

The news of Spion Kop came as a great blow. He wrote a hurried pencil note to his wife:

Very bad news from Buller, my dear child – I am in despair at all our misfortunes. God seems to be with the Boers and against us.

Warren abandoned Spion Kop after 200 were killed and about 300 were wounded, mostly badly wounded.

Yours G

For weeks he had been threatening to resign, but the disaster ensured that he got all he wanted. Lansdowne implored him not to write a letter of resignation and self-justification to the Queen, and the Government, unhappily aware that practically the whole of the Regular Army was out of the country, capitulated completely to him. This was some satisfaction to Wolseley, although it did not lessen his chagrin at the appointment of Roberts. He relieved his feelings slightly by sending a pedantic telegram to Roberts on receipt of dispatches from Methuen, which contained explanatory reports:

A despatch should be a complete account, and should not contain reports from subordinate commanders, or other documents.

In Britain the Spion Kop defeat accentuated the determination to push the war to a victorious conclusion. It also, by that peculiar British logic which says that a defeated General must never be immediately dismissed because this would be an admission of failure, ensured that both Buller and Warren stayed in their commands.

Chapter Twelve *Anxiety in Ladysmith*

White's messages to Buller after the battle at Caesar's Camp and Wagon Hill, and before Spion Kop, were increasingly gloomy in tone. He had said immediately after repelling the Boer attack that his troops were much played out, and that he would rather not call upon them to move out of Ladysmith. On the 10th he said that he had a sick list of 2,000, and on the 16th sent a telegram that was almost despairing. He suggested that Buller should ask Roberts for more troops. 'If you are repulsed now, Ladysmith will be in a bad way... I think I could maintain this place until 5th February, but the sick would suffer badly. I have 2,400 in hospital, and many very weakly men at duty. Sickness increasing daily.' Buller told White that he could not get reinforcements in time, and that 'Every man in this force is doing his level best to relieve you'. He told Roberts, not without some relish, that he could expect very little help from White. Roberts was concerned. 'As this is the sole chance of Ladysmith being relieved, surely he must make an effort to co-operate with Warren as he approaches,' he wrote. But Buller, whose contempt for White equalled his dislike of Warren, did not press for co-operation. He kept White informed of his progress, and then of his retreat.

On the day after news of Spion Kop came through, Wolseley, desperate to obtain action of some kind, suggested to Buller that it might be possible for White to break out at night with his mounted men, as many of the others as he could carry in carts, and some of his guns, and join Buller. The same thought had occurred to White, who wrote to Buller on the 27th: 'I put it to you and the Government whether I ought not to abandon Ladysmith and try to join you. I could, I think, throw 7,000 men and 36 guns into the fight.' Roberts pointed out at once that this would be a desperate venture at best, and that even if it succeeded a severe blow to British prestige would be involved in the abandonment of Ladysmith with its sick and wounded. Buller added that he thought it would not be possible for White to break out now and Wolseley, who had probably regretted the telegram as soon as it was sent, said that he had intended this as a step to be taken only as a last resort and that, in view of Roberts' remarks, it had better be regarded as cancelled.

Roberts, whose faith in Buller was no greater than Lyttelton's, was now concerned to keep him from making another attack. His own advance had been delayed by the fact that he and Kitchener had totally reorganized the transport system devised by Buller, which gave each regiment its own transport and provisions, and provided a secondary supply column run by the Army Service Corps from which the regimental transport was replenished, and a supply park which fed the supply column. Roberts and Kitchener replaced this by a completely centralized system of transport depots, which removed all transports from the regiments and was designed to allocate transport from the depots to the points at which it was most needed. In practice the new system was found not to work well, and after a few weeks a return to something very much like the regimental system was tacitly permitted, but at this time Roberts and Kitchener were full of reorganizing zeal. 'I am much concerned that I cannot afford you direct assistance, but the want of a properly organized transport renders any forward movement impossible just at present,' he wrote to Buller, who cannot have been pleased by this description of his own system. Nor did he care for Roberts' advice that he should stay on the defensive, which he probably interpreted as an attempt to take from him the glory of relieving Ladysmith. He replied to Roberts' adjurations by saying that Ladysmith was in a bad way, and that therefore another attempt must be made to relieve it. He said that he felt 'fairly confident' but added, typically:

One can never safely attempt to prophesy, but so far as my exertions can, humanly speaking, conduce to the desired end, I think I can promise you that I shall in no case compromise my force.

In Ladysmith itself hopes had been raised high before Spion Kop. White's estimate that he could put 7,000 men into the field was thought by many war correspondents to be a great exaggeration. 'Men and horses crawl feebly about, shaken with every form of internal pain and weakness,' wrote Nevinson, who said that women suffered even more, and that fear of the shells had caused thirty-two premature births. Many of the horses were killed, a 'chevril' factory was started to make soup, jelly, marrow bones and sausages out of the meat, and a biltong factory was run to dry and utilize the flesh of horses which would have died of starvation. Coffee was made from mealies, and starch was used to provide the gluten for bread. Europeans and Kaffirs could rely upon getting a pound of horseflesh or mule meat every day, but the Indians, who did not eat such meat, were in much worse case, getting only maize meal and rice. To get even these rations it was necessary to present yourself at a barrier, produce an order, and move on through a gangway protected by barbed wire to the depot, where you received your package of meat, biscuit, sugar and tea. Officers, or at least a good many officers, suffered much less hardship than the men under their command. One of them records that members of his mess never failed to get a rasher of bacon for breakfast and that every Sunday night a bottle of some sort of wine was served round in egg-cups to drink the health of 'Absent Friends'. This differentiation between officers and men was not conducive to good temper, nor was the message which told them that Buller had 74 wagons at Frere for their relief, containing 50 cases of whisky, 11 wagons of rum, 5,000 cigarettes, milk, vegetables and forage. At Intombi several men died each day, of typhoid, dysentery or simple weakness. The Boers did not make any serious attempt to storm Ladysmith after the attack on Wagon Hill and Caesar's Camp. They were content to let hunger and sickness be the siege masters, although a half-hearted attempt was made to construct a never-completed dam on the Klip River which would flood the Ladysmith plain, cut off communication between Ladysmith and Intombi, and compel the town's surrender.

The garrison knew, of course, of Buller's attack, and were able to follow the course of the fighting. Very early on 25 January, Nevinson saw the Boer wagon laagers breaking up, and thought that Buller must be through and the Boers in retreat. Later in the day he saw bands of British prisoners, marching in step, being escorted away by groups of unorganized Boers. On the following day many of the Boer wagons had returned, and at 2 o'clock in the afternoon of the 27th the full, dismal news was known. It is a tribute to the courage of those in Ladysmith that after the immediate shock of the knowledge that they would not yet be relieved, there was no thought of surrender. They settled down to face more days or weeks of siege. There were no more sports or concerts, but there was determination to endure. Only occasionally did irritation with those outside the garrison show itself. On 2 February, after two days of rain and cloud the sun came through, and the heliograph began to work again. Perhaps there would be news of relief? The first message said:

Sir Stafford Northcote, Governor of Bombay, has been made a peer.

The other messages were merely dull, but this one seemed an insult. 'That peerage!', as Nevinson said, 'To a sick and hungry garrison!'

Chapter Thirteen *The Attempt on Vaal Krantz*

There were, truly, several keys to Ladysmith. The one at Spion Kop had been turning in the lock when Thorneycroft withdrew it, and this key Buller had no intention of trying to use again. There was the key that Buller himself had constantly wished Warren to use, that would be turned through the recapture of Bastion Hill and the rolling up of the Boer right wing, and there was the key of Hlangwane, which Lyttelton and others had favoured before Colenso. There was no reason why Buller should not have carried out any of these moves after assuming command, and one might have expected that he would have returned to his own favourite idea of turning the Boer right. Buller, however, was like a theatrical impresario who abandons a play after it has been tried out and unfavourably received in the provinces. His Generals did not approve of the attack on the Boer right, and so he did not attempt it. He accepted their views, but later showed that he was deeply resentful of their criticism. In the meantime he offered for their approval an entirely new presentation. He had given up the idea of turning the Boer right, the attack on the Boer centre had failed. Very well then, there remained the Boer left, and his new plan was to roll up the Boer position on their left instead of on their right.

The Boer left, thinly held, rested on a small hill called Vaal Krantz. Buller proposed to move his artillery on to Swaartz Kop, which dominated Vaal Krantz on the British side of the Tugela, make a feint attack on the Brakfontein heights from the position still held by Lyttelton on the Maconochie Kopjes, withdraw the

273

batteries from this position and use them to help the real attack, which was to be on Vaal Krantz and the adjacent Green Hill. Artillery would be established on Vaal Krantz, and the 1st Brigade of Cavalry would push out beyond the hill on to the plain leading to Ladysmith and 'bring the Battery RHA into action on any convenient target'. Lieutenant-Colonel Burn-Murdoch was given the command of this 1st Brigade, and Dundonald found himself with no other duty than that of protecting the right wing and rear of the force. He had been doubtful whether, after Spion Kop, he should reveal to Buller the great Secret Plan. Was this the national emergency in which the Plan should be used? It involved the creation of a dense smoke screen:

In my mind's eye I saw the great banks of smoke, producing an atmosphere – to use the words of the plans – 'dark as the darkest night'; then I thought of this same atmosphere impregnated with sulphur. I saw the lines of Boer riflemen in their trenches, waiting for our men, with Mausers useless, for those that held them could not see.

But, as Dundonald says, 'I restrained myself and kept the secret'.

Vaal Krantz was believed, on the strength of a farmer's description, to be a good artillery position, but in reality it was a narrow ridge, on which it would be difficult to mount or to maintain guns. The chief objection to the plan, however, was that it demanded speed in pushing through to the plain beyond the hill, and that all the British operations so far had been miserably slow. The idea of the feint did not promise speed, for the feint was not to accompany the real attack but to precede it, so that it would be a warning to the Boers rather than a deception of them. Perhaps it is too much to expect that the British commanders should have accepted the truth that in agility of mind and movement they were no match for the Boers, and at Buller's conference no objection was raised to the scheme. Even Lyttelton, who had received a telegram offering him a Divisional command under Roberts, was persuaded to stay. Buller urged him to do so, saying that he thought that he had found the way in to Ladysmith, and that Lyttelton's Brigade would carry out the plan.

The men, who had rested for a week and had been given good and plentiful rations of meat and vegetables, were in high spirits, and they would have been still higher if the position on the Boer side had been known. After Spion Kop the Boers, with or without approval, had gone on leave. The general expectation of peace had infected even Louis Botha, who had taken some deferred leave and gone to Pretoria. Facing Buller's army there were now no more than about 4,000 men, of whom some 350 were encamped on Doorn Kloof, to the east of Vaal Krantz and Green Hill. Spread out between Krantz Kloof and Doorn Kloof were 1,200 men under the command of a young newspaper editor named Ben Viljoen. At one time, according to Viljoen, he had no more than 400 men to defend a front one and a half miles long. When one thinks of the relative strength of the two forces, and of the lack on the Boer side of any plan more than determination to resist attack, it seems impossible that any attack against them by a force so much superior could possibly fail. Behind the assurance of Buller's bearing, however, was the gift for discovering the germ of failure in any possibility of success.

The attack began at 6 o'clock on the morning of 5 February. This time there was to be none of the confusion involved in a night attack. Buller's Chief of Staff, Wynne, had been appointed to the command of Woodgate's Brigade, and had been replaced as Chief of Staff by Colonel Miles, who had never seen a shot fired in anger in his life. The appointed feint was made, Wynne's brigade moving out slowly in very open order from the Maconochie Kopjes, followed by the batteries. The guns on Mount Alice and on Gun Plateau joined in the assault on the Boer trenches on the Brakfontein heights. The British guns on Swaartz Kop blazed away at Vaal Krantz. Wynne advanced so far in the direction of Brakfontein that á Court for one began to fear that he was too far up, but the Boers did not react to his advance for some while. At 9.30 the 63rd Battery was withdrawn from the attack, and sent round to support the engineers, who constructed a 70 yard pontoon bridge across the river in fifty minutes, with the loss of no more than eight wounded. Lyttelton's men were ready to cross, and the real attack could be made at once – must be made at once, if it were to surprise the Boers, for in the absence of any attempt to build pontoons elsewhere (a stroke of supreme subtlety that never occurred to Buller) the building of the pontoon bridge showed clearly enough where the attack was to be made. But Buller – it was Buller, for although the attack was nominally under the command of Clery, Buller took control from the minute it began – would have none of this unseemly speed. The attack was not to take place until the feint was over, and he sent instructions to the batteries engaged in the feint to withdraw at ten minute intervals. He was determined that the confusion on Spion Kop should not be repeated here, and certainly he achieved his end. The withdrawal was made in such perfect style that it strongly resembled a field day at Aldershot. As the account of the war by the German General Staff says scathingly: 'The purposeless and purely rule-of-thumb procedure of the troops engaged in (the demonstration) might have been suggested by reminiscences of old-time barrack-square duties.' At 2 o'clock the feint was over. Wynne had withdrawn, with one man killed and some thirty wounded, and the Boers had gathered in force to repel an attack across the pontoon bridge, which had been in place for nearly three hours.

With the demonstration finished, it was time for the real attack. Lyttelton was ready, had been ready for hours, but now Buller was afflicted by doubts. Perhaps after all, he thought, the whole enterprise had better be given up. 'It is too late,' he said to Lyttelton. 'You will never carry the kopjes before dark, we had better put it off.'

'Let me go at once, and I will guarantee I will be on the top of Vaal Krantz by 4 o'clock,' Lyttelton said. So Buller let him go, but it will be seen that he had again taken covering action. If Lyttelton succeeded, well and good, but if he failed Buller had disapproved of his action in advance. Yet there was surely some deeper ambiguity here than the mere wish to absolve himself from blame. Even more than at Colenso, Buller in command here showed a failure of the spirit, a terrible paralysis of the will. No sooner had he agreed to let Lyttelton attack than he regretted the decision. The Durham Light Infantry and the Rifle Brigade had crossed the pontoon, and Lyttelton with them. Now Hildyard's two battalions, which were to support the attack by capturing Green Hill, started to cross, and at this point Buller changed his mind, and decided to withdraw them. The Devons were already over, and they perforce joined Lyttelton. The other troops were halted on the bank of the river. Lyttelton was left to take Vaal Krantz alone. And if he did take Vaal Krantz, what was the use of it? The idea had been that Hildyard should capture Green Hill, and that the two forces would keep the defile between the hills open for the 1st Brigade of Cavalry and Hart's infantry. The withdrawal of Hildyard made nonsense of the whole scheme.

Nevertheless, Lyttelton went on. From Swaartz Kop Buller and his staff watched them. One of the war correspondents wrote:

> Hildyard's and Hart's brigades lay below me ready for every-thing. Lyttelton's brigade was half across the newly built bridge. The Durham Light Infantry lay under the sheer river bank on the other side… The most easterly ridge of Vaal Krantz stood obscured in dust and smoke. Above all were little white airy buttons of smoke from bursting shrapnel. Nothing, one thought, could live under that bombardment.
>
> The time was ripe. A handful of skirmishers from the Durhams climbed up the bank and ran into a mealie field, their bodies curved crescent shape as they ran. They dropped among the mealies. All shot? No, there they were, firing. Up again in a minute, on they went. Now some were out in the open, beyond the mealie field. Two men collapsed behind ant-heaps; then one rose up and ran back to the field. More men – a whole company – came out from the river bank.

The crossing, which might have been made unhampered at midday, was strongly resisted, but the Boers were too weak in numbers to stop the advancing force. The Durhams, Lyttelton says, were at first 'a bit staggered at the heavy fire, which greeted them'. He ran forward himself to join and encourage them, but before he had reached them they had pulled themselves together. The whole 66 guns under Buller's command, including those brought back from the demonstration, opened a tremendous fire upon Vaal Krantz. It was, Viljoen said later, the heaviest bombardment he saw during the whole war. A shell burst over his head, stunning him and killing four men nearby. The Rifle Brigade conquered the eastern side of the hill, and the Durhams charged the southern side with fixed bayonets, driving the few Boers before them. At 4 o'clock precisely Lyttelton saw Lascelles, a young officer in the Durhams, waving his hat on the crest. He was mortally wounded soon after.

The lodgement on Vaal Krantz was very much like that on Spion Kop, in that it urgently needed support. Instead Lyttelton received an order from Buller to withdraw, but he ignored it, thinking that after his success the rest of the action agreed on would be carried out. His position was uncomfortable, for the Boers still held the northern end of the hill, and also Green Hill. He found it impossible to keep control of the eastern side, up which the Rifle Brigade had clambered, and was compelled to place his men on the western side of the hill, where they crouched under stones and dug themselves in, scraping away at the ground with their bayonet points and with the blades of knives while they waited for help to come. In place of help Buller sent á Court, whose optimism about the Spion Kop position had proved so misplaced. á Court crossed the pontoon bridge under fire, reached the hill, which was being raked by pom-pom shells, and found Lyttelton. They agreed that the failure to assault Green Hill had been unfortunate, but that it might still be made successfully. They agreed also that another pontoon must be thrown across the river nearer Vaal Krantz, so that if the Boers closed in upon the first one reinforcements could go through, and Lyttelton would have a way back. á Court suggested too that guns should be pushed up on the British side of the Tugela, to help the defenders. Buller agreed to these last suggestions about the guns and the pontoon, which were essentially defensive measures, but he would have nothing to do with the assault on Green Hill which would have made sense of the operation. He decided – a decision which seems in retrospect even more extraordinary than it must have appeared at the time – to leave Lyttelton's men, exposed and unsupported, on the slopes of the hill, without making any attempt to help them. In the morning he would decide what should be done. While the Boers dragged round guns to Doorn Kloof and Doorn Kop, ran a telegraph line from the Twin Peaks to direct their fire, and brought up what reinforcements they had available, Buller slept the sleep of – what? The self-righteous, the anxiety-ridden, the well-fed? Perhaps all three.

He was up at dawn. The reinforcement of the Boers by men and guns had made the whole project a hopeless one. Their Long Tom on Doorn Kop and Creusots on Doorn Kloof now controlled the position completely, and but for Lyttelton's adroit placing of his troops they would have been in even worse case than those on Spion Kop. There was nothing now to be done but retire, but Buller was as unready to accept this necessity as he had been to give the troops on Vaal Krantz substantial support. He felt that he was committed to an attack, but he had in mind that promise to Roberts not to compromise his force. He vacillated between the ideas of withdrawal and attack, telling Lyttelton first that he would try to clear the northern end of the hill by artillery and howitzer fire, and that if he failed Lyttelton was to retire at 10 o'clock, then saying that he would place a pontoon over the river at the foot of Vaal Krantz to facilitate an attack, and later still asking Lyttelton to stay on the hill during the day, while he 'watched developments'.

Still the burden of responsibility weighed him down. Could it really not be shifted? During the morning he sent a telegram to Roberts. He said that he had pierced the enemy's line and held a hill which divided their position and would give him access to the Ladysmith plain. Now came the problem:

> To get my artillery and supplies on to the plain, I must drive back the enemy either on my right or on my left. It is an operation, which will cost from 2,000 to 3,000 men, and I am not confident, though hopeful, I can do it. The question is how would such a loss affect your plans, and do you think the chance of the relief of Ladysmith worth the risk? It is the only possible way to relieve White; if I give up this chance I know no other.

Roberts was just about to leave Cape Town. His plan of movement was bold and simple. He had scrapped completely the original War Office plan, and meant instead to assemble an army at

Orange River Station and then strike eighty miles across country to menace the Orange Free State capital, Bloemfontein, thus achieving the advantage of surprise. Because it was feared that there would be no water on this march, the point of departure was changed a little, with the effect of bringing Roberts' force much nearer to the Boers under General Cronje. Occupied as he was with his own plans, Roberts must have been infuriated by Buller's telegram. Buller had refused to accept his suggestion that the Natal Army should stay on the defensive, and now here he was asking a man hundreds of miles away to answer problems that were essentially those to be solved by a General in the field. But Roberts was not a man to shirk making decisions. If Buller wanted to have his mind made up, Roberts was prepared to do it for him. He replied unambiguously that 'Ladysmith must be relieved, even at the cost you anticipate', and said that if Buller would let the men know that 'the honour of the Empire is in their hands' he had no doubt that the attack would be successful. After sending this telegram, Roberts set off for the front in as secret a manner as possible. His headquarters staff had gone earlier in the day.

So Buller had his answer, but it was not the answer he wanted, one which would permit him to retire while placing the onus of retirement on Roberts. He had occupied the day of 6 February in an exchange of artillery fire, while he waited for a reply to his telegram. The fire had been ineffective upon both sides, although a lucky shot from one of the British naval guns blew up the ammunition wagon of one of the 6 inch guns on Doorn Kop, and silenced it for several hours. In the afternoon the Boers made an unexpected attack from the northern part of the hill. Part of the British line wavered, but a charge by the King's Royal Rifles restored the position within a matter of minutes. Late in the afternoon, after their many hours of dull waiting in the blazing heat, Lyttelton's battalion was relieved by Hildyard's, this move being carried out across the pontoon bridge which had been put over the river in the morning. Hildyard's men spent part of the night in improving their entrenchments. Lyttelton and his Brigade Major, Henry Wilson, returned to report to Buller. They found him at dinner, and he asked what sort of time they had had.

Lyttelton was angry at the failure to support him. 'Very bad,' he said. 'Shot at day and night from nearly all sides.' He added that their own return fire had been perfectly innocuous.

'Wait a bit,' Buller said. He went into his tent and came out to offer them what Lyttelton calls a large jorum, and Wilson a horn, of champagne. We do not know positively that it was Veuve Clicquot, although this was Buller's favourite, but we do know that it was good champagne. 'The best of anything is good enough for me,' Buller was fond of saying, adding in explanation, 'The best of anything is not the same as the best of everything. Bread and cheese by all means, but not inferior champagne.' Both Lyttelton and Wilson said afterwards that this was the most refreshing drink they had ever tasted.

Even the best champagne solved no problems, and Buller woke on Wednesday 7th February, to find the position unchanged. Hildyard's men were safe enough on Vaal Krantz, but what was the point of keeping them on the hill to be shot at? Roberts had said he should attack, but his own fear of defeat and dislike of risking a large number of casualties made him reluctant to do so. Perhaps if he went on firing and made some sort of further demonstration, the Boers would go away? With this in mind he borrowed Warren's two brigades on the morning of the 7th, and had them marched round from Potgieter's to Swaartz Kop. It was Warren's sixtieth birthday, and he volunteered to go over the top of Vaal Krantz to see what the country was like on the other side. Buller readily agreed to this, saying only (a remark into which it is tempting to read a subconscious wish), 'Be sure you don't get killed.' Warren set out with his scout, Lieutenant Schwikkard, and an ADC. They crossed the pontoon, and advanced under shell-fire up the hill. Some of Hildyard's men were asleep or dozing; one was reading a penny dreadful; they did not appear to be worried by the bullets. Up near the top they found Colonel Kitchener, and with him made a tour from boulder to boulder. Then Kitchener left them.

We now got pretty well out of the shell zone, and had only to face bullets coming over the hill. Not a soul to be seen. We crawled and rushed and at last got into the firing line at the top

281

of the hill... I pulled a sleeping man out of the schanz by his heels, and crawled into his place. Then by lifting up my head fitfully, as the least movement caused a patter of bullets, I looked out and reconnoitred the country, and made little sketches and notes.

Upon his return Warren took these sketches and notes to Buller, who remarked (again, is one detecting or imparting a note of irony?), 'See what it is to be an Alpine climber'.

For a day and a half now, Buller had done nothing. On the afternoon of the 7th, still looking for somebody to decide a course of action for him, he called a meeting of Generals. They met in Clery's tent, for Clery had been ill since the morning of the 6th with blood poisoning which affected his knee. Buller, Warren, Lyttelton, Hart, Wynne and Colonel Miles attended the meeting, at which Buller told them that Roberts wanted to continue the advance, without communicating the exact terms of his telegram. He then asked whether they were in favour of attack or retirement. Lyttelton, Wynne and Clery were for retirement, Lyttelton feeling that the original plan had been hopelessly bungled and must be given up. Hart, who had been nicknamed by his men 'General No-Bobs' because he never ducked a shell, wanted to attack. Warren wrote afterwards:

Hart was splendid. Nothing would induce him to retire except a direct order. Hart would be a great man if he could learn to extend his brigade, but he always works the battalions in close order as though he were on board ship or in a cattle kraal.

Warren also was in favour of going on. This seems strange, because he had been completely opposed to the attack on Vaal Krantz in the first place, but his changed opinion had no strategic grounds. He was simply convinced that he had 'taken the pulse of 20,000 men', and that they would get through. They should go on, he said, unless Buller could suggest a better line of advance. When asked what he would favour himself, he said: 'Hlangwane.' They were back to the plan which Buller had rejected before Colenso.

There was a murmur of assent, Buller looked relieved, and the decision was unanimous. It was to be Hlangwane.

In the meantime the younger staff officers had held an informal Council of their own. They were equally unanimous that the attack should be continued, and they looked at each other in amazement when they learned of the order to retreat. The meeting of the Generals, á Court said caustically, 'confirmed the truth of the venerable maxim that a Council of War never fights'.

Happy to have the retreat democratically agreed on and a new line of advance settled, Buller sent off telegrams at once to White and Roberts. To White he said that the Boers were too strong for him at Vaal Krantz, and that his plan was to 'slip' back to Chieveley and take Hlangwane. 'I hope to be at Hlangwane on Saturday,' he said, adding optimistically, 'Keep it dark.' He also, as he had done before, asked White if he could think of anything better. White naturally replied that he did not know the country, and so could not offer suggestions. The telegram to Roberts was much less cheerful. At Vaal Krantz, Buller said, the Boer positions were much superior to his own, and he was outclassed by their guns. He would try to capture Hlangwane and then make a 'desperate effort' to take Bulwana Hill, about four miles south-east of Ladysmith, but 'desperate' was the appropriate word, for he said that he thought he had 'a forlorn hope chance at both places'. Having thus, as it might be put, washed his hands of the whole distasteful Vaal Krantz affair, Buller left for Chieveley. He did not trouble to see Warren, but left a message asking him to withdraw the whole force to Springfield, and thence to Chieveley.

Amery says that the Vaal Krantz operation was even feebler than Spion Kop, although it was much less costly. The British losses were thirty odd men killed and some 350 wounded, against the Boer losses of thirty men killed and about fifty wounded. Amery wrote with the post-war knowledge that the Boer defences were so thin that 'almost any reasonably planned attack anywhere along the Tugela would have succeeded if pushed with the least promptitude and resolution', but it should be remembered that Buller and all his Generals believed that they were opposed by many thousands of men. Nor was this belief confined to the Generals, as can be seen from the reports of newspaper correspondents with the force, and of such intelligent men as Henry Wilson, who wrote in his diary:

> Poor Sir RB, it must be bitter work for him, and they won't like it at home, but Buller is right. I am certain in my own mind that if we pushed on we would probably have to lay down our arms. It's quite impossible with 15,000 men to turn 8, 10 or 12,000 out of lines and lines of entrenchments.

Buller had more than 20,000 men, and the force opposed to him, even after the time he had given them to obtain reinforcements was never more than 5,000 but his generalship was so singular that he had again managed to manoeuvre a British force much superior in numbers into a hopelessly untenable position.

The Boers, with their customary courtesy, did not attempt to disturb the British retreat. Hildyard got his men across the river again without trouble, and the pontoon troop dismantled the bridges. Warren was in his element during the retreat, which, as he saw it, provided a splendid opportunity for more practice and rehearsals. He encouraged his men to have what he called games of skill with the Boers. These involved, as he said, many exciting adventures and some really good fun, perhaps the most notable of which was his order to some of his rearguard to strip naked but for ammunition and rifles, recross the Tugela, and destroy some schanzes on the north side which had not been razed and might provide cover for advancing Boers.

The men were depressed at first by the retreat – Churchill said that only perfect discipline enabled them to control their grief and anger – but cheered up when they got back to Springfield, had a good meal and a bathe in the Little Tugela, a bathe which á Court described as 'worth anything in the world'. They had not in any way lost confidence in Buller. His officers might behind his back call him 'Sir Reverse', and Wolseley say that his nickname should be the Ferryman, because he had crossed and recrossed the Tugela so frequently, but the ordinary soldier's faith in Buller was well expressed by Winston Churchill:

A great deal is incomprehensible, but it may be safely said that if Sir Redvers Buller cannot relieve Ladysmith with his present force we do not know of any other officer in the British service who would be likely to succeed.

Chapter Fourteen *The Last Push*

Buller got back to Chieveley in a very gloomy mood. It was all very well to say to White that he hoped to be at Hlangwane on Saturday – a day which he changed almost immediately to Monday – but such words involved the obligation of action and for action, in his periods of depression, he felt himself to be quite unfitted. From Chieveley he sent two telegrams to Roberts on 9 February which are explicable in terms of a depressive neurosis rather than of military strategy. In the first of them he said that he had seriously overestimated the power of the Ladysmith garrison and that the Boers were practically neglecting Ladysmith and turning their whole force on to him. If Roberts could send him reinforcements, something might be done, but otherwise he thought his chance of success was very small. His second telegram, sent on the evening of the same day, began: 'It is right you should know that, in my opinion, the fate of Ladysmith is only a question of days, unless I am very considerably reinforced.' He complained that he had not received all the reinforcements he had expected, suggested that all forces arriving at the Cape should have been sent up to him, and ended by saying that if it was thought that anybody else could do better he would willingly be sacrificed, and that he would like Roberts to forward this telegram to the Secretary of State.

These telegrams reached Roberts at the Modder River just as he was about to begin the great flank march which was to end in the battle of Paardeberg, and the patience and courtesy of his reply cannot be too much admired. It was inevitable, however, that he should remind Buller that he had never before asked for reinforcements, that he had rejected the suggestion that he should stay on the defensive, and that he had known perfectly well that the troops arriving at the Cape after Roberts assumed command would be used by him. Sending considerable reinforcements, Roberts pointed out, would mean abandoning his own operations, and he 'requested' that Buller would now, 'while maintaining a bold front act strictly on the defensive'. He sent all the telegrams to the Secretary of State for War. In London these telegrams disturbed Lansdowne and infuriated Wolseley. He wrote to his wife: 'I have been thoroughly disappointed in him (Buller) for he has not shown any one of the characteristics I had attributed to him; no military genius, no firmness, and not even the obstinacy which I thought he possessed when I discovered he had no firmness. He seems dazed and dumbfounded when he loses men.' Even Wolseley could not deny that in relation to what he called these 'silly telegrams' Roberts had acted well, but he could not resist saying hopefully that 'if Roberts fails and follows in Buller's footprints, I can see nothing for it but to send me out, old as I am'.

In the meantime Roberts had thought further about these extraordinary telegrams, and had realized that they came from a man who had temporarily lost his nerve. He had not yet received the Spion Kop despatches in which Buller so severely criticized Warren, and it occurred to him that he ought to obtain Warren's opinion of the situation. Warren, after all, had been appointed second in command to Buller, and so was the third senior officer in South Africa. He therefore sent a further telegram, asking whether Warren shared Buller's views. It is quite possible that if Warren had said that no reinforcements were needed, Roberts would have placed him in command, but this was not Warren's way. In a statement whose confusion must have been almost more maddening than Buller's downright pessimism he said that his views 'closely coincided' with Buller's, although 'the matter involves an immense number of considerations and investigations of detail in which I may or may not share (Buller's) views'. This statement, with all its qualifications and hints of varied possibilities, cannot have been of much help to Roberts, and he must have been completely baffled when in response to his adjurations Buller said, 'As you value the safety of Ladysmith, do not tell me to remain on the defensive'.

Roberts answered this telegram on 15 February. On this day the threat to the Boers involved in his flank march, together with a dashing cavalry charge by French, effected the relief of Kimberley, the first real success that had come to the British in four months of warfare. On this day also – and this was really of greater importance – Roberts suffered at Waterval Drift the loss of four days' supplies and a third of his transport when the Boers swooped on his supply park. His telegram to Buller shows for the first time the strain under which he was working. He had only asked that Buller should act on the defensive, he pointed out, because 'it appears to me to involve useless waste of life for you to again undertake an enterprise which you regarded as hopeless', but Buller must do what he thought best, so long as he did not compromise his force.

During this exchange Buller had been considering his course of action. He had managed to side-track another request by Lyttelton that he should be allowed to join Roberts. Buller told Lyttelton in confidence that Sir Frederick Treves had examined Clery, and had discovered a blood clot on the brain which rendered the General quite unfit for the field, and possibly imperilled his life. Since Clery stayed in South Africa for another nine months, and lived until 1926, Treves' diagnosis (if he made it) was markedly inaccurate. However, it was certainly true that Clery was unfit for duty, and Buller offered Lyttelton command of his Division. 'This was a tempting offer, a fine Division including my own and Hildyard's Brigades,' as Lyttelton says, and his final hesitation disappeared when Buller described his new plan for reaching Ladysmith, by moving much further east than he had done before, and making a wide sweep round the Boer left which would be executed by Lyttelton's Division and Dundonald's mounted troops. These ideas 'appeared so sound that I doubted if they were his own, and I decided to stay on with him on these terms'.

The Boer positions on the southern bank of the Tugela were now established far beyond Hlangwane, which was the only point they had occupied at the time of Colenso. Their trenches now extended for some two miles further, and were then drawn back north-eastward to the range of hills known as Monte Cristo. It was this position that Buller decided either to penetrate or to turn, as opportunity should serve, but he showed none of that eagerness or rapidity in doing so suggested in his telegram to White. Rejecting as too precipitate a suggestion of Barton's that he should march directly on Monte Cristo and Cingolo, the nearest hill to it, he sent Dundonald on Monday 12 February, to occupy Hussar Hill, some five miles from Chieveley, and still a good way distant from the Boer positions. After a brief skirmish Dundonald occupied the hill, and Buller then carried out a lengthy reconnaissance with his telescope. The result of this was that he ordered the whole force back to Chieveley, whence it returned under Boer rifle fire. The Colt guns, mounted on the specially light gun-carriages designed by Dundonald, proved extremely serviceable in this operation. The carriages enabled the guns to be run back by hand instead of by horse power, so avoiding casualties to both men and horses.

That was 12 February. On the 13th – well, the 13th was very hot, and so Buller decided to do nothing on that day. On Wednesday, the 14th, however, there was action of a kind. Dundonald occupied Hussar Hill again, and Lyttelton's 2nd Division moved out, going two miles further east than Dundonald. They were promptly recalled by Buller, who was intent on those instructions that he should not compromise his force. For three days the British crawled eastwards along a line which was more or less parallel to the Boer positions. Warren held the left of this line, which was unlikely to see heavy fighting – the right, which was extending eastwards, was Lyttelton's Division. It was very hot, so hot that, according to Buller, no infantry movements on any scale were possible.

Lyttelton may have been annoyed by the fact that his men had covered only five miles in as many days, but Warren was never at a loss for some small touch of comic invention. He found that a commander on Hussar Hill had put his men under cover, but had left his arms exposed in the open, so that Warren and his staff were in effect standing guard over them. Warren then tried to induce this commander to enact with him a little playlet. Warren would be the sentinel, the commanding officer would come up, and the password on which Warren gave up the arms to him, would be: 'Allow no Boer to touch any of the arms.' Warren thought that this would have turned the lapse into fun, and he was disappointed that the commander concerned would not participate in the playlet. He had to content himself with an exhibition of his indifference both to the heat and to Boer shelling, by ordering that water should be heated and put into his mackintosh bath. He then stepped into the bath with the men all around him, curious and amused. As luck, good or bad, had it, Buller and his staff appeared while Warren was in the bath. He covered himself with a bath towel and received the Commander-in-Chief's orders, while the men looked on. 'I felt,' Warren says, 'that I had done what I could for the day to amuse the men.'

On the 17th Buller ordered Lyttelton to attack Cingolo Nek and Monte Cristo. He did so, with some success and at little cost, but the weather was still hot, the ground was extremely rocky, and there was little water. Lyttelton halted his troops in the afternoon, ready to make the final assault on the following day. In the meantime, Dundonald had again exceeded his orders with good effect. He had been told to keep in the rear of Lyttelton, but he saw the chance of capturing Cingolo itself, and so turning the Boer position. Churchill, who went with Dundonald's 650 men, described the difficulties they encountered.

The Cavalry Brigade marched ten miles eastward through most broken and difficult country, all rock, high grass, and dense thickets, which made it imperative to move in single file, and the sound of the general action grew fainter and fainter. Gradually, however, we began to turn again towards it. The slope of the ground rose against us. The scrub became more dense. To ride further was impossible... So scattered was our formation that I did not care to imagine what would have happened had the enemy put in an appearance. But our safety lay in these same natural difficulties...besides which war cannot be made without running risks. The soldier must chance his life. The General must not be afraid to brave disaster.

Dundonald's enterprise paid a rich dividend. His men, pushing along the summit, completely surprised the Boers and captured the whole summit of Cingolo. They were followed up by the Queen's Regiment, and although the Boers kept up a hot fire from Monte Cristo and from Green Hill, this had little effect. Buller, for once, did not order a retreat from a position unexpectedly gained, and Dundonald bivouacked that night on Cingolo Hill, after making a positional sketch, which he sent to Buller.

At dawn on the 18th, the attack was resumed. In the night guns had been dragged up the western slopes of Cingolo, and the whole line moved forward against the Boers, who were nervously conscious that they had their backs to the river. As Dundonald on the right went forward and captured the extreme end of the Monte Cristo ridge, Hildyard on his left advanced more cautiously, but with equal success. They were fired on from Green Hill, but when Barton's 6th Brigade attacked this hill frontally and at the same time Hildyard's men reached the summit of Monte Cristo and opened fire on the Boer laagers on the open ground below them, the effect was immediate. The Boers abandoned their positions on Green Hill and elsewhere, and fled in something like disorder. Four miles of mostly rolling plain separated them from the river, and the opportunity of converting their retreat into a rout was ideal, but Buller had no intention of taking what he would have considered to be this unnecessary risk. He was fighting not only the real Boers but also the ghost army of his imagination, and no sooner had the Boer positions been captured than he sent messages to all commanders to stand on the defensive, as the Boers were receiving large reinforcements. For fear of these imaginary reinforcements the Boers were allowed to make good their passage across the river. They left their camps standing, with thick blankets, coats, waterproofs, entrenching tools and ammunition. The soldiers would have slept in the Boer tents had they not been so disgustingly dirty and stinking. As it was they were able from Monte Cristo ridge to look down at last on Ladysmith, eight miles away, a twenty-acre patch of tin houses and blue gum trees. Soon, surely, they would be there.

The next two days, however, were spent by Buller in bringing up the rest of his army. The Boers made some slight resistance at Hlangwane, but recognised that they would now have to abandon altogether the south bank of the river. They did so during the night of the 19th, and on the following day Buller had command of this bank for a stretch of several miles and could have crossed at any one – or preferably three or four simultaneously – of a dozen positions. But success had completely changed his state of mind. Where before he had feared the advance of substantial Boer reinforcements, he now felt certain that nothing but a rearguard remained between his army and Ladysmith, a rearguard which could be driven gently before him while the last long miles were covered. He was warned by White that, so far from the Boers retreating further, reinforcements appeared to be coming up. If Buller would tell him which way he was coming, White said, the Ladysmith force would do its best to co-operate. Buller ignored all this. On the 21st he told White: 'I hope to be with you tomorrow night. I think there is only a rearguard in front of me.' With the conviction that there was no more serious fighting to be done, he had just one bridge made across the Tugela, about a mile west of Hlangwane, and started to push his army across it. No more unsuitable position for battle – if there was to be a battle – could have been thought of, for this way across the Tugela led into a deep hollow surrounded, although at some distance, by hills. When á Court heard where Buller had decided to cross he could hardly believe it, and said to Winston Churchill that they were going to 'march into the arena of the Coliseum and be shot at from all the benches'. Buller took no notice of such criticism, gratified perhaps by Warren's opinion that to cross at this point was a masterly tactical stroke. During the course of the 21st he got 11 battalions and 40 guns across into the open space on the other side of the river, and in the morning of the 22nd four more battalions crossed. If anything more than a rearguard faced them, they would be in the worst sort of trouble.

And there was something more. The Boers were depressed, it is true, and their depression was well based. At Paardeberg Cronje's army had been surrounded and, after a costly and unsuccessful attack by Kitchener, was being slowly starved into a surrender which took place on 27 February, with the capture of 4,000 prisoners. Nevertheless, when Kruger received from Botha the gloomy news of the British success at Monte Cristo he sent back a reproachful message saying that it seemed as if Botha's faith and that of his burghers had been replaced by unbelief. Steadfastness, he said, must bring victory. 'Even if they have no earthly rock behind which to seek cover, they shall win on the open plain,' he said. All the more encouraging was it to have earthly rocks for cover and to find the British on the open plain, and the Boers, collected and rallied by Botha, poured rifle and gunfire into the crowded British troops. Reluctantly Buller acknowledged that he was not dealing with a rearguard, and that a telegram he had received from Roberts, saying that special trains were being run from Natal to divert Boers from Ladysmith to the Western front was not accurate. He had now somehow to get out of the position into which he had placed his fifteen battalions, and Wynne's brigade was sent to make a push to the right and capture what was later known as Wynne Hill. The unfortunate Lancashire Regiments were engaged in this attack, and they suffered heavily from the Boer rifle fire. Wynne himself was shot in the leg and had to be temporarily replaced by Colonel Crofton, of Spion Kop fame. The hill was taken, but its capture was useless, for the British on it were surrounded on all sides by the Boers. During the 21st and 22nd the British casualties, on Wynne Hill and in the hollow beside the bridge, numbered over 500. Buller, who had ordered that his own headquarters should be brought across the river into the hollow, found it badly shot up by the Boer guns. He showed the coolness under fire, which Lyttelton said he had never seen surpassed, but was furious at the destruction of his tents.

He was determined to push on, and to do so by the line of the river and railway which he had chosen. Since the capture of one hill had failed to dislodge the Boers, he would take the next. On the morning of Friday the 23rd he told Hart to advance under the cover of Wynne Hill and take the next hill in the range, later known as Inniskilling Hill. To Churchill, who saw him on this morning, Buller showed his usual composure, inquired after the wound suffered on Hussar Hill by Churchill's brother Jack, and said that he had ordered Hart's Brigade, supported by two of Lyttelton's battalions, to take the hill. 'I think he can get round to their left flank under cover of the river bank,' Buller said, 'But we must be prepared for a counter attack.'

What happened was not a counter attack, but something like slaughter. Churchill, eager to see the progress of the attack, cantered along the railway by the line of stretchers, and joined Lyttelton in a position from which they could watch. The gallant General No-Bobs moved off his men at about 12.30, the Inniskilling Fusiliers leading, followed by the Connaught Rangers, Dublin Fusiliers, and Imperial Light Infantry. For some time they were able to go along the line of the river under cover, but as they emerged past Wynne Hill on to open ground the 'brown dark face of Inniskilling Hill, crowned with sangars and entrenchments', which had been silent, was suddenly active. All along the rim of the trenches Churchill saw through his telescope 'a crowded line of slouch-hatted men, visible as far as their shoulders, and wielding what looked like thin sticks', and heard above the average fusillade the roll of Mausers, which sounded like the fingers of both hands drummed hard on a wooden table. It was now 5 o'clock. Hart's march had taken more than four hours, and he was faced with the prospect of spending the night in what was later known as Hart's Hollow, which afforded some cover but was subject to fire from above, or of attacking. There could be no doubt of General No-Bobs' choice. Ordering the bugler to sound the 'Double' and the 'Charge' to encourage the men, he led them up the bare and steep hillside. An artillery bombardment accompanied this advance, which had to negotiate a barbed wire fence, move up and down a cutting, and then climb the hill. The Boer rifle fire was pitiless, but as Churchill and Lyttelton watched with straining eyes they saw 'the leading companies rise up together and run swiftly forward on the enemy's works with inspiring dash and enthusiasm'.

The British artillery fire was tremendous. 'Again and again whole sections of the entrenchments vanished in an awful uprush of black earth and smoke, smothering the fierce blaze of the lyddite shells from the howitzers and heavy artillery. The cannonade grew to a tremendous thundering hum.' But the Boers did not move from their parapets.

As the charging companies met the storm of bullets they were swept away. Officers and men fell by scores on the narrow ridge... The survivors hurried obstinately onwards until their own artillery were forced to cease firing, and it seemed that, in spite of bullets, flesh and blood would prevail. But at the last supreme moment the weakness of the attack was shown. The Inniskillings had almost reached their goal. They were too few to effect their purpose; and when the Boers saw that the attack had withered they shot all the straighter, and several of the boldest leapt out from their trenches and, running forward to meet the soldiers, discharged their magazines at the closest range.

Another correspondent called the struggle a frenzy, a nightmare. When it was over the attackers, or what was left of them, had been driven down the hill. They built a large curved wall as some sort of shelter, and stayed there during the night. Their losses had been some 450 in killed and wounded, more than half of them from the Inniskillings.

Hart was not deterred by these losses. He put in a request for stretcher bearers and told Warren, under whose command he was, that he proposed to renew the attack in the morning with the new troops sent him, the East Surreys, half the West Yorkshire Regiment, and half the Scottish Rifles. Buller was distressed, as he was always distressed, by the losses, but he could think of nothing fresh to do except to take the hill beyond Inniskilling Hill, that is Railway Hill, round which the railway ran. It seemed to him, however, that General No-Bobs was not an ideal leader for a strategy which involved an attack upon two points at once, and he sent for Warren to go to Hart's Hollow and direct the attack. Warren's sense of humour did not fail him even in these trying circumstances. He went across and saw Buller, with his staff and clerks, pinned down by the shell-fire. Warren, in a safe nook, shook with laughter at the sight and when Buller sent across to know why he was laughing, said, 'Come over and see'. Buller crawled over to him on all fours. 'Look at your staff,' Warren said, and pointed out that as each shell came over the senior officers scarcely moved, but a wave went down the line in descending order of seniority, and as each rank was reached the heads were more and more lowered.' Buller was not pleased or amused. He went back and told the men to hold their heads steady. Warren reflected cheerfully: 'A good laugh does one's inside so much good.'

Warren went over to Hart, but by the time the two had arranged that Hart should himself attack Railway Hill with two battalions while Colonel Cooper of the Dublin Fusiliers led a new attack upon Inniskilling Hill, the time was 4 o'clock, and it was agreed by everybody that the attack had better be postponed until the following day. So on this day nothing happened on either side except an occasional exchange of gun and rifle fire. The British clung to the sides of Wynne Hill and Inniskilling Hill, the Boers remained above them. Many of the wounded still lay out on the hills unattended, and Buller's staff had been urging him to ask for an armistice so that they might be brought in. He had rejected this idea, but now he changed his mind, and Sunday February 25th, was observed as a day on which there was no fighting. Botha and Lukas Meyer refused to agree to an actual armistice and troop movements were made, although no fighting took place.

By noon the wounded had been brought down and the dead buried, and there was a good deal of fraternization between British and Boers. The British soldiers examined their enemies with astonishment: old men with tobacco-stained white beards, young farmers, big boys in ill-fitting suits, and not one of them wearing uniform except the Boer commandant Pretorius, who wore a smart khaki suit with silver buttons and stars. Pretorius was much shaken by a talk he had with Lyttelton, who said that the war was obviously going to last a long time, and that he was going to bring out his wife and family. The Boers' casualties were not much more than a tenth of the British, but they had been rattled by the heavy artillery bombardment, and were amazed by Lyttelton's acceptance of this as a mere everyday matter.

'A rough time?' he said to some of them. 'I suppose so. But for us, of course it is nothing. We are used to it, and we are all well paid for it. This is the life we always lead – you understand?'

'Great God', said the farmer soldiers listening to him.

On this Sunday Buller evolved, either in his own head or through talking with others, the plan that was to bring relief at last to Ladysmith. He would take almost all of his artillery and most of his baggage back across the river, put a pontoon bridge over to the rear of Hart's Hollow to support the attack there, and enlarge the front so that he attacked for the first time with his full force. He had lost 1,300 men in a series of purposeless attacks. Now authority and energy seemed suddenly to return to him, and by the morning of the 26th he had 76 guns in position on the south bank of the river. Later on that day he rode out with á Court along the whole line of heights as far as Monte Cristo, and then dictated orders to him for the following day. 'He had suddenly become the old War Office Buller,' á Court says, 'and dictated so rapidly that I could scarcely keep pace with him, but as he went on I saw that he had a complete grasp of the operation, and that everything that I had hoped would be done was in the orders.' The plan was in essence a simple frontal attack, designed to take the three hills, Inniskilling Hill, Railway Hill, and Pieter's Hill to the right of it. Beyond Pieter's Hill was the plain, and Ladysmith. The attack was to be supported by an overwhelming weight of artillery, and would be directed at an enemy who were weary from continuous fighting, and who had hopefully misinterpreted Buller's recrossing of the Tugela as a prelude to his retirement. On the afternoon of the 26th, Botha wrote to Joubert in Pretoria that it was quite possible that the British were retiring because of their heavy losses.

Day broke behind a cloudy sky. The 100 yards long pontoon bridge in its new position was across the river by 10 o'clock, and half an hour later a 'clear the line' telegram from Roberts announced Cronje's surrender, which was told to the troops as they were advancing to attack. They were greatly heartened by the news, and stirred also by the fact that this was Majuba Day, a day to avenge. 'I never saw infantry strain at the leash as they strained this day,' wrote one of the war correspondents. The attack was begun by Barton, whose brigade crossed by the new pontoon bridge and then made their way along by the river in single file to the foot of Pieter's (or as some rechristened it afterwards, Barton's) Hill. Dundonald's mounted men, with two battalions of infantry and the Colt machine gun company, had been told to occupy the rough and rocky ground on the south-bank, and to cover Barton's advance with gun and rifle fire. Churchill, who was with them, had a wonderful view of the advance:

Deep in its gorge below our feet flowed the Tugela, with the new pontoon bridge visible to the left, just below a fine waterfall. Behind us, on a rounded spur of Monte Cristo, one of the long-range batteries was firing away busily. Before us, across the river, there rose from the water's edge first a yellow strip of sandy foreshore, then steep, scrub-covered banks, and then smooth, brown slopes, terminating in the three hills which were to be successively assaulted, and which were surmounted by the dark lines of the Boer forts and trenches. It was like a stage scene viewed from the dress circle.

On this stage scene Barton's infantry, the Scots, Irish and Dublin Fusiliers, moved to the attack, climbing the 500 feet to the edge of the Pieter's plateau. The Irish Fusiliers rushed across it, captured the nearest kopjes, and opened fire ahead of them and on Railway Hill to their left. This was the limit of their success. Very heavy fire was opened on the Scots Fusiliers, who were trying to extend the line of the Irish Fusiliers to the right, and their advance came to a halt in a sheltered donga. Barton had been slightly wounded, and the Scots had lost many killed and injured.

After this check there followed the kind of pressure that Buller had never before put upon the Boers, as the attack upon the next hill in the range, Railway Hill, began. It was upon this hill that the artillery fire from the southern bank had been most fiercely concentrated, and now the West Yorks captured the east end of it with little opposition. The rest of the 11th Brigade stormed up the hill in face of rifle fire, right into the Boer trench. The Boers had no time to run. Several of them were bayoneted in the trench, some fifty or sixty taken prisoner. To the watchers, painfully used to assaults that failed, what happened seemed almost beyond belief. They saw the infantry storming up the hill, as they had done up other hills, enter the trench – and there, coming out of the trench and in panic flight, were tiny black figures. Then a British soldier was on the topmost point of the trench, waving his helmet on his bayonet, and down the sharp and stony slope on the other side the Boers were fleeing headlong. By 5 o'clock in the afternoon Railway Hill had been captured, and now the pressure was further increased by the assault on Inniskilling Hill, carried out by the Rifle Brigade and the East Surreys. This too was successful, and as night fell the kopje on Pieter's Hill from which the Scots Fusiliers had been repulsed, was taken also. As a result of the day's fighting the British had captured all three of the hills. Their losses for the day had been some 100 killed and 400 wounded. The losses of the Boer defenders were naturally less, but they were still considerable. In one Pretoria corporalship every man was either killed or taken prisoner and, as Deneys Reitz says, 'their going at this calamitous time was scarcely noticed', so great was the confusion and distress.

So Buller had won his victory. Gunfire continued throughout the night, but the Boers' resistance was broken, and Botha's attempts to rally the burghers were made in vain. The morning of the 28th found them fleeing across the plain in total disorder. Reitz spent a gloomy hour or two watching the tide of defeat roll northward, Botha tried to introduce some order into what was happening, but uselessly. Men, wagons and guns streamed over the plain. There were fierce quarrels between teamsters about the right to cross a spruit or nullah, and whole groups of vehicles got their wheels interlocked, so that movement was impossible. 'Had the British fired a single gun at this surging mass everything on wheels would have fallen into their hands,' Reitz says.

No gun was fired. Buller resisted the attempts of his Generals and his staff to induce him to pursue the Boers or try to fight them. His job was not, as he saw it, to fight Boers but to relieve Ladysmith, and besides, his view was that 'retreating Boers are very difficult to catch'. He knew, he told them, a little more about Boer rearguards than anybody else in his army, from his experiences in 1879, and it was his belief that 'unless there is some paramount object to be gained, an attempt to force a Boer rearguard is merely a waste of time'. Warren, Lyttelton, á Court, all implored him to harass the Boers by cavalry attack or gunfire or both, but he would have none of it. He was indeed the old War Office Buller, and he told them that he would not lose a single man to capture the whole Boer camp and transport. The most he would permit was that Dundonald should cross the river and 'reconnoitre the enemy'. His orders were strict, and although á Court tried to circumvent them he was unable to find any pretext on which the cavalry might attack. Years afterwards á Court said, 'I cannot think of that day even now without rage'.

In the morning Buller had received a telegram from White, telling him that they were down to half a pound of very inferior bread a day, and that he could hold out no longer than 1 April. Buller replied with two telegrams, the first confirming that he had many wagons of supplies for Ladysmith, and the second giving the smell of victory:

> I beat the enemy thoroughly yesterday, and am sending my cavalry as fast as my bad road will permit of, to ascertain where they have gone to. I believe the enemy to be in full retreat.

Slowly, slowly, since there were still Boers in the vicinity of Ladysmith, he moved forwards to his goal.

Chapter Fifteen *The Relief of Ladysmith*

These last days of the siege were miserable. The Boers still shelled the town, but made no attempt to capture it. There was very little fighting. Sickness increased continually, and the lucky ones were those who did not go to the hospital at Intombi, but managed to stay in the line or, if they were civilians, in their quarters. Far away, a distant promise, they heard the sound of Buller's guns. Nevinson suffered badly from what he called sunstroke, and when the fever subsided he could get only 'a tiny ration of tea, a brown compound called rice-pudding, flavoured with the immemorial dust of Indian temples, and a beef tea which neighs in the throat', to help his convalescence. When he tried a bit of bread he found it uneatable. Few had the strength, and none now had the heart, for playing cricket or for holding concerts. There was no defeatism in Ladysmith, but there was hunger, and the depression that hunger accompanied by inaction brings. It was decided not to issue any more horse as rations until the last of the tough oxen had been killed. When, on the morning of the 28th, the Boer retreat could be seen in the distance, a silver snake of wagons moving across the veldt, the sight seemed too good to be true. Then, later in the day, it was seen that the great gun on Bulwana was being removed.

At about 6 o'clock in the evening of the 28th the still feeble Nevinson had gone out to watch the tail-end of the Boer wagons disappear.

On returning I found all the world running for all they were worth to the lower end of the High Street, and shouting wildly. The cause was soon evident. Riding up just past the Anglican Church came a squadron of mounted infantry. They were not our own. Their horses were much too good, and they looked strange. There was no mistake about it. They were the advance of the relief column.

The actual arrival of the relief squadron was almost fortuitous. Captain Gough who had joined Dundonald's staff as an Intelligence Officer, had been put in command of the Composite Regiment, and at about 4 o'clock in the afternoon he found that the ridges between his men and Ladysmith seemed to be unoccupied. He asked Dundonald if he might push on but Dundonald, who had promised another officer that he should lead the advance into Ladysmith, was undecided. Finally he said 'yes', and Gough went on. As he approached the town he was fired on, and Dundonald ordered him to retire. Ignoring this, and a second order that he was not to advance, Gough went on. At 6.15 he sent back a message to say that the road was clear, and two squadrons of horse rode down into Ladysmith, among increasing crowds and cheering. One of Gough's troopers came galloping up to join him at the head of the column. They had been at Eton together, and now the trooper said: 'An Eton boy must be first into Ladysmith.'

And so it was. Gough was taken to see White, a grey-faced, stooping, pathetic figure weakened by illness, who walked with a cane. Dundonald, annoyed that glory was passing him by, followed as quickly as possible. Churchill, who went with Dundonald, found the ride on this deliciously cool evening unforgettable. As they neared the town they were challenged:

'Halt, who goes there?'

'The Ladysmith Relief Column.'

At these words a score of tattered men, thin and pale, came out of trenches and rifle pits feebly cheering. The relievers gave what was in their wallets, slabs of chocolate, cigarettes and tobacco, to the soldiers and civilians. One of Dundonald's staff officers broke down and wept as he saw the wretched, emaciated men standing in the street cheering them. That night Dundonald and Churchill, and Gough too, dined with White and his staff. 'I was placed next to Hamilton, who won the fight at Elandslaagte and beat the Boers off Wagon Hill,' Churchill said, 'and next but one to Hunter, who everyone said was the finest man in the world. Never before had I sat in such brave company nor stood so close to a great event.' Dundonald sent back a message to Buller: 'Am in Ladysmith, Dundonald.'

During the next two days Buller tried to discover the presence of Boers in the neighbourhood. He planned an attack on Bulwana, but found that it had been completely evacuated. He made cautious gestures a mile or two away from the town, and still discovered no enemy. He sent Dundonald forward almost to Van Reenen's Pass, nearly twenty miles distant: no Boers. On 3 March, satisfied that they had really gone, he made his formal entry into Ladysmith, characteristically going first to Intombi Hospital to visit the sick and wounded. The contrast between the besieged garrison, ragged and attenuated, and the well-dressed well-fed relieving force was very striking. Sir Frederick Treves, who arrived on the 2nd, a few hours before the food convoys came in, found the place still unrelieved as far as the misery of hunger was concerned:

I had no food at my disposal, but I had fortunately a good quantity of tobacco, which was doled out in pipefuls so long as the supply lasted. It would have taken many pounds, however, to satisfy the eager, wasted, trembling hands, which were thrust forward on the chance of getting a fragment of the weed.

On walking into 'Starvation City' one's first impression was that of the utter emptiness of the place. Most of the villas were unoccupied, were closed up, and, indeed, barricaded. The gardens were neglected, and everything had run wild. All the people we met were pallid and hollow-eyed, and many were wasted. All were silent, listless, and depressed. There were no evidences of rejoicing, no signs of interest or animation, and, indeed, Ladysmith was still unrelieved.

By the time Buller came in some of the food had been distributed, and both soldiers and civilians were looking and feeling more cheerful. Buller wrote home to his family, 'As I passed each company of the garrison who were lining the street they gave three cheers for Sir RB, and in the middle there was the photographer fiend with his cinematograph, so I suppose it will all be in the Alhambra or some other house of entertainment as soon as may be. I dare say it was all right, but I should have been glad to have dispensed with it'. He praised the courage of the men, and followed this praise with some significant words:

> It has all seemed to me like a dream. Every day some new complication to meet, and every day the same roar of guns and rattle of musketry, with, alas, every day the long list of killed and wounded, which is what I cannot bear.

He was in Ladysmith at last, and he had no intention of leaving it for the sake of chasing the Boers, as some of his own and White's officers wished to do. He told Roberts that his own well-fed troops needed a week's rest, boots and clothes. The Ladysmith garrison would need at least six weeks before they could move. He concerned himself a good deal with the task of getting the sick and wounded to the hospital ships prepared for them. His recovery of self-confidence showed itself in brusqueness to Lyttelton and to White. The Ladysmith commander, who had been unwell during most of the siege, was invalided home on 9 March, and with his usual concern for the health of others, Buller agreed that he should be accompanied by the Staff-surgeon who had been caring for him.

It was in Ladysmith that Buller's Generals and staff learned for the first time of the 'surrender' telegram he had sent after Colenso. Ian Hamilton, writing to Spenser Wilkinson in England, said that a hundred of Buller's officers had talked to him, and that from General to subaltern they had all lost confidence in 'Sir Reverse, as they call him'. What especially angered Hamilton, Rawlinson, and their colleagues at Ladysmith, was Buller's conviction now that everything he had done was for the best. Hamilton wrote Roberts a letter on 14 March, which can hardly have been conducive to the maintenance of good relations.

> Buller was very rude to Sir George and spoke to him in the vilest way of you and Kitchener, whom he appears to dislike and to attribute dishonest motives to, almost as much as he does you. I never gave him the chance to be nasty to me, but contented myself with a very distant salute.

Hamilton also told Spenser Wilkinson of the 'surrender' telegram:

> After the battle he wired us that we had better fire off our ammo and make the best terms we could. We thought at first our cypher and helio must have fallen into the hands of the Boers, it seemed so incredible the great Buller of all men could be giving such unworthy counsel. He recovered himself in about 3 days and then became as boastful as ever.

Hamilton, suffering from what he called Peshawar fever, concentrated on the point, which he chiefly wanted to impress on Wilkinson:

> *Buller is no use*... It is a question of life or death of our selves here as well as of the empire in general, and I write to beg you to use all your influence to get the man recalled before he does more mischief.

EPILOGUE

THE TRIUMPH OF ROBERTS

Chapter One *The End in South Africa*

Buller was not recalled. He remained in South Africa, as second in command to Roberts, until October, when he returned to England. During March and April a tremendous flurry of telegrams passed between the two men on the subject of Buller's future movements. Buller was anxious not to have any men taken away from him, and he countered all Roberts' plans for him to advance with objections about his lack of cavalry, guns, boots and remounts. The upshot of this long, comic series of telegrams was that early in April Roberts took from Buller Hunter's Division and the Imperial Light Horse, and more or less left the Natal Army to its own devices. He also shunted Warren off to the post of Military Governor of the Cape Colony, north of the Orange River. Lansdowne congratulated Roberts on this move. 'It struck me that, after what had passed, he and Buller could not with advantage remain together.' The Spion Kop dispatches still remained unpublished when Warren parted from Buller, and when they did appear later in the month the sharpest criticisms of Warren were omitted. Warren was still under the impression that he and Buller were on good terms, and when he received the appointment he went to see Buller. They discussed the course of the campaign, speaking as Warren said, 'in very strong terms', yet remaining 'in the best of humours'. That Buller's humour was good is doubtful, nor is it likely, as Warren thought, that he was unwilling to let his subordinate go. Lansdowne suggested, after reading some of the telegrams sent by Buller to Roberts during March and April, that Buller's mind was unhinged. 'It is certainly a misfortune that we should any of us be called upon to transact business with such a personage,' he said. Yet Roberts did not like to suggest, nor Lansdowne care to consider the idea of Buller's removal.

Between April and the end of September he occupied himself with clearing Natal. Opinions of the capacity he showed in doing so varied. Lyttelton, who after all remained with Buller, thought that upon the whole he fought a well-planned and well-executed campaign, which he carried through vigorously. Dundonald, on the other hand, when he found Buller one day extremely irritable, said to him: 'You are a changed Buller, you are not the Buller I knew in the Sudan.'

Buller's manner changed at once. He said, in what Dundonald calls 'a broken voice': 'It is true, my dear Dundonald, I am changed, and what changed me was the indoor life at that cursed War Office, those long hours, day after day, without exercise, for I used to work there long after others had gone.'

At any rate he suffered no more defeats, and when in June Roberts captured Pretoria, Buller went there and the two met in apparent amity. It seemed to everybody that the war was over. Histories of it published in 1900, Conan Doyle's among them, said as much. Roberts had had his checks and defeats – in a surprise attack on Sannah's Post at the end of March, De Wet captured seven guns and a whole convoy and killed or took prisoner 600 men, and a few days later part of the unhappy Gatacre's force was ambushed, and surrendered with the loss of another 400 men. Such losses were a risk inherent in the speed with which Roberts moved, and the force he had at his command, of nearly 100,000 men with half that number in reserve, was so strong that these defeats were comparatively unimportant. He never, after Paardeberg, defeated the Boers in battle, although Hunter compelled the surrender of some 4,000 of them in July, but he took Bloemfontein, Johannesburg and Pretoria. What more could there be to do? Some Boer commandos remained in being, but nobody supposed that they would go on fighting for more than a few weeks. Roberts was to return home to succeed Wolseley as Commander-in-Chief and Lansdowne, writing to congratulate him and to announce his own departure from the War Office said: 'If Kitchener remains behind to "sweep up" after your departure, I should not think that he need stay very long.' Roberts was in favour of Lyttelton being given the supreme command as his successor, but Kitchener was preferred. Buller left for home early in October, and at the end of November Roberts handed over command to Kitchener for the sweeping-up process. The Government took the opportunity of the war's apparent end to hold a 'khaki election', which sent them back to office with a slightly reduced but still very handsome majority.

Roberts, and the British Government acting on his advice, had made a gross miscalculation both of the kind of men they were fighting and the kind of war they would fight. Ahead lay another eighteen months of bitter struggle, which ended in the Boers' submission through starvation. Ahead lay the miseries and inhumanity of the concentration camps in which the Boer women and children were placed, the burning of farms (which had been begun by Roberts), the establishment of the system of 'blockhouses' by which the commandos were much subdued. Ahead there was no glory, but the systematic subjugation of a small nation by a large one, a process which made Britain appear in the role of a swaggering, inefficient bully. Ahead, further ahead still, lay the task of reconstructing South Africa in the Imperial image, which was undertaken by Milner and his band of devoted young men.

All these matters are no part of this book. Both Buller and Roberts left South Africa trailing clouds of military glory. When Buller said goodbye to the 3rd Mounted Brigade at Machadodorp 'the men cheered him and cheered him again', as Dundonald says, 'for Buller was loved by all'. The men's belief in him, Lyttelton says, was extraordinary. One of the speakers at the farewell banquet given for him in South Africa said that he had saved Natal, South Africa and the British Empire. Roberts' departure was also marked by scenes of great enthusiasm, less demonstrative perhaps than those that speeded Buller. Their arrivals in England caused much excitement. Buller's reputation with his men had preceded him, as those invalided from South Africa came home. When 40 officers and 300 men came home on the *Majestic* they were loud in Buller's praise. One of the officers said, 'General Buller is a remarkably hardy man, and can have as good a night's rest on the veldt as Tommy Atkins. He does not favour garden parties at Pretoria when the troops are actively engaged, nor would he allow my Lady So-and-so to volunteer as a hospital nurse for any base hospital in his division'. One of the privates from Ladysmith said, 'It is all Buller out here. He is the man'. He landed at Southampton on 9 November. The Corporation gave him the freedom of the Borough. Wolseley was there to meet him, large crowds gathered wherever he went, and the Queen received him with the utmost cordiality. Roberts also, of course, was received with great acclaim. A nineteen gun salute was fired for him when he landed at East Cowes, and from Cowes he went straight to Osborne. There the Queen created him an Earl, and a Knight of the Garter.

Nothing was yet known publicly of the surrender telegram, little of the true story of Spion Kop. In this unanimity of acclaim for Buller there was no hint of the wrath to come.

Chapter Two *The End of Wolseley*

Power and influence had passed decisively from the hands of Wolseley on the day when the Government appointed Roberts to the supreme command in South Africa without consulting him. For some while he did not understand this, but gradually it was borne in upon him that his suggestions now had no more than a nuisance value, and that Roberts was to have the last word in the long struggle between them. In South Africa the solid, indomitable, imperturbable Buller, his nominee for success, had failed; Roberts, the advertising Roberts, the little Hindoo man, had succeeded. It was with deep dissatisfaction that Wolseley saw himself passing into the shade. His tenure of the office of Commander-in-Chief, towards which he had moved for so many years, had been neither happy nor successful, and now it was almost over. On 1 August 1900, he wrote to his wife:

> Three months hence – 1st November – I retire into private life. It will be a curious sensation, that of feeling that my public life is over. I shall have worn the Queen's uniform for 48 years and nearly 8 months. An end to all my once fierce ambition. But it is high time I went, for since Roberts was sent to South Africa I have lost all interest in my work... It was a great experiment sending out Roberts, a very *cute* man; but although not a great General, he has proved himself to be politically, and, so far, ostensibly, in a military sense, a success... I have had my chances, and I have been too independent, too careless of

public opinion and done too much to hurt old prejudices, and too indifferent as to what men for whom I had no respect thought of me. Roberts on the other hand, although according to my notions with much less ability has passed me in the race because he was much cleverer, *cuter* than I was in understanding public opinion and in playing upon its unworthy strings a tune that suited human vanity.

He nursed a hope, even though he knew it to be illusory, that his term of office might be extended, but with the election safely over the Government made their intentions known. He was to be succeeded – sharpest stroke – by Roberts ('Remember, I have no grievance, and you and I must be most careful as to what we say of my little Hindoo successor', he told his wife.) Lansdowne was going, but that was little consolation, for he was to be succeeded by St John Brodrick. Now, in his fury at being replaced by Roberts, with which was blended anxiety at the amount of his pension, Wolseley lashed out at them all. Lansdowne was 'very civil and grinning, but never says he regrets my departure or is obliged for my work, etc etc, and nothing hinted at, even, as regards pension'. A letter from Salisbury, in which the Prime Minister said he looked back with pride and pleasure on their relationship, made him even angrier. It was, he said, 'from either a disremembering humbug or from a man whose mind is either going or gone'. On 1 December he left the War Office forever and said goodbye, no doubt with his usual slightly exaggerated courtesy, to the new Secretary of State for War. 'I went into Brodrick's room, shook hands with that underhand and tricky prig and bid him goodbye... I hope never to have any relations in life with him again.' Thirty years earlier he had written to his wife that soldiers should never marry, because they had to leave their wives so often and for so long. Now he longed for nothing beyond her company, and the farmhouse at Glynde. 'I never want any other society – I find none so pleasant, none so witty and amusing as you are.'

It cannot be said that the Government were ungrateful to Wolseley. He complained that his pension was '£200 or more less than the Session Clerk who leaves as Permanent Under-Secretary', but he and his wife received from the Queen not long before her death the gift of an apartment in Hampton Court Palace – an arrangement which Wolseley did not much care for, although his wife delighted in it – and in March 1901, he was sent on a tour to announce the accession of King Edward VII to the Emperor of Austria, the Kings of Romania, Serbia and Greece, and the Sultan of Turkey. This was perhaps done to get him out of the way as much as for any other reason, for in March there had been an embarrassing interchange of speeches in the House of Lords between Wolseley and Lansdowne. Wolseley carefully abstained from any personal criticism of Lansdowne, and went so far as to say that 'No disagreeable incident of any sort that I can recall ever marred the pleasant relations which marked our intercourse', but he made vigorous criticisms of the divided authority through which the Commander-in-Chief's action was often paralysed and his office 'blocked with routine papers passing backwards and forwards to and from the office of the Secretary of State'. Lansdown's reply was a personal attack, which enlisted much sympathy for the former Commander-in-Chief, and the Government must have feared that Wolseley would make one of his imprudent public speeches.

His grip upon public affairs, although not upon life, failed rapidly. For a long time he had refused to admit his lapses of memory, but now he acknowledged that he simply could not recall recent events, or put a date to those that were a little further back. He went, with some disgust, on a sea voyage 'in search of health', and there met Thorneycroft the Spion Kop hero, and Methuen who should never, he thought, have been made a General. He brooded often on what had gone wrong, as he saw it, with his career. He felt that it was a pity he had not been sent to Eton or Harrow, but even without those advantages he had done well enough until he fell into the clutches of Lansdowne, 'half Frenchman, half sneak'. When he returned from the sea voyage he gave evidence before the Royal Commission established to consider the facts about the War. The Commissioners treated him gently, but it was plain that he was a mere shadow of the Wolseley of old. For eleven years he lived on, with his memory failing more and more, so that he shrank from any contact with society and became wholly dependent upon his wife. This failure of memory he accepted as an edict from God, 'perhaps to punish me for neglect of Him, or for some selfishness in dealing with men who deserved better treatment from me'. To most people he was little more than a name when he died in March 1913, and was buried in the crypt of St Paul's. Roberts was among the pallbearers.

Chapter Three *The End of Buller*

The publication of the Spion Kop despatches in April 1900, was mishandled by Lansdowne. There was a division of opinion in the Cabinet about the wisdom of publishing any dispatches at all, since any sort of publication must reveal the disharmony prevailing among the Generals in Natal. The Queen was against publication; Wolseley, while regretting that Roberts had found it necessary to censure Buller, thought that it was impossible not to publish some report of a battle in which so large a British force had been engaged, and Lansdowne apparently misinterpreted the feeling of the Cabinet meeting at which the question was discussed. At all events, he annoyed both the Queen and the Prime Minister by publishing an edited version of the dispatches. This included almost the whole of Roberts' adverse comments on Buller, but cut out altogether Buller's savage attack on Warren which had been written, as Buller said at the time, 'not necessarily for publication'. Warren's report on the capture and evacuation of Spion Kop was printed almost in its entirety, with some of Buller's comments, but the reports of Coke and Thorneycroft were omitted, together with any statement of casualties. Altogether, enough was published to make it clear that the operation had been profoundly unsatisfactory, yet there was a feeling, which was expressed in Parliamentary questions, that more remained to be said. Warren was astonished and deeply indignant at the comments made by a man with whom he had thought himself on friendly terms in relation to a battle which he thought he had managed rather well. He sent a despatch to Roberts supplementing

317

his previous report, but this was never published, and in response to further letters he received a curt instruction not to discuss the matter further.

The effect of the publication was distinctly unfavourable to both Buller and Warren, and the Government awaited Buller's return to England with some nervousness. What would he say, what would he do? Almost everybody was afraid of his temper, which Buller spoke of rather as a malady from which he had suffered all his life. 'Since old Eton days,' he once told Lord Esher, 'I have had a formula for myself, "Remember Dunmore".' This referred to an occasion at Eton when he had been playing football and had had a chance of taking a kick at goal. He had not taken it because he was too busy kicking Dunmore. Would he remember Dunmore now? It seemed so. To the Queen's request that there should be no recriminations he said that they would never come from him. In November Lansdowne wrote to Roberts, who was still in South Africa, 'Buller has been tremendously fêted and, so far, has bridled his tongue in public. He looks well, but has lost his sleek "fit to kill" look – and no wonder'. Buller attended a number of club and regimental dinners as guest of honour, and resumed his command at Aldershot, where the men for South Africa were being trained.

Roberts found himself almost as much hampered as Wolseley had been when he took up office as Commander-in-Chief. In theory his powers were in some ways enlarged, but in practice Brodrick proved to be even more determined than Lansdowne to keep essential power in the hands of the civilian Secretary of State. Brodrick proposed to effect a total reorganization of the home Army into three Army Corps. It was intended that these formations should stay together so that the General in command, his staff, and the various units should know each other well, when and if the time came for them to fight. This scheme could not possibly be put into effect while the war continued, but it was pointed out in the press that Buller would be the General in command of the First Army Corps. On the count of age, quite apart from that of ability, it was most unlikely that he would ever command this Corps in the field. Since the scheme remained on paper while the war went on, the point was not important, but it was pursued pertinaciously in the press, with many references to Buller's defects as a commander. This obviously was a potent source of future trouble, but in the meantime Roberts found the energetic Brodrick taking decisions on all sorts of matters without consulting him. He found also that where there was a difference of opinion between them it was almost always he who was expected to give way. When Roberts first assumed office Brodrick had told him that Wolseley had never been fit for his work since his illness in 1897, that he had come in at 11 and left for Glynde at 2 o'clock, and that there had been no fault in the system but only in the man. Perhaps Roberts believed this at the time, but Brodrick's constant interference, particularly in matters relating to discipline, soon made him change his mind. A climax to their arguments came in August 1901, when Roberts rejected altogether a surprising suggestion that Buller should be made Quartermaster-General, showed his resentment of Brodrick's view that he was too lenient in matters of discipline, and threatened to resign:

> I accepted the Commander-in-Chiefship with no light heart, but with every desire to assist you to the best of my ability in the very difficult task you had before you, but I confess eight months' experience has not made me feel sanguine as to there being any successful result. For some reason or another War Office work is unsatisfactory. It is too hurried, and there are too many ramifications, too many masters... If I am to remain I must feel that I have your entire confidence. I cannot work unless I am trusted, and if this is not to be, I would far rather make way for someone else whom you can trust.

Brodrick replied pacifically, the suggestion about Buller was dropped, and within a couple of months the Commander-in-Chief and the Secretary of State for War were standing side by side, as the storm about Buller broke.

The 'surrender' telegram had never been made public, but its general nature was known to all of White's staff officers, and rumours about the telegram appeared frequently in the press. It seems also that White told a woman friend about it, and that she gossiped. After the relief of Ladysmith, Buller had written home, 'What I really like most is to get abuse of myself; sometimes it makes me laugh, and sometimes it really helps me, so I am always pleased to get it', but the press attacks and innuendoes made him steadily angrier. His anger was increased by the fact that he had been more or less passed over in the distribution of honours, being awarded only the GCMG. He attributed this comparative slight to Roberts, quite wrongly, for with his usual generosity Roberts had suggested that Buller should be given a peerage, an idea which was immediately rejected by both Lansdowne and Brodrick. 'Buller must remain in the cold,' Lansdowne wrote to Roberts, 'and Brodrick is quite prepared to "face the music", which will be loud.' But Buller had reached a point where he attributed almost all of his misfortunes to Roberts. In July he had been formally rebuked because he had appeared at a bazaar for War Charity in plain clothes, although troops were present in uniform. The King was displeased, and Roberts communicated this displeasure. Buller's apology was grudging. 'I confess your letter surprised me: but of course if the King thinks I ought to have been in uniform there is no more to be said, and I am very sorry I was not.' In October the chief of Wolseley's lieutenants forgot Dunmore, and rushed to his doom.

The occasion was a luncheon given by the Queen's Westminster Volunteers. Sir Howard Vincent was in the chair, and he coupled the toast of the Regiment with the name of Buller. The reply to the toast was made in terms which suggest that Buller had, as Wolseley put it, too much champagne on board. He told how he had been visited at Aldershot by an international spy, who first talked mysteriously about the Transvaal Secret Service, and then suggested that Buller should give up the Aldershot command. The conversation between them continued:

BULLER: Thank you very much. I do not know that I need to do so. Why should I do so?

SPY: I will tell you. You have got enemies, men who mean to get you out of the way, and they will get you out of the way, and you had better get out of it quietly.

BULLER: I am a fighting man, and if what you say were really so, I am much more likely to stop here than to leave. If it is necessary for me to use that information, I shall.

SPY: You can.

Buller went on to say that *The Times* had said he was not fit to be in command of the First Army Corps. 'I assert that there is no one in England junior to me who is as fit as I am. (Cheers). I say so. I challenge *The Times* to say who is the man they have in their eye more fit than I am.' He told in detail his version of the 'surrender' telegram, which had been mentioned in *The Times* by Amery, writing pseudonymously. 'I challenge *The Times* to bring their scribe "Reformer" into the ring. Let us know who he is, by what right he writes, what his name is, what his authority is. Let him publish his telegram. Then I will publish a certified copy of the telegram I sent and the public shall judge me. I am perfectly ready to be judged.'

He was judged, but not as he had expected. Brodrick, who was on holiday in Scotland after the death of his wife, sent a telegram immediately to Roberts, and on his return showed that he was eager to take this chance to get rid of Buller. If *The Times* took up Buller's challenge, he said, 'Telegrams which I have promised Parliament not to produce, and a discussion which I had pledged myself to the late Queen not to allow, would have been made public'. Buller must first be asked to admit that he had made the speech; next, the substance of it must be telegraphed to Balmoral; and third, he must be replaced in his command. King Edward agreed, and Roberts said that after the speech either Buller or he must go, but it did not prove easy to get rid of Buller. 'He will fight to the death,' Brodrick warned Roberts, and certainly he fought to the furthest point possible, that of dismissal. He asked first of all for five minutes in private to tell Brodrick 'one thing, which I do not think you know, and which I think material to the issue, and it is a point that I should not like to bring out before others unless obliged to do so'. Brodrick flinched from this interview, but in the end granted it. The five minutes extended to an hour and a quarter, during which Buller complained of Roberts, of White, and of the way in which he had been treated in the publication of despatches. Buller had tried to obtain an assurance that Roberts would not be present, and when he eventually came into the room, Brodrick had 'much difficulty in keeping the peace'. The intransigent General refused to resign, and appealed to the King. In this final appeal he said that he regretted making the speech, but that he thought this speech alone should not be made the ground of 'depriving me of my position, and of driving me from the Service in which I have served for 43 years'. The King was unmoved. On 23 October 1901, it was announced that Buller had been relieved of his command and retired on half pay.

The decision had been expected, yet it still came as a shock, and it had the effect of rallying public (as distinct from military and press) opinion behind the dismissed General. *The Times*, which had been completely hostile to him, reported on 25 October that 'Government House, Aldershot, was inundated with letters from all parts of England, expressing sympathy with Sir Redvers and Lady Audrey Buller, and unshaken confidence in the General. These messages, which come from all classes of society, numbered many hundreds'. He was replaced at Aldershot by Hildyard, and arrangements which had been made for him to present war medals and clasps to the 1st Devon Yeomanry were hurriedly cancelled. In the West Country there was great and long-lasting indignation. The mayors of several Devon boroughs, meeting at Exeter, expressed their confidence in him, and he was given a hero's homecoming when he retired to Downes. Brodrick wryly noted that it was said that he could turn out the candidate of any party in the West Country, simply by going down to speak for him. Buller's prestige in the West survived the publication of the full Spion Kop despatches which revealed the whole of his wrangle with Warren, survived even an unhappy debate in the House of Commons when a Liberal attempt to censure the Government action was shattered by Brodrick's reading of the 'surrender' telegram, which was now made public for the first time.

None of this did anything to impair his popularity as a national figure. He was in great demand to unveil memorials to the war, and wherever he went he was cheered. His infrequent visits to London were signals for expressions of public sympathy and affection. On one occasion he had to escape down a side street from a demonstrative crowd, and on another the footmen at a reception lined the way as he left the house specially to cheer him. Most of his time, however, was spent at Downes, where he installed new machinery and sawmills. He remained, as he had always been, a benevolent father figure to his tenant workers, and took a great deal of interest in local education. A public statue of him was commissioned and Captain Adrian Jones who executed it, remarked upon his good humour while the work was being done. At the first sitting he said, 'We have now to reverse the order of things. I am entirely at your command'. In September 1905, this equestrian statue, which showed him in full uniform and greatcoat, was unveiled by the Lord Lieutenant of the County in the absence of Wolseley, whose health was too indifferent for him to endure the fatigue of the occasion. In June 1908, he died after a long illness, which he bore with his usual stoicism. 'I am dying,' he said on the day of his death, and added, 'I think it is about time to go to bed now.' He was buried in Crediton churchyard.

Even for Roberts the South African War, which had seen such an extraordinary upward turn in his fortunes, brought bitter disappointment. His tenure of the War Office was a most unhappy one. He unwisely agreed to the hushing-up of the 'Cape Ragging Case', in which a group of officers forcibly unclothed another of their number, photographed him, cut off part of his hair and moustache, and in other ways humiliated him. The affair was revealed when the officer brought and won an action against his fellows, and the resultant publicity had a bad effect on Roberts' reputation. Soon there were accusations in Parliament that it was impossible to obtain promotion in the War Office unless you were a member of the 'Roberts Ring'. It was pointed out that the rise of both Hamilton and Nicholson had been meteoric (against the wishes of Brodrick, Nicholson had been made a Lieutenant-General as soon as he was appointed Director of Military Intelligence, whereas Ardagh had remained a Major-General for years), and that every one of Roberts' ADCs had received quick promotion. Brodrick defended him in Parliament, but the relations between the two men became almost as strained as had been those of Wolseley and Lansdowne. This was partly because Roberts had far less administrative ability than Wolseley or Buller and, accustomed to the leisurely routine of India, continued to answer in his own hand the many letters he received from private soldiers, so that the time he had to spare for larger matters was strictly limited. But he was also the victim of the fact that the office of Commander-in-Chief was now a mere troublesome appendage. The end came for him late in 1903, as a result of the deliberations of the Esher Commission on War Office reorganization. Roberts worked with the Commission compliantly, and agreed with their decision that the office of Commander-in-Chief should be abolished and that the Army should be run by a Council of seven members, four military and three civilian, with an Inspector-General who would co-ordinate the work of the various executive commands. Brodrick, who disapproved of this plan, resigned in September 1903, and thereafter Roberts seems to have been the victim of a deliberate plot to humiliate him and strip him of power.

He was told by Balfour, who was now Prime Minister that, with the abolition of the position of Commander-in-Chief, he would be appointed Inspector-General for the rest of his term of office. After that he heard nothing, until he was called to Buckingham Palace for an interview with the King, who said that he hoped Roberts would not accept the position of Inspector-General, which would be derogatory to his dignity after he had been Commander-in-Chief. 'I don't think he made much impression,' Esher wrote in his Journal. 'The little man is very tenacious. Roberts promised to think over the question, but two days later he saw in the papers the announcement of the members of the Army Council, with nothing said about the Commander-in-Chief and the Inspector-General. He went to the War Office, and there learned the brutal discourtesy with which the replacements had been made. Stopford, who had been Buller's Military Secretary, knocked at the door of Hildyard's office and told him that he had come to take over the department of military Education and Training, and Nicholson was similarly called on without warning to hand over his office. 'Our torpedo has exploded, and the little C in C has left the War Office for good, in a devil of a temper,' wrote Esher, whose machinations had been responsible for the way in which the affair was handled. Roberts had been treated atrociously, but he was not a man to feel anger for long, even against Esher. His last years were spent in urging without success the doctrine of compulsory national service. His views on this subject were held to be so extreme (although they were very similar to Wolseley's) that they isolated him even from his greatest military friends, Hamilton and Nicholson. He died in 1914, just after the outbreak of the First World War, too soon to see the acknowledgement of the truths he had preached.

In the years that followed the war, commentators on the Ladysmith campaign placed the responsibility for its failures upon Buller's military incapacity, or upon the shortcomings of the War Office. Such criticisms were true enough, yet they are not fully adequate as explanations of battles, which are among the most absurd in British history. Roberts is not now thought to have shown high talents as a General in South Africa. He won a single victory in the field, he drove back the immensely inferior Boer forces, he captured cities, he substituted energy for Buller's procrastination: but essentially he was the same kind of General, one accustomed to personal command of small forces and unable to recognize the need to delegate responsibility when handling tens of thousands of men over a large area. Twenty years earlier Buller might have done as well as Roberts, and his failures must be explained less in terms of military or intellectual inferiority than by reference to psychology. The fragments of his correspondence that remain give us little data, but it is obvious that some great psychological change had transformed 'the Bayard of South Africa' into the man, irresolute and stupidly stubborn by turn, who relieved Ladysmith. That he was the prey of some deep neurosis is certain, and it is tempting to speculate on its nature and origins, to link it with his unhappy childhood and the death of his mother, with his voracious eating and drinking, and with the tender-heartedness that increased as he grew older. But there are not sufficient facts to build even a card-house of theory. Behind the tragi-comedy of the lost guns at Colenso and the confused command at Spion Kop there stands his figure, 'huge, heavy, solid, and reliable to look upon...impassive as Helvellyn, yet notoriously tender with heart bleeding for his fallen soldiers', capable of the most unselfish devotion to Wolseley and of savage unfairness to Warren and Coke; impatient, irascible, unreasonable, too frequently forgetful of Dunmore, but far more intelligent and sensitive than history has allowed; aware of his own faults, yet powerless to check them; arrogantly overconfident yet neurotically inhibited from decisive action: an enigma.

Bibliography

Amery, L S (Editor) *The Times History of the War.* 6 vols. 1900–1909

Amery, L S *A Political Life.* Vol. 1. 1953

'An Average Observer' *The Burden of Proof* 1902

Arthur, Sir George (Editor) *The Letters of Lord and Lady Wolseley. 1870–1911* 1922

Aston, Major-General Sir George *His Royal Highness the Duke of Connaught and Strathearn* 1929

Atkins, J B *The Relief of Ladysmith* 1900

Atlay, J B *Lord Haliburton* 1909

Barrow, General Sir George *Life of General C C Monro* 1931

Biddulph, General Sir Robert *Lord Cardwell at the War Office* 1904

Birdwood, Field-Marshal Lord *Khaki and Gown* 1941

Boscawen-Wright, Charles *With the Imperial Light Infantry through Natal* 1903

Buchan, John *Lord Minto* 1924

Burleigh, Bennet *The Natal Campaign* 1900

Burne, Lieutenant R N *With the Naval Brigade in Natal* 1902

Buller, Sir William *Autobiography* 1911

Callwell, Major-General C E *Field-Marshal Sir Henry Wilson* 1927

Chapman-Huston, Major Desmond and Rutter, Major Owen *General Sir John Cowans* 1924

Charlton 1931

Churcher, Major D W (Diary of) *With the Irish Fusiliers from Alexandria to Natal (ND)*

Dawson, Brigadier-General Sir Douglas *A Soldier-Diplomat* 1927

'Defender' *Sir Charles Warren and Spion Kop* 1902

Dickson, W K-L *The Biograph in Battle* 1901

Doyle, A Conan *The Great Boer War* 1900

Dundonald, The Earl of *My Army Life* 1926

Dunlop, Colonel John K *The Development of the British Army 1899–1914* 1938

Esher, Viscount *Extracts from Journals.* Vols 1 and 2. 1914 and 1932

Fortescue, Sir John W *Following the Drum* 1931

Garvin, J L *Life of Joseph Chamberlain, Vol 3* 1934

Gleichen, Major-General Lord Edward *A Guardsman's Memories* 1932

Gordon, Hampden *The War Office* 1935

Gosse, Edmund *Aspects and Impressions* 1922

Gosse, Edmund 'Sir Redvers Buller' *North American Review,* January 1900

Grenfell, Field-Marshal Lord *Memoirs* 1925

Hamilton, Lord George *Parliamentary Reminiscences and Reflections* 1922

Hamilton, Ian *Listening for the Drums* 1944

Headlam, Cecil (Editor) *The Milner Papers*, 2 vols. 1931

Hurst, Colonel Godfrey Thomas *History of the Natal Mounted Rifles* 1935

James, David *Lord Roberts* 1954

Jones, Captain Adrian *Memoirs of a Soldier Artist* 1933

Knox, E Blake *Buller's Campaign* 1902

'Linesman' (Captain M H Grant) *Words by an Eyewitness* 1901

Lyttelton, General Sir Nevile *Eighty Years* 1927

MacDiarmid, D S *Life of Lieutenant-General Sir James Moncrieff Grierson* 1923

MacDonald, Donald *How we Kept the Flag Flying* 1900

McHugh, R J *The Siege of Ladysmith* 1900

MacReady, General Sir Nevile *Annals of an Active Life* 1928

Malmesbury, Susan, Countess of *Life of Major-General Sir John Ardagh* 1909

Marling, Sir Percival *Rifleman and Hussar* 1931

Maurice, Major-General Sir Frederick (Editor) *Official History of the War in South Africa.* Vols. 1 and 2 1906–7

Maurice, Major-General Sir Frederick (Editor) *Life of Lord Rawlinson of Trent from his Journals and Letters* 1928

Maurice, Major-General Sir Frederick and Arthur, Sir George *Life of Lord Wolseley* 1924

Maxwell, Raymond *Diary of Contemporary Review*, Dec. 1901

May, Major-General Sir Edward *Changes and Chances of a Soldier's Life* 1925

Melville, Colonel C H *Life of Sir Redvers Buller* 2 vols. 1923

Midleton, Earl of K P *Records and Reactions, 1856–1939* 1939

Milner, Viscountess *My Picture Gallery, 1886–1901* 1951

Montgomery-Cunninghame, Sir Thomas *Dusty Measure* 1939

Musgrave, George Clarke *In South Africa with Buller* 1900

Neligan, T *From Preston to Ladysmith with the 1st Battalion South Lancashire Regiment* 1900

Nevinson, H W *Ladysmith. The Diary of a Siege* 1900

Newton, Lord, P C *Lord Lansdowne* 1929

Pearse, H H S *Four Months Besieged. The Story of Ladysmith* 1900

Reitz, Deneys *Commando* 1929

Repington, Lieutenant-Colonel Charles á Court *Vestigia* 1919

Robertson, Field-Marshal Sir William *From Private to Field-Marshal* 1921

Romer, Major C F and Mainwaring, Major A E *The 2nd Battalion Royal Dublin Fusiliers in the South African War* 1908

Royal United Services Institute Journal, March 1899. *The Official Report of the Salisbury Manoeuvres* 1898

Salt, Lieutenant G S *Letters and Diaries* 1902

Smuts, J C *Jan Christian Smuts* 1952

Spender, Harold *General Botha* 1919

Steevens, G W *From Capetown to Ladysmith* 1900

Tobin, R F *A Memoir of the late Lieutenant-Colonel Charles Dalton, RAMC* 1915

Verner, Willoughby *Military Life of the Duke of Cambridge* 1905

Viljoen, General Ben *My Reminiscences of the Anglo-Boer War* 1902

Warren, T Herbert *Christian Victor* 1903

Waters, Colonel W H H (translator) *German Official Account of the War in South Africa* Vol. 1 1904

Wilkinson, H Spenser *Lessons of the War* 1900

Wilkinson, H Spenser *Thirty-Five Years, 1874–1909* 1933
Wulcocks, Sir William *Sixty Years in the East* 1935
Williams, Watkin W *Life of General Sir Charles Warren* 1941
Wood, Field-Marshal Sir Evelyn *Winnowed Memories* 1918

Unprinted and Other Material Consulted

Hansard and Newspapers for the period
Buller and Ardagh Papers in the Public Record Office
Milner Papers at New College
Letters of Lord and Lady Wolseley in the Royal United Services Institution
Correspondence of Lord Roberts
Letters and Papers at the Ogilby Museum
Official publications relating to the War. The most important of these are Cd. 1789–1792, the Report of the Royal Commission on the War in South Africa (1903)
Other important papers are Cd. 987, the Ladysmith telegrams (1902), Cd. 155, which relates to the omission of part of the Spion Kop Despatches (1900) and Cd. 968, the Spion Kop Despatches in full (1902). Cd. 457 (1901) contains Roberts' despatches, and Cd. 458 (1901) the despatches of the Natal Field Army. Also of interest are Cd. 3127–3130, the Report of the Royal Commission on War Stores in South Africa (1906), Cd. 9404, which relates to the Bloemfontein Conference (1899), and Cd. 9415, 9507, 9518, 9521, and 9530, all of them relating to political reform in South Africa (1899)

JULIAN SYMONS

THE BROKEN PENNY

An Eastern-bloc country, shaped like a broken penny, was being torn apart by warring resistance movements. Only one man could unite the hostile factions – Professor Jacob Arbitzer. Arbitzer, smuggled into the country by Charles Garden during the Second World War, has risen to become president, only to have to be smuggled out again when the communists gained control. Under pressure from the British Government who want him reinstated, Arbitzer agreed to return on one condition – that Charles Garden again escort him. *The Broken Penny* is a thrilling spy adventure brilliantly recreating the chilling conditions of the Cold War.

'Thrills, horrors, tears and irony' – *Times Literary Supplement*

'The most exciting, astonishing and believable spy thriller to appear in years' – *The New York Times*

JULIAN SYMONS

THE COLOUR OF MURDER

John Wilkins was a gentle, mild-mannered man who lived a simple, predictable life. So when he met a beautiful, irresistible girl his world was turned upside down. Looking at his wife, and thinking of the girl, everything turned red before his eyes – the colour of murder. Later, his mind a blank, his only defence was that he loved his wife far too much to hurt her...

'A book to delight every puzzle-suspense enthusiast'
– *The New York Times*

THE END OF SOLOMON GRUNDY

When a girl turns up dead in a Mayfair Mews, the police want to write it off as just another murdered prostitute, but Superintendent Manners isn't quite so sure. He is convinced that the key to the crime lies in The Dell – an affluent suburban housing estate. And in The Dell lives Solomon Grundy. Could he have killed the girl? So Superintendent Manners thinks.

JULIAN SYMONS

A MAN CALLED JONES

The office party was in full swing so no one heard the shot – fired at close range through the back of Lionel Hargreaves, elder son of the founder of Hargreaves Advertising Agency. The killer left only one clue – a pair of yellow gloves – but it looked almost as if he had wanted them to be found. As Inspector Bland sets out to solve the murder, he encounters a deadly trail of deception, suspense – and two more dead bodies.

THE PLAYERS AND THE GAME

'Count Dracula meets Bonnie Parker. What will they do together? The vampire you'd hate to love, sinister and debonair, sinks those eye teeth into Bonnie's succulent throat.'

Is this the beginning of a sadistic relationship or simply an extract from a psychopath's diary? Either way it marks the beginning of a dangerous game that is destined to end in chilling terror and bloody murder.

'Unusual, ingenious and fascinating as a poisonous snake'
– *Sunday Telegraph*

JULIAN SYMONS

THE PLOT AGAINST ROGER RIDER

Roger Rider and Geoffrey Paradine had known each other since childhood. Roger was the intelligent, good-looking, successful one and Geoffrey was the one everyone else picked on. When years of suppressed anger, jealousy and frustration finally surfaced, Geoffrey took his revenge by sleeping with Roger's beautiful wife. Was this price enough for all those miserable years of putdowns? When Roger turned up dead the police certainly didn't think so.

'[Symons] is in diabolical top form' – *Washington Post*

OTHER TITLES BY JULIAN SYMONS AVAILABLE DIRECT
FROM HOUSE OF STRATUS

Quantity		£	$(US)	$(CAN)	€
CRIME/SUSPENSE					
☐	THE 31ST FEBRUARY	6.99	11.50	15.99	11.50
☐	THE BELTING INHERITANCE	6.99	11.50	15.99	11.50
☐	BLAND BEGINNINGS	6.99	11.50	15.99	11.50
☐	THE BROKEN PENNY	6.99	11.50	15.99	11.50
☐	THE COLOUR OF MURDER	6.99	11.50	15.99	11.50
☐	THE END OF SOLOMON GRUNDY	6.99	11.50	15.99	11.50
☐	THE GIGANTIC SHADOW	6.99	11.50	15.99	11.50
☐	THE IMMATERIAL MURDER CASE	6.99	11.50	15.99	11.50
☐	THE KILLING OF FRANCIE LAKE	6.99	11.50	15.99	11.50
☐	A MAN CALLED JONES	6.99	11.50	15.99	11.50
☐	THE MAN WHO KILLED HIMSELF	6.99	11.50	15.99	11.50
☐	THE MAN WHO LOST HIS WIFE	6.99	11.50	15.99	11.50
☐	THE MAN WHOSE DREAMS CAME TRUE	6.99	11.50	15.99	11.50
☐	THE NARROWING CIRCLE	6.99	11.50	15.99	11.50

ALL HOUSE OF STRATUS BOOKS ARE AVAILABLE FROM GOOD BOOKSHOPS OR
DIRECT FROM THE PUBLISHER:

Internet: www.houseofstratus.com including author interviews, reviews, features.

Email: sales@houseofstratus.com please quote author, title and credit card details.

OTHER TITLES BY JULIAN SYMONS AVAILABLE DIRECT
FROM HOUSE OF STRATUS

Quantity		£	$(US)	$(CAN)	€
☐	THE PAPER CHASE	6.99	11.50	15.99	11.50
☐	THE PLAYERS AND THE GAME	6.99	11.50	15.99	11.50
☐	THE PLOT AGAINST ROGER RIDER	6.99	11.50	15.99	11.50
☐	THE PROGRESS OF A CRIME	6.99	11.50	15.99	11.50
☐	A THREE PIPE PROBLEM	6.99	11.50	15.99	11.50
	HISTORY/CRITICISM				
☐	THE TELL-TALE HEART: THE LIFE				
	AND WORKS OF EDGAR ALLEN POE	8.99	14.99	22.50	15.00
☐	ENGLAND'S PRIDE	8.99	14.99	22.50	15.00
☐	THE GENERAL STRIKE	8.99	14.99	22.50	15.00
☐	HORATIO BOTTOMLEY	8.99	14.99	22.50	15.00
☐	THE THIRTIES	8.99	14.99	22.50	15.00
☐	THOMAS CARLYLE	8.99	14.99	22.50	15.00

ALL HOUSE OF STRATUS BOOKS ARE AVAILABLE FROM GOOD BOOKSHOPS OR
DIRECT FROM THE PUBLISHER:

Hotline: UK ONLY: **0800 169 1780**, please quote author, title and credit card details.
INTERNATIONAL: **+44 (0) 20 7494 6400**, please quote author, title, and
credit card details.

Send to: House of Stratus Sales Department
24c Old Burlington Street
London
W1X 1RL
UK

Please allow for postage costs charged per order plus an amount per book as set out in the tables below:

	£(Sterling)	$(US)	$(CAN)	€(Euros)
Cost per order				
UK	1.50	2.25	3.50	2.50
Europe	3.00	4.50	6.75	5.00
North America	3.00	4.50	6.75	5.00
Rest of World	3.00	4.50	6.75	5.00
Additional cost per book				
UK	0.50	0.75	1.15	0.85
Europe	1.00	1.50	2.30	1.70
North America	2.00	3.00	4.60	3.40
Rest of World	2.50	3.75	5.75	4.25

PLEASE SEND CHEQUE, POSTAL ORDER (STERLING ONLY), EUROCHEQUE, OR INTERNATIONAL MONEY ORDER (PLEASE CIRCLE METHOD OF PAYMENT YOU WISH TO USE) MAKE PAYABLE TO: STRATUS HOLDINGS plc

Cost of book(s): .... Example: 3 x books at £6.99 each: £20.97

Cost of order:.. Example: £2.00 (Delivery to UK address)

Additional cost per book: .... Example: 3 x £0.50: £1.50

Order total including postage: .... Example: £24.47

Please tick currency you wish to use and add total amount of order:

☐ £ (Sterling)   ☐ $ (US)   ☐ $ (CAN)   ☐ € (EUROS)

VISA, MASTERCARD, SWITCH, AMEX, SOLO, JCB:

☐☐☐☐☐☐☐☐☐☐☐☐☐☐☐☐☐☐☐☐

Issue number (Switch only):

☐☐☐

Start Date: **Expiry Date:**

☐☐/☐☐   ☐☐/☐☐

Signature: _____

NAME: _____

ADDRESS: _____

_____

POSTCODE: _____

Please allow 28 days for delivery.

Prices subject to change without notice.
Please tick box if you do not wish to receive any additional information. ☐

House of Stratus publishes many other titles in this genre; please check our website (**www.houseofstratus.com**) for more details.